LATIN AMERICA IN THE YEAR 2000

LATIN AMERICA IN THE YEAR 2000

Edited by
JOSEPH S. TULCHIN
University of North Carolina at Chapel Hill

Translated by Paula Hazen and issued under the auspices of the
Sociedad Interamericana de Planificación

Addison-Wesley Publishing Company
Reading, Massachusetts
Menlo Park, California • London • Amsterdam
Don Mills, Ontario • Sydney

This book is in the
ADDISON-WESLEY SERIES IN HISTORY

Robin Winks,
Consulting Editor

ISBN 0-201-07603-9
ABCDEFGHIJ-DO-798765

PREFACE

At the Seventh International Planning Congress held in Lima, Peru, in October, 1968, with the general theme "America in the Year 2000," the Interamerican Planning Society (Sociedad Interamericana de Planificación, SIAP) called on all those interested in the progress of our continent to present their vision of our reality, in its different aspects, with a view to eliciting forecasts and expectations of what Latin America will be at the beginning of the twenty-first century, now only a few years away.

The papers presented before this Congress are scientific and honest expositions of present-day problems and those solutions considered viable. Taken together, these documents make a broad and objective examination of Latin America and of the factors that condition the development and integration of that great nation extending from the Straits of Magellan to the Baja California peninsula.

The members of SIAP and those who participated in the Congress at Lima believe that all Americans should have a comprehensive knowledge of the hemisphere's problems and of the politically conscious contributions of intellectuals, especially the ones who have joined the liberation efforts of their peoples. Such knowledge is essential for overcoming the alienation produced by economic and political dependence, and the destruction of moral values and cultural traditions which provide social cohesion and awareness to the various Latin American collectivities. It is necessary to combat the aggressions and narrowing of democratic paths of expression of the popular will, the dictatorships, and in general, all those elements which limit democracy and the exercise of national sovereignty and self-determination.

In extending this invitation to discuss common problems, SIAP felt that it was fulfilling its responsibility to heighten consciousness among the hemisphere's intellectuals and students so that their actions, in whatever field they move, redound to the benefit of the peoples of the hemisphere—facilitating closer relations among the different countries, the development of cultural and economic collaboration, and the interchange of experiences.

By presenting the papers from the Lima Congress to English-speaking readers, the Interamerican Planning Society believes that a better understanding of the ideals and needs of our peoples can be provided, thereby forging stronger intellectual links and ties of friendship among North Americans and Latin Americans interested in authenic development, democracy, justice and peace in this continent.

August 1973   *Cuauhtémoc Cárdenas*
Mexico, D.F.   *President, Interamerican Planning Society*

EDITOR'S FOREWORD

The Interamerican Planning Society (SIAP) is one of the most prestigious non-academic groups of intellectuals in the western hemisphere. From modest beginnings at the First Interamerican Technical Meeting of Housing and Planning in Bogotá in 1956, it has extended its range to include all of the social sciences and the vast area of public policy. Its diverse constituents are held together by a common aim: to promote the development of principles and practices of comprehensive planning as a continuous and coordinated process at international, national, regional and local levels, in order to direct and accelerate the development of the American countries.

Since its creation and up to the present time, SIAP has held eight technical congresses jointly with its Biennial General Assemblies, where themes of continental significance were discussed. These meetings were attended by professionals, technicians and planners of international prestige. These Congresses have helped to bring the professionals and planners of America closer together and have fostered the exchange of experiences and techniques in comprehensive planning.

The Seventh Congress, held at Lima in 1968, under the auspices of the Instituto Peruano de Estudios del Desarrollo, was organized around the topic "America in the Year 2000." Here was a fit challenge for professional planners—not visionaries, but people concerned with practical realities. Aside from straightforward efforts at prediction, the organizers of the Congress focused on two related issues: how to select elements from the present to formulate projections into the future; and how public policy might be shaped to achieve selected goals and avoid undesirable elements in the future.

The Congress was organized into five symposia, each with a chairman, as follows:

I. The Social Situation in Latin America in the Year 2000. Horacio Godoy, Chairman

II. National and International Politics in Latin America in the Year 2000. Kalman H. Silvert, Chairman

III. Integration and Development. Claudio Véliz, Chairman

IV. The New Culture. Harvey Perloff, Chairman

V. Demography and Planning. José Donaire, Chairman

Thirty-three papers were presented to the Congress and discussed at animated sessions. The proceedings of these sessions were edited by the chairmen of the five symposia and prepared for publication by the Instituto Peruano de Estudios del Desarrollo under the supervision of its President, Carlos Zuzunaga Flórez. The original publication, in Spanish, with each symposium in a separate volume, was distributed to the members of SIAP.

Many of the hemisphere's leading social scientists participated in the Lima Congress and their papers provided a wealth of information on contemporary affairs and a unique compendium of proposals for the course of future development in the area. Given the importance of the theme and the high quality of the proceedings it seemed vital that the papers be made available to an English-speaking public. We were convinced that students and the general public would benefit from reading these varied approaches to the broad problem of development, a problem which concerns all Latin Americans and all North Americans interested in the so-called Third World and in the future role of the United States in world affairs.

To make the proceedings of the Congress accessible to the widest possible audience they had to be condensed in a single volume. While I was responsible for editoral decisions, articles were selected for publication in consultation with Luis E. Camacho, Executive Secretary of SIAP, and Jorge E. Hardoy, the Chairman of the SIAP Publications Committee. In choosing the papers to be published in this volume we were guided by the intrinsic interest of the piece, the potential interest of the subject to North Americans, the need to avoid unnecessary repetition of material, and a preference for general treatments over specific studies. Additional editorial interventions, in the form of deleting or condensing certain sections, were prompted by a desire to create a balanced volume and by budgetary limitations. Despite the long delay in publication, we decided to leave untouched the references to the timing of the original conference. In a sense the intervening years are a partial test of the predictions made in 1968.

In ordering the contents of the volume, our aim was to enhance the utility of the book in the classroom, and the materials are arranged in units to allow the teacher maximum flexibility. Insofar as the arrangement by subject units permits, there is a progression in the subject matter from the general to the specific and from the familiar to the technical.

We hope this collection will find a place in a wide variety of undergraduate and graduate courses. We believe it offers a valuable resume of contemporary problems in Latin America and fascinating projections for the future. Perhaps most important of all, it makes a broad spectrum of Latin American views, none previously published, accessible to an English-speaking public. These articles—by both Latin Americans and North Americans—are recommended to those interested in history, politics, public policy, demography, urbanism, the multinational corporation, economic integration, and dependence. They are recommended both for their substance and for their prescriptive value.

An editor incurs many debts in the course of his labors and I am no exception. I want to thank Larry Wilson and Roger Drumm for encouraging me to take on this project. Luis Camacho was un-

failingly helpful and ensured the cooperation of SIAP. My good
friend Jorge Enrique Hardoy was indefatigable in his efforts to see
the manuscript through its various transformations. Finally, Paula
Hazen was a cooperative translator and delightful colleague.

Chapel Hill, N.C.   J.S.T.
October 1973

CONTENTS

1 INTRODUCTION

1. LATIN AMERICA SEEN FROM THE YEAR 2000

HORACIO H. GODOY
Director of the Latin American School of Political Science and Public Administration of the Facultad Latinoamericano de Ciencias Sociales

I. INTRODUCTION

Futurology studies being carried out at institutions around the world are examining possible alternatives for world organization in the year 2000.[1] Some methodologies employ diagnoses of current circumstances based on indicators such as GNP, population, and per capita income, to formulate what has been called a "surprise-free projection."[2] Another approach elaborates a model based on a preferred value system, specifies the phases of the transition period, and defines the means for achieving desired changes. The project "World Order Without Nuclear War for the Year 2000," sponsored by the World Law Fund and conducted in various centers, is an example of this approach.

These methods begin with an analysis of the present, from which they project toward the year 2000. As an intellectual exercise, this study proposes forsaking the prospective method to examine a new technique which may facilitate practical analyses of the future.

A certain world order for the year 2000 will be proposed, and the current Latin American situation will be considered from that perspective. Contrasting the hypothetical world order and the current situation can show how Latin America might effectively participate in decisions leading to that future order.

3

This exercise is similar to conventional studies in projecting a future on the basis of contemporary conditions. It differs from the model-building technique in that the hypothesized world situation does not necessarily correspond to a preferred value system. It is rather a "surprise-free projection" of current tendencies. Both approaches stress analysis of the transition period.

Speculation regarding the future—speculation understood not as attempts to predict, but rather as exercises in preparing and constructing future conditions—can take several forms:

1. Study of the present and projection of essential tendencies and features toward the future—the present as anticipation of the future.
2. Study of the present from a past perspective; for example, how the sixties might have been foreseen in 1930. This method involves "retrospective futurology"—analysis of the present as the past's realized future.
3. Study of the present from the future, postulating a future order from which the present is examined as the past.

II. THE WORLD SITUATION IN THE YEAR 2000

We will postulate these conditions for the year 2000:

1. A world united in fact and made smaller by new transportation and communications technology.
2. Because of this unification, no corner of the world is excluded from advances in health, nutrition, education, and housing.
3. Satellite communication, supersonic transportation, computerized knowledge, new construction materials and energy sources, maximum utilization of food resources, and new medical products, all constitute the technical infrastructure for social development.
4. The United Nations has been transformed into a coordinating center for world organs with effective but strictly limited powers. These organs operate in the following areas.

a) *Nuclear disarmament and world arms control.* The discussions carried on by the superpowers for over fifty years ended with a disarmament accord.
b) *Outer space.* Its peaceful use is assured.
c) *World trade.* This key activity is entering a final phase of regulation.
d) *Food.* Increased food production and nutritional discoveries allow a worldwide market to continuously satisfy food demands from even the most isolated areas.
e) *Education.* New techniques have minimized illiteracy.
f) *Human rights.* The universal declaration of human rights, approved by the United Nations' General Assembly over fifty years ago, is now enforced by local tribunals; its application is guaranteed by the World Court of Human Rights.
g) *Financial assistance.* Financial resources are distributed in proportion to the populations and needs of underdeveloped countries; industrialized nations contribute 2% of their GNP.
5. World population totals about 6.3 billion, with 4.7 billion in the less developed countries of Asia, Africa, and Latin America. Continental groupings hold sway over individual states in various basic matters.
6. The world system remains stratified, and the gap between pre- and post-industrial countries has increased enormously. For example, while the GNP of underdeveloped countries (Africa, Latin America, and Asia, excluding Japan) grew from $306.7 billion in 1965 to $1.5 trillion in 2000, that of developed countries increased from $1.8 to $9.2 trillion. Average third world per capita incomes grew from $135 in 1965 to $325 in 2000, while the increase among advanced countries was from $1675 to $5775.
7. The importance of the public sector continues to grow; economic resources for large-scale industry are concentrated in activities outside the public interest. The only fields remaining open to private national sectors are those involving neither the state nor multinational industries.

8. Nuclear war is no longer a danger. Global authorities function in various spheres, and the great pressures of hunger and misery have been minimized. But world regions differ significantly in socioeconomic development and political potential, as do countries within each region. There is no war, but neither is there peace; the terrible injustices of 1968 no longer exist, but the world is still far from ideal levels of social, economic, and political justice.

III. LATIN AMERICA IN 1968

A retrospective analysis for Latin America in 1968 can be formulated on the basis of the institutions and sectors of activity proposed for the year 2000.

Latin America in a Stratified World

With international factors exerting increasing influence on national politics, considering Latin America in its global perspective can be of great value. Such analysis highlights the growing interdependence of countries, due to the modern science and technology which have drawn the world closer together.

This overall analysis differs qualitatively from the classical international focus, which regards individual states as autonomous agents. One effect of the atomic age in world politics has been to diminish the independence formerly characteristic of nation states.

In 1968, world power is concentrated in two superstates. New nations have tripled the number which originally composed the United Nations. The superstates' material wealth lies in financial, economic, scientific, and technological power—and, consequently, in military and political capacity. The stratified world of 1968—with economic, power, and prestige dimensions—displays enormous national variation in the distribution of social and economic benefits. International stratification is thus synonymous with injustice; although each nation has its own status, the quality of life in most is below acceptable standards.[3]

Two-thirds of humanity is hungry, miserable, and illiterate, lacks access to either science or technology, and is barred from greater economic returns by the unjust terms of international trade. Countries aligned with the industrial powers benefit most from these commercial relations.

Nuclear power is distributed as follows: nuclear superpowers (US, USSR); nuclear powers (England, China, France); near-nuclear powers, with access to nuclear energy (such as Sweden, Switzerland, Japan, West Germany, India, Israel, and Brazil and Argentina in Latin America); non-nuclear powers. All countries wish to define a nuclear arms policy. Agreements to denuclearize outer space, the poles, and the oceans have been negotiated primarily by the superpowers, with only limited participation from other countries. The major nations have also dominated in discussions on arms control and a general disarmament treaty. They have even offered to protect countries without atomic weapons in the event of nuclear attack.

The First Conference of Non-Nuclear Countries was held in Geneva to air views on such matters as disarmament and arms control. What was Latin America's position on nuclear arms? How many meetings were held between area Ministers of Foreign Affairs, with their scientific advisors, to define a nuclear policy which could benefit the region? Brazil became the spokesman for a so-called independent nuclear policy, supported primarily by India. Was this policy adequately discussed and analyzed in the rest of Latin America? Why were the possibilities of only two or three countries taken into account rather than those of the entire continent? Certainly the peaceful utilization of nuclear energy, as well as disarmament and nuclear arms control, were important issues for all of Latin America—as became clear in 1968.

Latin America was backwards in terms of international trade. Calculations made by the United Nations Conference on Trade and Development (UNCTAD) revealed that in 1968 the world was stratified into core and peripheral countries, with the terms of world trade benefiting industrialized countries and discriminating against developing ones. These projections indicated that exports of the developing or peripheral countries, excluding the major oil producers, would grow at 5 percent per year; this would generate a potential trade deficit of about $24 billion in 1975, of which Latin America's share would be around $8.2 billion.[4] The trade gap had been predicted and analyzed by The Economic Commission for Latin America (ECLA), by UNCTAD, and by international economists.[5]

The gap between rich and poor countries has increased steadily. In 1968 Latin America's gross national product fell between those of the industrial powers and of Africa and Asia. Latin American GNP was about $59.4 billion in 1965, while Africa's was $43.9 billion and Asia's $287.4 billion. Corresponding per-capita incomes were estimated at $357, $141, and $152, respectively.

The United Nations Conference on Trade and Development, in which members discussed ways to achieve a more equitable world trade policy, was an invaluable instrument for the underdeveloped world. The conference at Alta Gracia, Argentina, kindled hopes that Latin America would contribute significantly to redefining this policy, primarily because of the region's apparent concern for world trade, as manifested in the actions of various officials and experts.

Latin America in 1968 was incapable of effective participation in the world's scientific and technological development. Her deficiency in these fields became apparent every time an important decision had to be made—the denuclearization pact, use of outer space, satellite communication, assignment of priorities for industrial development, introduction of new production processes, and so on.[6] Neither area countries nor the continent as a whole had any significant influence in these critical decisions.

Conditions Hampering Latin American Development

The papers delivered at this congress show that Latin America is in crisis, dangerously ineffectual and incapable of organizing itself in a just, moderate, and efficient fashion. Rapid population growth is a major contributing factor. Area population is predicted to jump by 400 million in thirty years, with annual growth of over 12 million (as much as Peru's entire population in 1968). If current tendencies persist, half of Latin America's population could become "marginal" by 2000; 300 million Latin Americans would live in *barriadas, favelas,* or *callampas* (Peruvian, Brazilian, and Chilean terms for "shanty town"). Urbanization would become even more intense, while demands for jobs, education, public services, and the like would burgeon.

Under these chronic pressures, political structures would remain unstable, inefficient, and unrepresentative, and military interventions would probably be more and more frequent.

The discrepancy between population growth on one hand and productivity increases on the other would continue to retard economic development; Latin America would consequently become increasingly dependent on external powers. Weak governments would be at an increasing disadvantage confronting the ever-stronger major powers, with their concentrated financial and technological resources.

Finally, the inability of the upper and middle economic sectors to create viable models for accelerated development will stimulate serious political tensions, aggravated by larger and more concentrated urban populations.

The following conditions would persist: unintegrated countries; unstable, weak, isolated, and mutually jealous governments; twenty separate republics, each attempting to obtain meager benefits by pretentious—and dangerous—bilateral agreements with the superpowers.

This is a picture of near chaos which, hopefully, will not come about. Is this Latin America's only and inevitable alternative for 2000? If present patterns are not altered, the outlook for the future is at least as gloomy as that described. We have not even mentioned violence or the potential explosiveness of mass misery, beyond noting the perhaps unconscious violence of the powerful against the dispossessed.

We must, then, search for alternatives to allow Latin America authoritative participation in the great decisions affecting humanity's future. How can a distracted and disorganized Latin America define and defend positions on world commerce, international financing, disarmament and arms control, outer space, science and technology, human rights, and world education?

IV. AN ALTERNATIVE FOR THE TRANSITION
PERIOD [1968–2000]

Integration

Obstacles and advantages. Latin American integration must unfold within and be shaped by the larger process of world power, organization, and change. Integration could answer the challenge of our times, though there are many risks and difficulties. Dangers arise out of strong leveling tendencies, which can affect both the surface and the spirit of third world countries. Integration must allow for the expression of diverse cultural values and behaviors. Difficulties arise because sectors with vested interests resist integration, defending national sovereignties to maintain the status quo.

Continental integration will not be achieved just by resolving critical economic problems in the Latin American Common Market. World unification could alter Latin American culture and superimpose foreign currents, discordant with or contrary to our ways of life. These are the opposing forces that must be reconciled in any integration movement: the irreversible processes of world unification and the need to conserve the fundamental values of our culture.

The concept of "liberating integration" must be encouraged, rather than "dependent," "colonizing," or "satellizing" integration. Until the Latin American countries define their basic policies, in full awareness of the modern world's historical opportunities, they will neither carry influence in world power centers nor be able to participate effectively in decisions establishing the future world order.

Awareness in the modern world implies an objective and consistent understanding of the global situation and of formal organization and real structures of power. Such awareness allows assessment of the influences of international factors on national life and the possibility of defining realistic and efficient national policies.

Universalization advances relentlessly—all countries must define new policies in accord with actual possibilities, distinguishing areas in which they can initiate action from those already fixed by circumstances beyond their control.

The Latin American Common Market.   The Latin American Common Market, as envisioned by continental leaders in the meeting of Heads of American States (Punta del Este, April 1967), could be the instrument to implement continental economic action for mutual benefit, and to allow regional participation in world politics. Signs of progress on this front include the following:

1. the situation of the Latin American Free Trade Association (LAFTA) and the need to determine its future functions, including the possibility of closer ties with the Central American Common Market;
2. Interamerican Development Bank activities to promote and finance integration;
3. the new Organization of American States' (OAS) efforts to fulfill the Declaration of Hemisphere Presidents (including the United States), signed in Punta del Este in April 1967;
4. creation of the so-called Andean Group—including Venezuela, Colombia, Ecuador, Bolivia, and Chile—as a sub-regional integration project;
5. organization of the Rio de la Plata basin, a huge undertaking involving Bolivia, Paraguay, Uruguay, Argentina, and Brazil;
6. such specific projects as Peru's frontier Amazon highway and the formation of an Argentine, Bolivian, Paraguayan, Uruguayan, and Peruvian group to build a highway system and thus expedite the continent's physical integration;
7. creation of regional air transport and ocean fleets;
8. installation of a modern telecommunications system.

The dynamism of Latin American integration is thus manifest as are the areas—both public and private—in which our countries need clear ideas to establish coherent and constructive policies. But these new policies must reflect Latin America's position in the stratified international system, so that joint effort can check the region's seemingly permanent deterioration.

The Prospects for Integration.   The process of Latin American integration is at low ebb in 1968. Various governments and interest groups have voiced reservations and doubts. In a recent Buenos Aires meeting of the Interamerican Press Society, the Argentine president asserted that Latin American integration would bring chaos under present circumstances.

In the face of an economic and political process of such historical import, it is understandable that people react cautiously, and even with alarm. Some factions are acting in good faith; others, ignorant of the real nature of the process, fear the unknown; some are simply masking concern for their own interests. The progress of integration and the growth of opposition to it seem directly related. Those favoring the status quo will become more and more intransigent as the concept of "liberating integration" gathers momentum.

Latin American integration despite these temporary setbacks, is inevitable. It is neither a technocrat's caprice nor a tool of malevolent international forces. Continental integration can be our generation's answer to the challenges of the times. That is why it must conform to a model we create, inspired by our own realities and values, and employing highly efficient means to obtain new resources, enlarge our markets, and plan continental actions of worldwide impact. Only thus can we vanquish the dependency and underdevelopment which afflict all our countries.

Of course some sectors, hoping to turn integration to their own interests, would transform Latin America into a continent of consumers. But integration is an open process. Government and non-government sectors can jointly outline, orient, and establish a Latin American common market corresponding to our necessities and goals—which, of course, Latin Americans would determine for themselves.

Latin American governments have already initiated the integration process. Latin America's presidents, meeting in Punta del Este in April 1967, solemnly agreed " . . .to progressively create the Latin American Common Market over a fifteen year period, starting in 1970." They also stated: "This great undertaking will reinforce our historical ties, promote and fortify industrialization, stimulate more efficient production, and open new employment opportunities, permitting the region to assume a distinguished international role....Finally, it will strengthen the bonds of friendship between all our nations."

The presidents also decided to establish multinational transportation, telecommunications, and energy projects, and to develop international river basins and border zones to facilitate economic integration. They agreed to collaborate to increase income from foreign trade; augment agricultural and livestock production; boost education; expand national programs in science and technology; enlarge health programs; and terminate unnecessary military pacts. Finally, the presidents expressed their common desire to ban nuclear arms on the continent as quickly as possible, once treaty requirements are met.

The following undertakings, among others, attest to the growing intensity of integration: the work of the Executive Secretariats of LAFTA and the Central American Common Market; the Interamerican Development Bank's financial support, as well as investigations and courses it sponsors through the Instituto para la Integración de América Latina (INTAL); ECLA studies; the continued activities of various national organs common to almost all Latin American states; creation of the Action Committee for Latin American Integration; and finally, on a more modest scale, a preliminary draft project for installing the Latin American Economic Community, presented to the Latin American Parliament by FLACSO's Latin American School of Political Science and Public Administration.

CONCLUSION

The world order described in the first part of this article is based on an extrapolation of the current situation and of tendencies which appear harbingers of the future. However, the subsequent diagnosis and prognosis of Latin America's situation are in total disagreement with the first section. Why is this so? Are we seeking to relate two qualitatively different tendencies, one global and positive, the other regional and negative? Are not some global tendencies also negative and dangerous? Or is Latin America so poor and miserable as to have no future?

First, more rigorous selection and analysis of variables would be necessary to permit consideration of different alternatives; we were forced to work with only one possibility. Time limitations precluded analysis of alternatives like thermonuclear war, worldwide federation, division between the superpowers, and so on. But our prediction for Latin America would remain the same in other cases.

This merits emphasis: *If* current tendencies continue, Latin America's future, our future as individuals, will run all the risks mentioned, and we will suffer the consequences of our inability to organize more effectively. Our prediction is not, however, inevitable or fatalistic. Even now, Latin American leaders in all fields are seeking new directions for the future.

I have chosen to propose and analyze only one of many possible paths, that of continental integration. If it can unfold as we have described—and as this generation is already beginning to accomplish—we will witness a truly historic gesture. It will be the second phase of our fight for independence, begun at the dawn of the last century; it will be a crucial step in the struggle for development and effective participation in the world of the future.

NOTES

1. See *Étapes de la Prospective*. Bibliothèque de Prospective. (Paris: Presses Universitaires de France, 1967).
2. Herman Kahn and Anthony J. Wiener, *The Year 2000* (New York: The Macmillan Company, 1967), pp. 5, 65.
3. See *International Stratification and Underdeveloped Countries* (Chapel Hill, N.C.: The University of North Carolina Press, 1963), p. 10.
4. See the report of the General Secretary of UNCTAD, *Toward a Global Strategy of Development* (New York: United Nations, 1968). Doc. #TD/3/Rev. 1, p. 15.
5. Louis J. Zimmerman, *Poor Lands, Rich Lands; The Widening Gap.* (New York: Random House, 1965).
6. See the study on Latin American scientific and technological policies prepared by Jorge Sábato and Natalio Botana and presented at the Bellagio (Italy) meeting held under the auspices of the World Law Fund in September, 1968, to consider "Models of World Order," by the directors of the Latin American Group, Horacio Godoy and Gustavo Lagos. The study was published in *La Revista de la Integración* No. 3 (Nov. 1968).

2. LATIN AMERICA IN THE WORLD IN THE YEAR 2000

KALMAN H. SILVERT
Department of Political Science, New York University

The weakness of history is that it has no future. And the trouble with the future is that we do not know what its history will be. Sending the mind into the future is consequently a chancy business, but the only way of getting there short of clairvoyance or patient survival.

Rational projections into the future should not be leaps to a single predictive point, but rather attempts to paint differing historical situations within which probabilistic ranges of social events can occur. Even with this limitation, simulations must be created within systems of constraints; the soothsayer must decide what range of change he is willing to allow for. For example, there are those scientists who argue that the history of the future may well be lived and created by humanoids biologically different from contemporary humans. They do not mean merely the biological "manufacture" of supermen, but rather the use of genetic control to change the very mechanics of our physiological construction. If future men have eyes that enable them to see in a 360° arc, one might expect intellectual reflections of such perceptual difference. Other scholars maintain that as we learn more of "biological imperatives" such as "territoriality," we can decide to what extent the nobility of the savage can be promoted, to what extent a search for social peace may be hopeless, and perhaps even how to engineer "instinct" out of our systems if we deem it ethically desirable to do so. I intend to avoid arcane discussions of this nature. Instead, we shall hold constant man's physiological and instinctual apparatus, assuming that no scientific control over them will have significant social effect before the end of this century. Much more important to this paper, I shall also assume that the available choices of the forms and justifications of human organization will not be increased. That is, no totally new kinds of societies will emerge, and no completely new ideologies will be generated. I do not mean that ideas and procedures and systems will not change, but rather that those changes will be variations on existing themes. Socialism, capitalism, communitarianism, and other such code names for mixed economic systems will still be with us. Democracy, communism, falangism, fascism, and caudillismo will remain possible political forms. Social class will not go away. Special interests will continue to press their cases. Ethnic diversity and class distinctions will continue to perturb the integration of national communities. And national communities will continue to have difficulty reconciling internal and international interests. The freshness and uniqueness of coming situations will arise from the interactions of these elements, not from entirely new elements. The implications of this construction, then, are that this paper must deal with innovation through an examination of possible syntheses, and not through presuming great change in the building blocks of political thought and action.

The most easily measured changes in society are likely to come in the related areas of technological innovation brought to bear on economics and communications. Automation and the automatic factory are certain to continue their advances. The variety, speed, and social penetration of communications systems will continue to increase, but the content of communications and their significance in social organization and idea-systems are variables that do not depend directly on the mere existence of the systems. To recognize economics and communications as two areas of almost certain crucial technological change does not imply that we must accept a set of ineluctable qualitative consequences as inevitable products of those material changes.

The introduction to this paper would remain incomplete were I to neglect a statement of my approach to the study of societies. The preceding emphasis on the necessity of synthesis as well as analysis, and the suggestion that material change varies somewhat independently of qualitative consequences, imply a multivariate approach—a denial of lineal and deterministic theories. I presume that the explanation of social change can be covered reasonably well by indicating the conditions necessary for any given occurrence, and adding the sufficiency through examining their interrelations. In macro-social analysis, for example, one should know the power of the actors in any given circumstance, their normative systems, their relation to the institutional structures of society, and the idiosyncratic factors of personality. Proper analysis is not attained by holding three of these elements stable, and varying one. Rather, it is their simultaneous variance, measured by the differing patterns into which historically they fall and potentially can fall, that permits the perception of the necessary as well as sufficient conditions leading to social happenings.

I do not mean to say that those four elements are the only ones, or that they could not be expressed in much greater detail. I am suggesting, however, that as one cannot think of data without theory, one also should not think of analysis without synthesis, of necessity without sufficiency, or of causation as other than a statement of probabilities of the play of elements *within* complex independent and dependent variables, as well as between independent and dependent variables.

Another element in my personal view is that I see politics as the study of the distribution and uses of public power. Naturally, the creation of power is related to social class, the uses of it to normative systems, and the channels of its application to institutional orders—all affected by the personal idiosyncracies of the actors involved in their differing positions. The particular study of international relations may at first blush appear simpler than intra-system studies, for international affairs *par excellence* reflect the facts of power relatively unsullied by other considerations. Scholars in the field have long sought to relate internal to external matters, giving rise to such well-known schools of thought as geopolitics, present attempts to see the world as the scene of international class conflict, and such racist arguments as those of Gobineau or the exponents of a softer "white man's burden" argument. I shall attempt to relate the expression of power internationally to the patterns of generation and maintenance of internal power through an analysis of the prime variables I have already mentioned.

It has often been said that to know what groups or individuals will do in the future, the most relevant data are what they have done in the past. The control one must put on such a construction is to remember that there is no logical necessity that what has happened before must somehow happen again. The fact that the sun rose yesterday is not proof in itself that it will rise tomorrow. The point of looking at the past for clues is thus not to predict a recurrence of events, but rather of their patterning, of how they have taken place as a clue to asking how future probabilities will unfurl themselves. We will not attempt to predict the sun's rising in itself, but rather the array of circumstances that (all other things being equal) will bring with it yet another dawn.

I shall now turn to an analysis of United States–Latin American relations in the past, as a test of the analytical model I shall later attempt to employ in discussing the array of future possibilities. This procedure will make explicit my presumptions, and permit the reader more ably to defend himself against the projective portion of this paper.

**HEMISPHERIC INTERNATIONAL RELATIONS:
A HISTORICAL ANALYSIS**

Let us consider first the power the United States has exercised over Latin America, and then the Latin American side of the influence balance. North American power is not a constant, of course. It has varied with time and place, and the places have varied through time. Let us not tarry for any description of the emergence of the United States from its colonial period through the critical period of the Civil War to its present position as a dominant world power. We all know that this growth has been quite constant and particularly so since the onset of the second industrial revolution after the Civil War. We also are all aware of the shifting world power patterns that have affected the relative standing of the United States in the global scene. Two axioms of American power in the hemisphere are obvious: first, United States influence has increased steadily through time; and second, the influence has spread further and further down the South American continent through time. Less obvious is the probability that the nature of the influence has changed. During the Latin American Independence Period, United States power was felt largely in ideology and law. As has so often been noted, many early Latin American constitutions were modelled on the American document; even in statutory law, such as Guatemala's Livingston code, such appropriate models as the Louisiana Civil Code were adapted to the needs of the new Latin nations. Ideologies of libertarianism, republicanism, and nationhood drew on French and American precepts, while they in their turn relied heavily upon English doctrine. But American political and economic penetration was relatively small and was concerned principally with neighboring states such as Mexico and Cuba, from the earliest days objects of attraction to North American expansionist notions of Manifest Destiny. Within half a century of the establishment of the United States, Mexico felt the use of overt power. But as late as the Second World War, the United States still drew its defense perimeter only through the bulge of Brazil.

Through time both the pace and the extent of United States involvement in Latin America have increased. For example, prior to World War II Great Britain, Germany, and Japan outstripped the United States as Latin trading partners. For a generation after the war, however, the United States held an almost monopolistic position in Latin American trade. Now, even though the classical partners have reappeared, the United States still holds hemispheric preeminence. But these trade patterns have always been unequally distributed. Major American investments were long concentrated in Cuba and Venezuela; the latter still represents the major single cluster of American economic investment. From the Latin American point of view, of course, even small foreign investments in such countries as the Central American republics may have contributed importantly to political events in those countries. From the North American point of view, however, the unevenness of investment has not been directly reflected in politics. The evidence appears to be that the political interest has washed slowly and relatively evenly down through the Caribbean to the northern tier states of South America, and now embraces the entire hemisphere.

To these variables of time, place, and economic and political influences, let us add two integrating concepts: types of United States influence, and the groups within the Latin American countries reacting to those influences.

Types of United States Influence

Direct Intervention. The most obvious and public influence is direct intervention—military or paramilitary. The cases are many: Haiti, Nicaragua, Panama, Honduras, Mexico, the Dominican Republic, Guatemala, Cuba, and certainly many others known, suspected, or unknown. Overt military occupations have more often than not ended in the establishment of a "safe" dictator with some military or police training (Trujillo, Somoza) and eventual withdrawal of the overt investment. Then long periods of despotic rule of a traditional type have usually followed. It is impossible to know whether the development of such countries as Honduras, the Dominican Republic, or Nicaragua would have been substantially different without this kind of intervention. But Panama and Guatemala certainly have been fundamentally affected, the former in its very existence, and the latter in its present decay into a decade of violence directly related to American assistance in the overthrow of the Arbenz regime in 1954. In line with what I have said above about unevenness, however, it should be added that this kind of action is sporadic and even to a certain extent casual. The 1965 intervention in the Dominican Republic, for example, was "accidental" in the sense that the particular United States leaders involved took an action that was "inevitable" for them, but that would probably seem remote for other leaders. Thus, direct intervention is the influence most susceptible to variability.

The extension of national interest policies. The second level of effect may be said to be the reflection of the long-term national interests of the United States as defined through explicit or implicit policy statements. These views tend to build whatever stability there is into the hemispheric policy of the United States. The best known example is the Monroe Doctrine. Although its meaning and effectiveness have changed over time, the Doctrine's basic sense is that the United States has a special interest in and responsibility for Latin America. This particularity of concern is not necessarily to the exclusion of that of other states, but is considered to override other nations' interests in times of stress. Another example—of implicit policy this time—stems from North American beliefs in a modified capitalistic market system. When translated into the private ownership (but not capitalistic market system) of most of Latin America, American private enterprise tends to social Darwinism. Business operating in an ambience without effective political and social constraint, and equipped with a high capacity to compete, can degenerate into rapacity. The common result is that United States business is looked upon with great suspicion by many Latin Americans simply because of its power relative to that of local institutions and groups. (This statement can be modified by type of enterprise; there is an important difference between reactions to public monopoly and extractive industries, on one hand, and to light industrial and commercial activities on the other.) The United States commitment to a particular type of economic organization defined as "correct" also exemplifies a kind of moralism in our international stance that may be highly offensive to other nations, whether led by conservatives or liberals. Thus, when the United States cuts off foreign aid to Argentina and Peru (the latter is presently under an interdict) because those governments threaten to cancel oil contracts or to engage in other disapproved economic activity, a strong conflict of values is involved. For the United States, the motivations stem from conviction of the correctness of given economic beliefs, the sanctity of contract and private property, and surety in the virtuous use of power. Many Latin Americans see such action as violations of their sovereignty in its most profound sense—that is, as sovereignty somehow reflects the being and becoming of a people.

National interest, thus, should not be seen as a mere military or defensive question. It is that, as well as a desire to see others live in accord with whatever world-view a people may have—by one's values, with one's institutional referents, and one's ways of conducting affairs. Clearly this latter view has been denied by some United States leaders; but it has also been expressed in deed as well as word. It is the rare culture that can prevent itself from seeing others in its own image. Given the facts of international power, few nations have not attempted to impose certain elements of their own image on others when able to do so. And yet, American public demonstrations against the Philippine campaign of Theodore Roosevelt, the nonintervention policies of Franklin D. Roosevelt, and the succeeding years of Good Neighborism and the Alliance for Progress have all reflected a counter-desire—the containment of this aspect of American power. This dialectic reflects domestically what have in truth been major differences in the United States approach to Latin America.

"Americanization": the diffusion of a dominant culture. The third level of influence is the most pervasive, and the least susceptible to control by anyone. It is the cultural influence of a nation that is powerful intellectually and technologically as well as militarily and economically. The most common examples of this weighty influence are linguistic: the "new" Spanish of *parquear, troque, breque, estok, estandard,* and so on—for *park, truck, brake, stock,* and *standard,* as in "standard of living." Much is also made of movies and television as contributors to the "revolution of rising expectations," or what may better be called the "bedazzlement effect" leading to social paralysis at least as often as to action. In any event, the influence is much broader than even these types of examples might indicate. Faulkner, Hemingway, and others have contributed much to a generation of Latin American novelists. The social science explosion of Latin America is a direct exportation of American theories, models, and techniques, and with them goes much ideology. The training in the United States of Latin American military officers, for example, is specifically designed to implant North American ideas of proper civil—military relations.

It is in this area that one must search for some explanation of the widespread grief felt in Latin America on the deaths of Presidents Roosevelt and Kennedy. The joke references may be illuminating. There is the hackneyed one, that when the United States catches cold Latin American contracts pneumonia. Or, that Latin Americans are vitally interested in the present American campaign because they want to know who their next president will be. What I think is being expressed is that the very posture, the "psychic" stance if you will, of the United States has an immediate effect on the choices made in many Latin American polities. For example, the Dominican intervention, when linked to Vietnam and certain military policies undertaken in Latin America, as well as to the general tone of the Johnson administration, persuaded many Latin Americans that the United States welcomes right-wing military movements. President Ongania of Argentina was reportedly bitterly disappointed that the United States did not welcome him as warmly as it did his Brazilian prototypes. They, earlier, had overthrown President Goulart to the apparent satisfaction of the United States. The result of this projection was that the Argentine and Brazilian armies mobilized during the Dominican crisis to intervene in Uruguay and Bolivia in the event the governments of those countries threatened to go leftist. Not all Latin countries react with this sensitivity, however. In general, it may be said that those in which the internal political forces are delicately balanced try to read into American policy the factor that will send the balance in one direction or another. This kind of anticipation is of long standing in Latin America, stemming from the last century, and will be discussed more fully below.

Some other recent examples of attempts to anticipate American favor may help to illustrate this point. In late 1947 in anticipation of United States approval and assistance, President Gonzalez Videla of Chile broke the Popular Front that had governed the country since 1938. (The approval was forthcoming, but not much assistance.) It is possible that the Castello Branco revolt in Brazil would not have occurred when it did had not President Kennedy been assassinated, an act leading in the first week of Mr. Johnson's presidency to the firing of Teodoro Moscoso and thus an indicated change in United States governmental attitudes toward revolts in Latin America. Center and center–left presidents (such as Raul Leoni of Venezuela and Eduardo

Frei of Chile) complain that they know the United States supports them, but they also fear that if overthrown by a military coup, the United States would also support the new military rulers. Their complaint is that adventurist military men are as certain as they of this American stance, and therefore emboldened in their ambitions.

These attitudes of Latin Americans are guesses. Sometimes they reflect real United States policy decisions that must be put in the first of the three categories in this list. But at least as often as not, the hunches are derived from feelings concerning whether the United States is in a period of liberalism and international confidence, or in a period of international insecurity suggesting the wisdom of "safe" governments of force in Latin America.

When cultural style and political choice thus interact, conscious choice becomes difficult. Some of the less recognized but still important defeats for United States policy in Latin America come from a disjunction between verbal expressions of desire and Latin American perceptions of basic United States posture. Thus, United States diplomatic pressure against recent military coups in Argentina and Peru, among other countries, were unavailing. The coups came, and indeed the combination of security considerations and the attitudes of United States policymakers supported the presumptions of the Latin Americans: their coups were recognized and normal relations quickly established. There have also been moves in the opposite directions. The Good Neighbor Policy and the Kennedy period of the Alliance for Progress strengthened Social Democratic and Christian Democratic elements in Latin American politics. These shifts in United States political posture, contained as they are within the standard range of our own political events, thus provoke wide swings in Latin American government and help to institutionalize political instability there.

LATIN AMERICAN INTERNAL POLITICS AND LATIN FOREIGN RELATIONS

A standard sociological way of stratifying Latin American populations is as follows: 1. the Indian populations, outside the stream of national politics entirely; 2. mestizo rural villagers, on the fringes of national consciousness and culture; 3. recent lower class migrants to the cities; 4. urban industrial lower classes; 5. middle class groups; and 6. upper class groups. A social psychological dimension is then normally added to these caste–class differentiations. The rural villagers and recent migrants are usually classified as "mobilized" but "unintegrated," meaning that they have lost their "folk" culture, but have not as yet taken on the routinized behavior patterns and identifications of a citizen integrated into the national society. The artisan and unionized lowers, the middles, and the uppers are then normally divided into "traditionals" and "moderns." The definitions vary, but I will give what I employ:

A *traditional person* is ritualistic in his reasons for behavior; he views his behavior as universal in effect, or "organic," as having an effect on all else and as being imbued with moral significance; he is resistant to change, for the existing order has moral sanction by definition.

A *modern* person is rationalistic in his reasons for deciding on action; he is relativistic in that he assumes his behavior has limited influence, in recognition of institutional and role differentiation; he is anticipatorily self-adjusting to change.

To the class and value breakdowns above may be added groupings of Latin Americans by institutional affiliations relevant to international politics, such as parties, pressure groups, interest associations, and so on. Now, if we combine these three elements, we can say something about the effectiveness (the power or class factor), the uses of that power (the value factor), and the customary behavior and institutions that add the style component to public behavior, as well as providing the organized means for its expression. Let me simplify what would otherwise be a long and arduous typology by presenting a composite of political party arrays to show how to think of the three elements simultaneously.

Fascists	Falangists	Corporativists		Conservatives

TRADITIONAL SCALE

Left   Right

Fidelistas	Trotskyites	Communists	Socialists	Christian Democrats	Radicals	Liberals

MODERN SCALE

The leadership of all these parties is upper middle and upper class in status, although the social origins of the leaders often reveal a high degree of upward mobility. The leftist groups are strongly influenced by leaders of urban origins; on the right, the Liberals are also urban. Conservatives, Radicals, and Christian Democrats count important contingents of rural influentials among their leaders. The followers scatter widely: Conservatives rally some rural labor to their banner; Liberals attract lower middle class entrepreneurs and some artisans in search of "stable and honest govenment"; the Radicals, Socialists and Christian Democrats appeal strongly to middle class groups, as do the Socialists; the Communists, Fidelistas, and Trotskyites are basically middle class parties with some trade union support; the leftist corporativist parties are the most populist of all the parties, appealing to limited middle sectors and to broad parts of the recent migrants to the cities, and semiskilled and unskilled labor. (*Peronismo* is an example.)

The ideological attitudes of these groups toward the United States are as follows: All groups on the traditional scale are culturally rejective of the United States, but support anticommunism and the Cold War. Thus, a minister of corporate leanings could say, "We reject that Liberal capitalism that leads to atheistic communism." The point is, of course, that to the eye of a counter-reformation man, the Soviet Union and the United States must look more alike than different. Thus we find rejections of capitalism, Protestantism, and Communism in the same breath. Nevertheless, such groups generally support United States foreign policy as they define it, and seek alliance with counterpart groups within the United States.

The Christian Democrats share many of the corporativist views of the Conservatives (from whose midst they sprang), but reject present United States foreign policy, support a progressive Alliance for Progress view, and in their turn also seek to make common cause with such elements as Kennedy Democrats, for whom they feel a special affinity.

The Liberals—much like Taft Republicans—support United States foreign policy as evidenced in its Cold War stance, applaud American industrial culture, and resist competitive American industry and business. These groups, usually strongest among industrialists, often oppose such specific United States policies as inflation control, for they see high but not runaway rates of inflation as permitting hidden profit-taking, and thus conducive to economic development. Liberals share many points of view with Radicals of the right, and in general the Radical parties even of the left spread between the types of pro–United States views of the Liberals and of the Christian Democrats.

The democratic Socialists are profound admirers of United States culture and resist the specifics of US foreign policy. The Marxist left sees the United States as inevitably imperialist and thus as an ineluctable political enemy. But they too may sometimes admire what they see as the cultural and technological victories of United States capitalism and seek a partial emulation. The greatest single difference between Christian Democrats, social democrats in general, and democratic Socialists on the one hand, and the Marxist left on the other, is the way they view the susceptibility of the United States to pressure and change. They all see the United States as imperialistic. But the former think imperialism is a policy and not a necessity, and the Marxists think it culturally determined and unsusceptible to change without social revolution in the United States. In practical terms, then, the former seek alliance with the United States government, and with sympathetic pressure groups inside the country, while the latter espouse nationalistic revolution in their own countries as their only genuine defense.

Nationalism is then linked to attitudes toward the United States in ways much more subtle than the workings of simple xenophobia. The Conservatives are anti-national, in the sense that they reject the supremacy of a secular nation state. This view is shared by the left traditionals, but the Conservatives substitute a nationalism of the right, a clericalist and xenophobic attempt to return to an idealized medieval state. The modern groups all accept the idea of the secular supremacy of a nation state, reject right-wing nationalism, and then divide on the imperialism question, as I have indicated.

These attitudes when run against power as class expression and power as institutionally specific comprise the minimum paradigm necessary to understand the internal roots of Latin American foreign policy. There is no time to spell out the full range of relations here, but the description of a few polar cases may help suggest the limits. In terms of class power, we have at one end a country like Guatemala, of whose 4 million population perhaps 350,000 form the entire core of what can be called national, participant citizenry—the civil service, the army, the professionals, the white collar employees, and so forth. The remainder of the population is Indian, illiterate, rural, below fourteen years of age, and so on. At the other end, we have Argentina, where perhaps 45 percent of the population is in middle income and occupation groups, two-thirds are urbanized, 90 percent are literate, and so forth. Over half the total population votes in national elections. Naturally, Guatemalan leaders can have few followers, but Argentine leaders have large committed or "available" masses (to use Aron's expression) as followers. In a real sense, then, Guatemalan leaders have license to choose widely among ideologies, but little power to recruit mass defenders. The opposite would seem to be empirically true of the Argentines in situations short of total crisis, when populations may be forced back to their basic social premises.

When these class groups are related to value systems, it becomes apparent that the patterns of conflict are not alone *across* class lines, but probably more importantly *within* them. That is, intraclass conflict as engendered by differing perceptions and thus differing definitions of group interest describes the major lines of political division. Thus, upper class groups fight upper class groups as well as other interest levels. It is in order to explain this phenomenon that one is forced to discuss class and values simultaneously. And then, of course, there should be added the experience of organization, the technology of politics, if you will. This ingredient is the institutional dimension of which we have been speaking. Again, space precludes detail, but in general the Radical parties and the Marxist left are the most professionally organized and impersonal groups. The traditional left corporativists tend to be conspiratorial and badly organized, while the Liberals and Conservatives have small, organized pressure groups but generally scorn stable and extended party organization.

What this complex picture implies for interAmerican policy is that no Latin American country has sufficient intraclass and inter-class cohesion to have the politics of a true nation-state. Nor does any one of them have a strong institutional structure that can subsume class and value conflicts. (The only possible exception to these two generalizations is Cuba, which for good or ill may be Latin America's first nation-state in the social sense of that term.) Thus, opposition to the United States remains largely at the verbal level, and the temptation to employ the United States as a force in internal political decision looms large in all countries. To be more explicit, Latin America's weak governments reflecting inter-nal schism make it possible for political groups to impute desires and attitudes to the United States that can be used to tip the balance of internal politics one way or another. It is through this mechanism that the cultural stance of the United States, men-tioned above as the most basic influence on Latin America, is incorporated into their internal power constellations. This artic-ulation of United States and Latin relations is what makes the post of United States ambassador such a critical and delicate and diffi-cult one in many Latin American countries.

The stigmata of schismatic politics are not spread equally among the Latin American republics, of course. Ideological identifications do tend to bleed across frontiers, naturally, but in ways tending merely to reinforce the general "feeling tone" of the continent as it is in the first place related to more general inter-American pressures. For example, at this moment the major Latin American countries are being ruled by relatively softly authori-tarian governments: the military, quasi-falangist regimes of Argentina and Brazil, and the single-party system of Mexico. There are small islands of Christian and Social Democracy (Chile, Venezuela, Costa Rica), and the remainder are rather traditional Latin American authoritarianisms of combined civil-military stripe. The democratic regimes worry that they will be infiltrated by the authoritarian ones, and the latter worry that the former are islands of Communist penetration. But little occurs other than verbal hostility, an occasional attempt to propagandize. There are a few cases of overt action, however: the attempt of Trujillo to assassinate Betancourt, the successful assassination of Trujillo with its international overtones, tension between the late President Somoza of Nicaragua and President Figueres of Costa Rica, the rumors of mobilization of the Argentine army on the Chilean frontier on the occasion of the last polarized presidential election in Chile, and so on. Nevertheless, these incidents are relatively rare, I repeat, and are not often taken into routine consideration in Latin American policymaking.

The verbal interplay of Latin American international politics naturally reflects the class facts of leadership and their ideological commitments. Formal and informal organization are both functions of these factors. For example, the Economic Commission for Latin America reflects a reformist, industrially-oriented, Keynesian approach to economic development. It has been a major factor in promoting the InterAmerican Development Bank (of similar ideological persuasion) and the Latin American integration movement. The latter, with headquarters in Buenos Aires, is consciously attempting to link Liberal industrialists, Radical politicians, and cooperative trade union leaders, among others, to the end of building a Latin American common market that can also eventually become a political union. The ultimate aim is to generate sufficient power so that Latin America can confront the United States not in enmity, but as equal partner, á la the Western European powers. The Organization of American States, on the contrary, has been widely seen as reflecting Latin American surrender to United States suzerainty in the hemisphere. Whether the OAS is entering on a new period of growth remains to be seen.

The Central American customs union and LAFTA are still entirely economic entities. In my opinion there is little chance for either to proceed in the near future to full common market status, let alone to any semblance of political union. It is not merely that vested economic interest in Latin America's growing industrial sectors is already far enough advanced to make economic collaboration difficult, but also that there is little experience in intra-Latin diplomatic collaboration except for the most formal variety in the United Nations, ECLA, and OAS. The critical task facing Latin America, however, is not the extension of markets by lateral international expansion, but vertically, by intranational social growth. The integration of Latin America is no substitute for the internal integration of the Latin American republics.

IMPLICATIONS OF THE LATIN AMERICAN SITUATION FOR AMERICAN FOREIGN POLICY

The politics of crisis has also come to the United States. As in Latin America, the United States is now witness to clashes among differing world views and differing social strata, interinstitutional conflicts, and resulting personality struggles. More subtly, Latin American styles and heroes have also become part of the United States political scene. The hirsute fad may well have begun with Fidel Castro, and the cult of Che is widespread among United States and European youth. Columbia University student leaders are informing themselves concerning the Latin American university reform of 1918. Black Power advocates find fraternal echoes in Havana as well as Algiers. The persistence of riot scenes in United States cities is rare even for Latin America, but it is creating the same kind of discussions about the tension between order and freedom. Among right and left groups, as a matter of fact, the terms of ideological discourse have become disturbingly Latin American—as they must, for elements of the crisis must be the same whenever the total system is put into question.

The parallels must obviously not be taken too far, for great gulfs still exist between a national society such as the United States, and most of Latin America except for the more developed urban regions. What true resemblances exist, however, are very relevant to United States foreign policy: they can assist us to an understanding of how foreign policy is linked to the *nature* of national community in its fullest sense, and they can also help us to find answers if we are willing to admit the relevance of at least some of the experiences of others. But whether we consciously will an awareness of the resemblances between some Latin American and some North American happenings, the nature of the modern world seems to be that certain groups in the United States, of both right and left, will in any event draw such parallels for themselves. The "new left" is an obvious example of the self-identification of international communities. The growth of the international corporation, the existence of hemispheric interest groups already referred to, and the effects of international, diplomatic, trade union, business, military, and other ties must all nave their impact on hemispheric policy. Benefits may well flow from a disciplined and intellectually controlled use of these many channels of access as well as communication.

And now, at a more prosaic level, let us turn to the more obvious policy effects of Latin American events. The usual assumption is that Latin America is, with Africa, the politically and militarily weakest of all major world areas. Certainly events in the Far East and Europe must have more effect on United States power than can Latin America in the foreseeable future. Nevertheless, it was the Cuban missile crisis that probably brought the Cold War closest to a warm conclusion. The reason, of course, has to do not only with Cuba, but also with the perceptions of the antagonistic powers involved, and the uses to which each wished to put the island. The United States has always reacted most sharply when the internal politics of any Latin country threaten to become entangled with Cold War considerations. And yet, it should be noted that the ultimate definition of such involvement rests much less with the Latin country than with the decisions of the United States—and of Soviet Russia, in the case of Cuba.

PROBABILITIES

In beginning the projective part of this paper, it will be useful to set the limits of probabilities by examining the indisputably marginal cases—those at each end that define absolute limits. Each of these polar cases in truth voids the possibility of effective international action. They are:

a) *Armageddon, the Wagnerian solution.* Nuclear warfare that destroys civilization would render the year 2000 moot.

b) *Frozen balance-of-power, the Orwellian solution.* The famous projection, *1984*, posited the division of the world into three great power blocs, each under the leadership of a central power—the United States, Soviet Russia, and China. All other states were divided as satellite dependencies of one of the three, with internal politics rigidly hierarchized and controlled, warfare ritualized and perhaps even the figment of manufactured news, and "international" relations reduced to playing out the formal rules of a charade.

In this strange world of ours one should be wary of labelling any alternative as impossible. But certainly these two pure situations are unlikely. The first presumes a suicidal lunacy on the part of the leaders of the nuclear powers. The second assumes the utter powerlessness of Western Europe, the impotence of the third world, and a failure of such internal dynamics as can be seen everywhere, but which are especially evident in the internal turmoil of the Eastern bloc. The Orwellian view also implies a desolate view of "human nature," denying the meaning of a possibly very long-range trend toward greater human rationality and social decency.

The more likely social solutions are in the realm of mixed siutations in which "greater" and "lesser" are more appropriate adjectives than "hellish" or "heavenly." Nevertheless, of course, some social conditions that may be acceptable or even positively rewarding for some can be devastating for others. Even in Nazi Germany, as close to hell as we have recently come, millions of good burghers pursued their ways in relative placidity, and the sounds of genocide did not stop citizens of Warsaw from parading in their Sunday finery on their way to worship. It is erroneous to examine mixed situations by thinking in terms of averages, and thus washing out the absolute misery they may cause in given social groups. Even though I have no time for such refinement of speculation in this paper, the reader should be urged to keep in mind differences in human benefit and deprivation inherent in the facts of stratification by race and class.

The dimensions of change that, as a minimum simplification, need to be taken into account in describing the limits of mixed situations are as follows: changes in the relations of the major and the secondary powers, changes within the major and secondary powers, changes of international relations among the Latin American countries, and changes within each Latin American country.

These elements are a crystallization and a justification of the previous sample discussion on the history of interAmerican relations. That section of this paper attempted to sketch the interacting effects on hemispheric relations of changes within the United States and within the several Latin American societies, and the manner in which international influence reflects momentary, long-range, and cultural factors. I presume a continuance of internal change within a definable limits, a continuation of the three levels of international interaction, and continuing pressure toward changing power balances by shifting alliance and integration patterns. That leaves for discussion the sets of internal changes in economic and demographic factors in Latin American societies that I presume to be likely, and the ethical judgment of alternative possible directions of change.

Changes in Economic and Demographic Factors

Latin America. I assume the following to be likely trends:

1. The rate of population increase will continue to be high for most of the remainder of this century, but tapering off in the more developed urban areas, as is already evident in Buenos Aires, Montevideo, and elsewhere. I do not assume that population pressure will become so acute as to be a cause for political action in itself.
2. Urban clusters will increase in size and in numbers, and percentages living on the farms will decrease. But absolute numbers will go up both on the farm and in the cities.
3. Sophisticated technology will increasingly be imported into Latin America, and industrial and service economic sectors will continue to grow absolutely and to absorb increasing percentages of the employed population.
4. Rates of literacy will climb, and especially sharply in the newly industrialized countries, such as Venezuela. In addition, access to higher education will grow even more steeply than it has in the past five years, especially with an increase in secondary school attendance.

A sharp implication of these points is that we should turn our attention to absolute numbers, instead of being mesmerized by percentages that blur objective achievements by per capita rates. The striking physical changes of the past forty years in Latin America are likely to continue. So is the increase in the absolute numbers of educated and economically reasonably well-off urban persons. These absolute changes will work relative changes in the realm of political organization, making possible alternatives only weakly felt at this moment. These demographic and economic changes, however, do not bring in their wake any one necessary kind of political change. Industrial urbanization and a literate population are equally compatible, in the relatively short run between 1968 and 2000, with totalitarian or with libertarian public systems. The same theoretical independence of socioeconomic from political factors must also pertain for the world powers.

The major powers.   We may expect the following in the United States, Western Europe, and its cultural counterparts (Canada, Australia, New Zealand, and so on), and to a more limited extent in Soviet Russia:

1. The ecological facts of urbanization will be qualitatively modified by technological advance in industry, agriculture, and communications. Those countries will be able to become nation-city-states. That is, national and urban lifestyles will permeate all regions of the countries, and make it possible to follow a modern way of life inside or outside of cities. No groups, whether ethnically or socially defined, will remain outside the polities: pariah groups and "underclasses" will not exist as such, although certain self-selected marginal groups and individuals may be ostracized for reasons of social style. Truly national societies will exist, in which all groups have some access to or some role to play in all institutions.
2. Economic factors will increasingly be seen as secondary to social and political decisionmaking. The harder facts of ideology, culture, taste, and style will become increasingly important in determining the course of national political affairs. I do not mean that class structures will not exist, or that more privileged groups will not coexist with less privileged ones. I am saying only that economic factors will come to be seen as only instrumental to other considerations in determining the value and purpose of life.

Japan will probably follow the same paths as the European countries. China and India will have continued their economic development, although the former will probably be more successful than the latter in achieving high rates of economic growth, still assuming no intervening major armed conflicts. Because these countries come late to industrialization, but also because both have for long had major urban concentrations, one should expect that their economic progress will take advantage of their late appearance by the employment of highly advanced production techniques and the organizational tools of modern team science. China will certainly continue to employ labor-extensive devices for quite some time, but such a procedure for the generation and employment of capital is not incompatible with a selection of other appropriate and highly advanced techniques of production.

Whatever the tone of the political orders that accompany these probable socioeconomic changes, the almost certain consequence is that the primary and secondary powers will be stronger than ever not only in terms of arms, but also with respect to their ability to mobilize major masses of citizenry and to count on their loyalty through periods of armed international crisis. Whether this power is based on freely extended legitimacy, or on coercion made exquisite through the employment of sophisticated control devices, effective "massification" of society will permit high levels of social mobilization.

Another consequence of technological sophistication and mass mobilization is that the administrative comity of centralization and decentralization will become apparent. That is, old arguments over the desirability of centralized as opposed to locally based administrations will be as passé as the arguments over whether city or country life is more desirable. In synthesis, then, we may expect more powerful political units buttressed by complexly interwoven local and national administrations, the conversion of economics into an institution clearly dependent on choices made on political and social bases, and the consequent emergence of an array of ideological and socially stylistic choices that can be more firmly defined for more people throughout society than ever before.

The international scene. Reflections of the greater specialization and social synthesis that will be apparent at the domestic
level are to be expected. That is, two essential directions are
possible:

1. The international community may be an interacting group of
    highly autonomous national units, their viability made ever
    more apparent by the self-sufficiency stemming from their
    strenthened national cohesion and the conquest of some of
    the problems of economic scarcity. Nations may choose to
    sacrifice the cultural and economic gains possible through
    rational international arrangements in order to gain security
    through autarchy and isolation, formalized by international
    agreement. This alternative is not impossible, especially if
    the proliferation of ultimate weaponry provides every major
    nation with the weapons of absolute offense. In a way, the
    Cold War was prevented from erupting by this kind of self-
    imposed isolation, in which the two major antagonists tacitly
    agreed to respect a geographical division of the world, to
    limit the spread of their atomic arsenals, to talk before
    shooting, and to avoid the physical confrontation of their
    armed forces everywhere except in Berlin.
2. The international community may be the scene of syntheses
    of loyalty beyond the nation state. As local and national
    interests are now becoming compatible, national and inter-
    national interests may also be put in a mutually reinforcing
    order. The specialized agencies of the United Nations and
    the drives for regional integration are all contemporary evi-
    dences of attempts to rationalize certain international func-
    tional relations. No law of social community necessarily
    impedes the simultaneous development of intercultural as
    well as intracultural and local loyalties in interacting pat-
    terns.

Let me once more state that even these administrative
arrangements can proceed within both politically restrictive and
politically libertarian environments. But the consequences of the
choice of each alternative are critically important to the ways in

which societies will proceed through periods of crisis and change. Thus, aside from ethical judgments of political orders, there is a hard empirical relationship between political processes in a relativistic and rationalist humanistic style, and those in a dogmatic, ritualistic, and absolutist style. The former permit self-correcting mechanisms restricting the effects of mistaken or imperfectly informed choice, while the second lead to rigidities and attempts to prevent change.

CONCLUSIONS

In providing a summary of the spread of possible mixed situations in hemispheric international affairs, I shall employ the labels "best possible" and "worst possible." The valorative adjectives, however, should not be understood as implying an unreasoning choice of one kind of political situation over another. In this choice, as in all other public ones, empirical results flow from normative evaluation.

The best possible mixed situation:

1. That most Latin American countries should achieve true nation state status, ie, that all persons should be within the national institutional structure.
2. That national institutions should be sufficiently differentiated to permit individuals to attain differing status levels within each, i.e., that there should be a merit system of selection through relative equality of individuals before educational, economic, political, and religious institutions.
3. That the facts of social class should be contained not only by the equality before the institutions mentioned above, but specifically in the political sphere, by genuine equality before the laws, and the periodic ability of citizens to make effective and rational choices concerning the direction of national political life at all levels—international and local as well as national.
4. That the strength generated by participant politics be reinforced by regional Latin American organizations permitting the area to make its voice felt as a block when necessary in international affairs.

5. That direct foreign intervention be a thing of the past, not merely because the major powers eschew such behavior, but also because the strength of Latin American public opposition can be translated into effective armed opposition if necessary, thus raising the price of such intervention to unacceptable levels.

6. That the long-term policies of the foreign powers come into confluence with consciously derived long-term Latin American policies to provide a ground for equality of international collective bargaining.

7. That the literacy levels of Latin American societies be so high, and the advanced education so sophisticated as to make it possible to pick and choose among the international cultural stimuli bombarding the area for the sake of deepening national culture by an adequate response to international currents, instead of diluting national culture by intellectual mimesis.

8. That the great powers achieve levels of libertarian politics that they recognize as valid for others as well as themselves, thus eliminating the double standards now currently employed in distinguishing permissible domestic from permissible international action. Such a determination can only become truly realistic when in fact the developing countries move into the category of national societies.

9. That the great powers turn away from block and naked power politics to a politics of diplomacy based on a denial of the use of force and violence in international affairs, except in the case of clear and present danger to the international community.

10. That all countries recognize that expansionist totalitarianism threatens all the previous arrangements, and should thus be contained by any measures appropriate to the immediacy of the threat and consistent with the maintenance of domestically free societies.

The worst possible mixed solution:

1. That the Latin American republics should become rigidly stratified societies of privilege and deprivation; that is, that

only selected groups should enjoy the full fruits of national life.

2. That institutional differentiation should be denied in the name of the organic unity of society, i.e., that position should be the result of ascription, the accidents of birth that confer class position throughout life and determine the advantages or disadvantages to be attached to individuals and families.

3. That the facts of social class be reinforced by the above devices in order to create a self-perpetuating governing class for the long-term maintenance of authoritarian control, relying increasingly on the techniques of modern repression.

4. That the strength of the governing elites in each country be reinforced by international collaboration among them for the destruction of any possible opposition from within or among the Latin American republics.

5. That direct foreign intervention be requested from sympathetic foreign governments whenever the repressive systems are threatened from within or without.

6. That the authoritarian Latin American republics recognize that internationally, as domestically, the rich must get richer faster than the poor, that the powerful must become more powerful faster than the weak, and thus that the proper international position of the Latin American states must be as client systems of the great powers.

7. That the Latin American elites recognize that their systems can be maintained stably on a small base of educated technocrats; therefore, cultural and scientific stimuli must be invited from the outside in order to avoid the creation of a self-stimulating intellectual community within.

8. That the great powers recognize a continuing double standard in international affairs, treating the developing nations as they would irresponsible children, i.e., applying the same standards internationally that the governing elites do domestically within each Latin country.

9. That the great powers recognize the uses of force, and proceed to military investment in order to nip potential disorder at the roots.

10. That all countries recognize that democratic libertarianism encourages disorder and threatens the morality and the sensibilities of decent people, and should be contained by immediate strict control.

I trust the reader will recognize the relevance of the individual points made above to much current ideological disputation, as well as to actual practice. It is depressing, as well as heartening, that evidence of the possibilities of both dimensions of the future can be found in the present. The lists are not intended to exhaust characteristics or possibilities, of course. Nor are they designed to intimate that all of Latin America will homogeneous, in either a libertarian or an authoritarian direction. I leave it to the reader to use these and other elements as a kind of a do-it-yourself kit for the construction of many possible combinations.

Whatever the world of 2000, from the vantage point of 1968 I am certain that it can be said that people today are more the master of their destinies than they have ever been before, or than they are usually willing to admit to themselves. What we will be in 2000 is to a great extent what we will have made of ourselves—whether that be automata or free people.

PLANNING AND
DEVELOPMENT

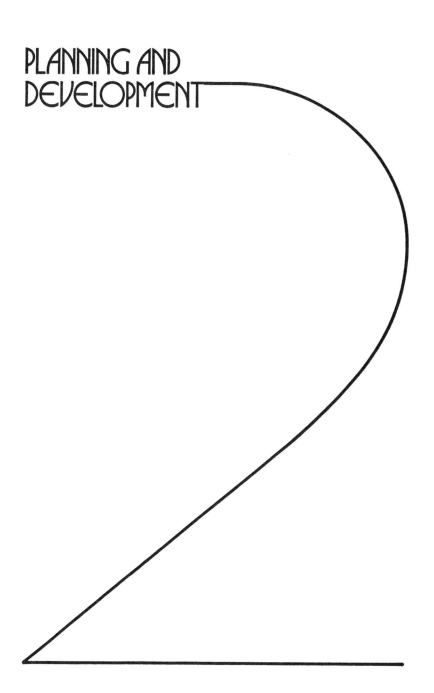

.

3. POTENTIALITIES IN LATIN AMERICA'S FUTURE

HARVEY S. PERLOFF AND LOWDON WINGO, JR
Resources for the Future

There are many reasons for looking to the future. One of the most significant—and appealing—is to highlight possibilities for the future which might otherwise be overlooked in coping with the pressing problems of day to day life.

We find ourselves stimulated by the focus on the almost magical year 2000. We have posed for ourselves these intriguing questions: In What fields might Latin America make a unique contribution to the remainder of the world by the year 2000? In what fields might Latin America lead the world? Here are some of the potentialities that we see, stressing the "might be" or "could be" rather than "necessarily will be."

DEVELOPMENT OF BROAD HUMANISTIC PLANNING

If we were to project the rate of improvement in planning that has taken place in Latin America over the past few years, we could expect, by the year 2000, to find a truly sophisticated type of developmental planning. Latin America has been taking some giant strides towards the development of the intellectual and institutional bases for planned development, with an emphasis on planning—for both national programs and external assistance—within the framework of the Alliance for Progress. While major emphasis has been on economic features, social development has also received attention because of the stress that has been placed by the Alliance on the educational reforms. While performance has not, as yet, equalled aspiration in this regard, it is of no small importance that social development has received open and official recognition within the framework of interAmerican arrangements.

It is also worth noting that the most important of the Latin American training institutes, the Latin American Institute of Political, Economic and Social Planning (ILPES) has for some years now had courses in social as well as economic planning and development and that it has focused on equity issues in both of these categories. Latin America's increasing concern with indigenous cultures is already reflected in some of the planning (in Peru, for example), and this could also signal an important direction for the future. Another factor, particularly among the less developed regions, is the emphasis on future possibilities of economic integration. In Central America, the process of planning on a region-wide basis has already gone some substantial distance, and in other parts of Latin America, where progress has been more limited, there are at least the beginnings of planning on a regional basis (such as the water basin development in the Plate River and the various border programs which sponsor development across national lines). While in each case performance has lagged far behind aspiration, the general directions revealed are significant.

These early steps might well provide a platform on which real progress could be made during the next thirty years towards the establishment of a hardheaded but essentially broad and humanistic planning. What we mean by this is planning which, while centrally concerned with the traditional problems of development, would also put stress on equity issues and on social and political as well as economic development. Thus, it would search for paths to broadbased development rather than relying on a filtering down process in which the returns reach the masses of the people long after the process begins.

There are reasons to assume that Latin America will lead the world in evolving this type of planning. It is hard to avoid the conclusion that the state of the art of developmental planning in general has been severely inhibited by 1) a simplistic view of economic development derived from a limited historical perspective; and 2) the tendency to extract economic development from the intertwined social, political, and cultural processes that make up a nation. The principal aim of development, according to this view, is to focus all efforts on the achievement of as rapid economic growth as possible. This, in turn, means that capital must be saved and employed to maximize national income at some assumed point in the future and that all other factors and processes must acknowledge the primacy of this purpose. The country, as a nation, should become as rich as possible as fast as possible.

Several assumptions are implicit in such a position. First, it assumes that the nation either has no significant values or aspirations competitive with the income maximization goal or, if there are such goals, that income maximization will at least never retard their realization. It seems to us that the record contradicts such an assumption. For many people in the developing countries, hard-driving economic development policies may well threaten ways of life and cultural values held dear; for others, they mean a dimunition of political freedom and civil rights. This kind of economic-growth-above-all planning tends in practice to be antihumanistic, to be impatient with values which appear to frustrate it, and to restrict social welfare calculation only to the easily demonstrated market effects.

Second, it is assumed that the manner in which the rewards of rapid economic development are to be shared among the various groups in the society is a question of little importance. Either an appropriate distribution of income will result from the market processes in the course of development, or public policy may in the future change the distribution of the rewards of development. In any event, the erosion of economic growth rates which egalitarian policies would produce should not be tolerated. Social development, in this view, is seen—with only certain exceptions—as an impediment to desirable economic evolution. It is reasonably clear that this view is not widely subscribed to outside academic circles. The political processes of most countries are deeply involved in issues of economic redistribution. It is naive to assume that this can somehow be put off to the future; it is going on all the time, either equitably or, as is usually the case, inequitably. The politicians and the general public quite rightly see that a continual struggle goes on over who gets what, and how. Thus, this planning dogma becomes something of a smoke-screen hiding from view the actual results being obtained through the continuous redistribution process, and if it continues there could very well be a widening of the gap between the middle and upper income groups on the one hand and a marginal population on the other. Developmental dualism could thus become an implicit part of national policy. In countries in which the rich spend richly, it is the height of naiveté to argue that unequal distributions of income of the type now in existence are conducive to economic development while a redistribution of income is a block to development.

It is in the resolution of this set of issues that Latin America can make a tremendously valuable contribution to the developing world. It can articulate and implement a new format of planning for development which is at once more realistic in its recognition of the complexities of the values and aspirations which have relevance to development, and more humanistic in its sensitivity to the issues of equity that underlie the tensions of the developing world today. Except where goals are truly mutually exclusive, the selection of goals is seldom an all or nothing proposition. Economic growth does not preclude a recognition of social and cultural values nor changes in the structure of income distribution. But it is probably true that realization of other objectives will involve the diversion of national resources from growth-maximizing activities. Other objectives will be paid for by somewhat slower rates of economic growth in the same manner that income maximization goals are now paid for by losses in the values attached to other social objectives. Once the tyranny of income maximization is overthrown, the really crucial planning question emerges: at every point in the developmental planning process, what mix of efficiency, equity and noneconomic goals is most desirable?

While the acceptance of multiple goals does imply ever-increasing pressures on the national resources, it does not simply

imply an increase in the volume of funds channeled into transfer of payments. Handled with rationality and goodwill, it means rather the channeling of funds into activities which will equip people and institutions to participate more widely and more effectively in the developmental process, and to the extent that such outlays increase the capability of the national and regional economies to grow and mature, they are in fact genuine investments. For some time now it has been recognized that expenditures in education which improve people's productive skills are among the most valuable of all investments and contribute to total national output as well as to the specific income they produce. But there are other tremendously important effects. Certainly literacy is an important condition for participation in the society and in the economy, and any program which extends or raises levels of literacy at least redistributes access to the returns of economic development. Broadening higher education expands the base of technical skills and professional competence, and in expanding the high skill cadre reduces the effect produced by shortages in these areas. Clearly, then, the ideal balance of investment in human resources for developing countries is not that which would produce the maximum increase in the rate of economic growth alone, but that which will have the "best" redistributional effect per unit of investment.

In addition, one must keep in mind that education is a desired good in its own right, and that a broad expansion of educational opportunities is itself a form of redistribution. Public health and medical care are even more clearly distributional in this sense. Reduction of morbidity rates, especially of chronic debilitating diseases, has important implications for productivity. At the same time, a reduction in the amount of working time lost is tantamount to an increase in income to the individual workers, and so again has redistributional impact. Above and beyond these effects, the simple enjoyment of improved health which such programs produce is by its nature redistributive.

However, while continued and rapid improvement in the quality and capability of human resources is crucial in this more complex set of development objectives, much more is needed than an expansion of public health and education services. The complexity of planning for some combination of efficiency and equity goals is well illustrated by the land reform problems which are faced all over the region. The agricultural sector in most Latin American countries is simply not producing at anything like its capacity, and the overwhelming majority of rural residents live at the subsistence level, so that income maximizing and distributional objectives are each key dimensions of the problem. If conservative and traditional values were to prevail in the debate over reform, new tenure and production systems would be left to evolve in response to market conditions. The dominance of income maximization goals might well lead to accelerated out-migration of rural dwellers to make way for a more land- and capital-extensive agriculture in the image of the large scale commercial agriculture of the United States. If redistribution were to be the sole planning objective, as proposed in the early agrarian movements, agricultural land resources would perhaps be redistributed among existing farm families with little attention to the impact on the agricultural output, and to viability during development of the new agrarian organization. Clearly no sensible agrarian reform program today can be organized around single-valued objectives.

What is needed is some balancing of the claims of these objectives. This requires planners to seek a more effective set of institutional relations to use the productive factors in agriculture in a manner more consistent with these objectives. Not only must land, labor, and capital be used in different proportions, but more attention must be paid to how they should be developed and adapted to the needs of the agricultural sector.

A healthy agricultural economy, implies a labor force and farm management which is sensitive to market opportunities, but it also implies an agricultural market for the goods and services produced in the urban sector. Such a market does not now exist in most of rural Latin America, from which it follows that some substantial redistribution of the returns to labor and management is a necessary condition for bringing the rural population into the market economy. As more efficient producers with greater access to land and capital resources, they will be able to command family incomes that will make them a force in the market economy of the nation as a whole, and as nations move up the

ladder of development, each succeeding step depends increasingly on the internal development of the national economy.

The achievement of these new conditions for agricultural
development will well depend on the emergence of a new type of
planning, capable of balancing many subtle considerations on a
fine scale.

This is a single, if crucial, example of how recognition of
these twin development goals might well result in a redirection
and restructuring of the planning process in developing countries.
For at every point planners will have to ask themselves not only
whether this act will improve the productivity of the economy,
but also whether it will result in a distribution of its consequences
among the population which is consistent with equity goals. The
world of the developing countries has not yet found the secret of
this kind of planned development and Latin America in the next
generation may well be able to lead the way.

A BALANCED CONCERN FOR RURAL AND URBAN DEVELOPMENT

There is a closely related contribution that Latin America might
well make to the world of the future. This is how to go about the
job of integrated areal planning and development. Here, again,
Latin America has already begun the intellectual probing and the
institution building which suggests that the region may soon be in
a position to make a highly significant contribution in this general
area.

One of the great intellectual failures of contemporary national planning is its tendency to treat rural and urban development as independent problems. This weakness is built into the
sectoral view of the national economy; it is perpetuated by the
way in which national governments are organized; it is augmen-
ted by the social isolation of rural and urban societies. The way in
which the terms *rural* and *urban* have come to be used to describe
mutually exclusive situations is an expression of this intellectual
dualism.

From the standpoint of policy, serious issues can be raised
vis-a-vis this unsophisticated view of internal development. Rigid

concepts of *rural* and *urban* describe archetypal situations which simply do not fit all of the significant developmental situations. How can one treat the social and economic problems of the rural hinterland of a large metropolitan area without reference to the social and economic conditions in the metropolis itself? How can a provincial capital cope with the problem of population growth without recognizing that a considerable part of its problem is rooted in the rural economy which surrounds it? Does one treat the small cities and towns in the hinterland provinces as urban or as rural problems? Should they come under the policy umbrella of the Ministry of Agriculture or under that of the Ministry of Urban Development? These are all key development problems which simply can't be dealt with through the old conceptual equipment suggested by the rural–urban dichotomy.

The key problem is the effective management of the critical integrated areal development. Most of these features have significant rural and urban dimensions. The quality of the urban services upon which the agricultural economy is dependent will have a great deal to do with how the whole vast region may develop. This is true of the communication and transportation services, of warehousing, of farm processing operations, of credit provision, and the like. When an effort is made to develop a Guayana or a Northeast Brazil, it becomes next to impossible to distinguish the impact of elements of the program on the countryside and on the urban communities.

Since almost all current building will be totally depreciated during the next thirty-two years, the cities of the year 2,000 will virtually be new cities, and this is great opportunity for Latin America: to demonstrate to the world how a country's settlement pattern can be an expression of its development aspirations.

It will be difficult to relate development objectives to characteristics of the settlement pattern, to be sure. We have never really been able to agree whether or not organization of the urban sector with the population concentrated in one or two centers complemented or retarded the maximization of income (or GNP, or rate of growth) goals implicit in many national plans. And if equity goals are to become more important in this coming period, as we think they will, additional questions have to be raised.

Some welfare redistribution may take place through the development of public services which have an overall progressive impact, and such a strategy is better served, for example, by an urban net of towns and cities which can bring an array of high quality services, both public and private, within reach of a large proportion of the population. While the large metropolitan center may have advantages in supplying such services to its own clientele, if one's objective includes the population of the entire country, a network dominated by such a metropolitan area may not be as effective as other organizations of the settlement pattern.

While efficiency goals are compatible with fairly decentralized economic decision making through many private and public units, there is no particular societal mechanism with decentralized decision-making characteristics which can be relied on to contribute to the achievement of redistributional goals. The government, through its agencies, will have to take the initiative in defining and implementing those goals. In this context Latin American countries can take the lead in the development of a new kind of planning which takes entire nations, with their problem resources and past mistakes as sets of plastic opportunities for realizing major goals. National planners will be concerned with filling in accounting tables and with the implementation of economic development models, since equity considerations are highly sensitive to the way in which things are organized geographically, and will require a close involvement with the location and distribution of activites.

Perhaps what is needed more than a better articulation of national and regional planning is a coalescence and interpenetration of the two. What does seem clear is that the old distinctions between the missions of the national planner, the regional planner, and the city planner would be unacceptable in this new kind of planning.

This new kind of planning will take the settlement pattern as one of the key instrumental variables in the development of the national economy and society. Since one of its principal objectives is likely to be to reduce the welfare disparities among groups in the economy, and since the largest disparities are traditionally those between the urban dwellers and the rural dwellers, it will have to be concerned with the ways in which new or existing settlements can be used to further this end. On the one hand, it might deliberately foster the development of growth centers in lagging parts of the country, but equally important it will be concerned with the ability of these centers to mobilize their hinterlands and integrate them into the national economy. The development of new towns, the improvement of marketing institutions between the city and the agricultural hinterland, the fuller development of public services in deprived areas, the organization of the national labor market to improve the distribution of skills and training with respect to the geography of new job formation, all these issues and many more need to become part of the national planning process, and not be left to chance.

Finally, such planning might turn a good part of its attention to removing the cultural and social barriers between the city and the countryside. While it is true that over the longer sweep of time, present rates of growth and the evolution of technology make it almost certain that within the next century 90 percent or more of Latin American populations will live in urban areas and engage in nonagricultural pursuits, it cannot be assumed that the welfare disparities that exist will be taken care of by time. If the problem *is* one of equity, it exists in greater degree now than perhaps it ever will again, and we must yield to the present some recognition of its claim on the long range development goals. The dualism of developing countries begins at the borders of the middle class neighborhoods in its large cities and embraces the remainder of the national territory. On one side of this barrier the middle classes live as do their peers in almost any large city in the world, secure in the enjoyment of their income, provided with exceptional services, having access to the highest products of their country's culture and indeed of the culture of the world, and controlling the commanding political portions of the country. On the other side of the line is chronic economic insecurity, poverty, social and cultural deprivation, and bewildered, if not angry, submission to governmental actions from which there is no effective recourse. Equity goals give a special quality of urgency to dismantling these barriers and to expediting the sharing of the highly desired elements of life. Educational and public health services need to be made more accessible in every part of the nation, economic security made more widespread, and opportunities to participate in the governmental processes vastly expanded. A good part of these changes will be best realized by a reorientation of economic, social, political and cultural institutions to cut across the urban–rural distinctions rather than to run with it, and a good part of this will be influenced by the way in which the city-*cum*-hinterland is designed in the future.

CONTRIBUTIONS IN SCIENCE AND TECHNOLOGY

Latin America may also contribute to world culture a sophisticated experience in the organized application of science and technology to the development problems of a large world region. As in the other fields to which we refer, there are beginnings which signal the great possibilities of the future. Thus, for example, the really remarkable success in the experimentation on corn and wheat in Mexico—with Rockefeller Foundation assistance—suggests some of the future possibilities. The products of the Mexican research in wheat and corn have been sent to many parts of the world and in large areas like India and Pakistan the seeds that have been sent have become the base of an agricultural revolution. At the same time, the vital interest in science and technology which has been shown by many of the Latin American nations and by the interAmerican organizations is an augury of the future possibilities. It is also of no small importance that in a summit meeting of the Presidents of the American Republics in April 1967, science and technology were singled out as among the few high priority items which were to receive the major attention of the Alliance for Progress and the interAmerican organizations. The cooperation among the Central American governments, symbolized by their support of the Central American Research Institute for Industry—of which Manuel Noriega Morales is director—is another indication of the promise that lies ahead. Of no less importance is the contribution already being made by individual Latin American scientists. But these, as we have noted, are all only beginnings. Latin America's great and unique contributions in science and technology are yet to come. When we refer to the organized application of science and technology to problems of the developing countries around the world, it should be kept in mind that we are not simply talking about hardware, but about software and institutional arrangements as well, for science and technology remain only potential until some group or organization applies them purposefully to the mitigation of a particular problem. A colleague of ours at Resources for the Future has been studying the factors which influence the rate at which new technical innovations are adopted, particularly in developing countries, and one of his important conclusions is that the rate depends very strongly on the way in which, and the scale at which, the potential users are organized. For example, a new machine which can be profitably employed by a firm producing, say, 100,000 units per year is not likely to be adopted very soon in a country in which the largest firm produces 15,000 units of that product per year. Similarly, innovations in specialized fields are not likely to be adopted at an early point in a country unless its scientists, engineers and planners have developed ongoing communications with the outside world and appropriate means of absorbing the necessary specialized know how. Thus, it is virtually impossible to talk about science and technology in the service of development without introducing the organizational variable.

Another point follows from this observation. The major sources of new technology and advancement in the natural sciences are the economically advanced nations, a fact which has advantages and limitations for the developing world. On the one hand, the developing world can avail itself of the products of the immense investment of human and physical capital in research and development at almost no cost; on the other hand, these developments are conditioned by the nature of the economies of the industrially advanced nations: they are designed to fit into small interstices in the technological superstructures of these nations and frequently do not relate well to the capital-poor production systems in developing countries. They are also designed for the production systems situated in temperate climates. This fact imposes a twofold responsibility on the developing nations in their search for appropriate technologies to fit their production requirements. Not only must they have an effective strategy to search out relevant innovations, but also they need to be prepared to adapt them to their specific needs. Both of these responsibilities can be translated into institutional roles.

While Latin America will certainly improve its strategies and institutional arrangements for introducing an increasing flow of innovation into Latin American productive activities during the next generation, it seems to us that there are several things that are not likely to get done unless some common strategies are developed and resources pooled to bring them off. Specifically, it is not likely that massive development of major natural resource regions will take place atuomatically. The tropical rainforests of the Amazon basin cover a large proportion of the continent of South America, and one-sixth of the total precipitation that falls on the earth's land surfaces flows to the sea. A large part of that precipitation reaches the Amazon Basin only after it has passed over the 2,500 mile sparsely developed desert that stretches along the West coast of Chile and Peru. Further to the south, the great rain forests and temperate plains of the near-arctic regions engage the development interests of both Chile and Argentina. These are among Latin America's most significant frontiers, and the doubling of the region's population during the next generation will put greater and greater pressure on their development. When they will be developed, in fact, will depend both on the build up of this pressure and on how fast technology can lower the thresholds of development feasibility fo these vast marginal areas. It is our hypothesis that concentrated efforts to apply the full leverage of technological potential to these problems will bring these thresholds down very rapidly and relieve the population and resource pressures in the presently developed portions of the region.

Consider the Amazon Basin for example. Its forestry, land and water resources would seem to be a likely base for a productive adapted tropical agriculture that could support millions. It has been argued many times, however, that the ecology of the rain forest is a delicate balance of natural conditions, the destruction of which would be irreversible. We have enough experience to know that conventional technologies do not make large scale production feasible. This is only to say that investment in tropical agriculture in the Amazon with present technologies simply cannot compete with land intensifying investment in agriculture in less rigorous regions and closer to the large cities which provide them with strong markets.

In a recent proposal, the Hudson Institute suggested the importance of treating the Amazon as a single development system in which not only Brazil, but Bolivia, Peru, Colombia, and Venezuela have significant stakes. Thus, a development strategy requires first of all an integrated international effort in which there is a sharing of the costs as well as of the ultimate returns from the progressive development of the region.

In addition, it seems that the key to early development probably lies in the achievement of a complex of technology and institutional innovations specifically adapted to the unique conditions associated with climatic and topographic characteristics of the region. An obvious dimension of this technological complex must be in the field of transportation. Goods must be moved to domestic or international markets quickly and inexpensively, for the Amazonas can only develop as fast as it can market its produce. The transportation system will have to knit this vast, formidable region into an effective economic entity, permitting a high degree of interlocal interchange. At this stage it seems unlikely that conventional surface modes of transportation can play the key role in this system. The river system itself penetrates every corner of the region, and although river transportation presents numerous problems here, it may eventually become the basis for a new transport technology of flexible, speedy craft, such as the ground effect machine or the hydrofoil. Airborne technology presents even greater potential in this field: recent developments in helicopters and vertical takeoff aircraft make it possible for any small clearing to become an entrepot in an airborne transportation system. The introduction of the jumbojet to Latin America will provide low cost airfreight from interior areas to the coastal markets for high value perishable products, such as prepared meat, beef, and specialty products. In short, the hardware elements of a transportation system technology are available now; the critical problem is institutional—how to apply them effectively.

A development strategy will also have to cope with the difficulties of land development where there may be severe ecological backlash for unwise policies. Recent experience in the *selva* of Peru dramatized the limitations of the best of our conventional land development technology under adverse conditions. Land clearing, the prevention of severe erosion and leaching where the rainfall exceeds one hundred inches a year, the development of an on-site infrastructure which will meet the needs of the new colonists—in fact, a new technology of living in the humid tropics—will require large scale experimentation, probably beyond anything we have yet experienced in economic development.

Finally, a considerable effort will have to be made in the development of a production technology which permits the exploitation of the region without severe damage to its ecosystem. Asia and Africa provide much experience with labor intensive tropical agriculture and forestry, but it seems to us that these provide limited lessons for the development of the Amazon. Crops will have to be developed which can be profitably produced through a land and capital extensive technology. We have already referred to major miracles created in Mexico with new varieties of wheat and corn. The development of a new rice variety in the Philippines promises to reverse recent trends in Asia in the annual per capita output of rice. These were both classic cases of the direct application of agricultural sciences to a crucial development problem. It is not unlikely that the same sort of experience might pace the development of the Amazonas. Given new crops with large potential markets, the costs of transportation are likely to make it economical to do some of the first stage processing of the products near the site of the production, so that in addition to a new agricultural technology, manufacturing technologies applicable to the processing of agricultural and forestry products will invite investigation and development as part of the overall effort. As a matter of fact, the key to profitability of a crop may depend in many cases on on-site, weight-reducing processing technologies.

Thus, it seems evident that science, technological innovation, and organization for development will be closely intertwined in any major assault on the obstacles to development of a large resource complex. Consider the problems of development of the arid lands of the west coast, the Pampas, and the Altiplano, or of the proto-Arctic areas in the far south. These are all similar to development problems already confronted in other parts of Latin America. Given such traditions, the new frontiers can be expected to yield to a great developmental thrust by the year 2000. In using such an approach and tackling the really difficult problems first, Latin America will be able to demonstrate to the rest of the developing world: 1. how to organize and carry off a massive multilateral regional development effort; 2. how to adapt and evolve appropriate technology as the critical part of a development effort; and 3. how to organize a development program that will encourage the participation of scientists and technologists.

CONTRIBUTIONS TO THE ARTS

In the next generation Latin America may well demonstrate to the world how to develop a regional fine arts culture with strong popular roots. This is a difficult and speculative area: who can predict the emergence of a great artist? Who even knows what it takes in the social environment and the life experience of the talented individual to permit him to realize his highest artistic capabilities? And yet, because the fine arts are such an important aspect of culture we should consider what directions they are likely to take in the future.

While we admit the impracticality of prediction in the fine arts, we know that in any field of human endeavor something of the future can be read in the past. The future of the fine arts in Latin America will undoubtedly be a product of the merging of its artistic traditions with the emerging themes and developments in the international environment of culture. Latin America's traditional artistic sources are ancient, humanistic, and richly complex. No textiles in the world have ever surpassed the fineness and the elegance of the *mantas* of Caracas, whose weavers died long before the Golden Age of Greece. City building and architecture have traditions whose beginnings are lost in the distant past. The city at Chavin de Huantar in Peru was probably flourishing while the first walls of Rome were being erected. By contemporary accounts, the size and glory of Tenochtitlan in Mexico on the arrival of Cortez must have rivalled all but the grandest of the cities of Europe and Asia. Certainly few cities of the ancient world ever achieved the elegance of Chichen Itza in the Yucatan, and few empires were ever united by a system of roads so planned and constructed as those which converged on Cuzco from Ecuador in the North and the Central Valley of Chile in the South.

The Spanish built the neatly planned, orderly colonial city on this tradition, whose legacy is to be seen in almost every provincial city in Latin America, with its key public buildings bordering its Plaza de Armas at the heart of a rectangular street system. These two historical traditions come together in much of the new urbanity of Latin America. While Brazilia is ultimately modern, it reflects the monumentality of the classic cities of Inca, Maya, and Aztec cultures, and its ultimate order is certainly in the tradition of the colonial city. The Museum of Anthropology of Mexico, one of the most impressive architectural achievements of the western hemisphere, memorializes the pre-Spanish world in an architectural environment which is both urbane and human. Not far away, the University of Mexico with its brilliant external murals on monumental structures joins history with the modern in a unique style. And everywhere the plazas and the parks with their decorative landscaping give Latin American urbanity a special style.

But what we see in the architectural or design qualities of Latin America's cities is only the most immediately perceived dimension of the artistic culture of the region. Its poets and novelists and men of letters have given Latin America a sonorous voice in the world culture. The American production of Ginastera's *Bomarzo* was the musical event of the year in the United States.

While economic integration is perhaps the highest priority item on the region's agenda, a contribution of tremendous significance that Latin America can make to world culture is in the demonstration that cultural integration can vastly enrich the cultural environment of the entire region, and provide levels of stimulation to the artistic imagination that the fine arts in an autarchic world can never enjoy. An active process of cultural integration might involve programs at three levels of concerted action: the region as a collectivity, the cultural relations among the individual countries, and intranational programs.

However crass an image it may convey, there is some virtue to casting the fine arts in a market analogy. We do not construe this figure narrowly in the sense that artists produce works of art which they sell to consumers who consume them by hanging them in their living rooms. Rather, we think of the artist's product, his work of art, as an item of collective consumption in which the whole public has an interest. Now this means something special to an economist, for a collective good is one whose benefits are difficult, if not impossible, to confine to the purchaser: a novel once published is a good to anyone who cares to pick it up and read it. While anyone who saw *Bomarzo* at the Metropolitan Opera in New York paid handsomely to do so, it is now on records which we can buy and which our friends can enjoy free of charge. While some part of this artistic production may be removed from the domain of collective enjoyment, few paintings are ever so hung as to confine their rewards to the gaze of the purchaser: for the most part, the artistic product of a society tends to permeate the experience of the society as a whole.

The reason for casting the fine arts in this framework is that it identifies some of the kinds of choices and opportunities that may confront Latin America in the next generation. In the first place, we are led to focus on the quantity and quality of the artistic output; in the second place, to examine the processes by which art is "consumed" by its public; and in the third place, we find ourselves thinking about the interaction between the artist as producer and the public as consumer of the region's output. Finally, one must speculate on the virtues and vices of the public's intervention in these market arrangements. It seems to us that opportunities in the field of the fine arts must ultimately make themselves known in one or more of these dimensions.

Consider the production aspect of the market, for example. The entire region has a stake in increasing the amount and quality of the artistic output of the region as a whole. Already the Fine Arts Division of the PanAmerican Union in Washington has carried on a splendid program of bringing Latin American artists and their work to the awareness of the world at large through exhibits and recitals. In this way it is creating an awareness that there is a powerful, regionwide Latin American style in the arts, especially in painting and sculpture. Of equal importance, its program has provided a new channel by which Latin American artists can come to the attention of the world; it is, in short, creating a powerful link between the artists as a member of the Latin American creative community and world cultural community. The opportunities thus created to reach a world audience must provide a powerful stimulus to ambitious young artists. It would be difficult to overestimate the importance of this function, and yet it has been performed by a handful of dedicated people with few resources at their disposal, and their tremendous success argues strongly that there is a significant opportunity for regional action in the future.

The cultural possibilities among the various nations of the region are parallel to the economic possibilities, and there are great gains to be had from joining the two efforts. It seems to us that nations of Latin America will have increasing opportunities to expand the array of artistic goods available to their populations and to encourage interaction among the artists themselves. Bilateral arrangements to provide fellowships and residencies for the artists of one country to work in another, cultural exchanges, joint institutions, all offer feasible ways of reducing the national barriers to artistic communication and production and of abating the tendencies toward cultural autarchy which are the companions of rigid nationalism.

Finally, every country in Latin America will find opportunities in their own internal policies which complement these regional and international chances to expand and elaborate the relationship between the Latin American artist and his consumers in the world, in the region, and in his own nation and city. We are, of course, very sensitive to the potential of governmental policies to do serious mischief to the delicate fabric of the artistic life of a nation. Censorship, political opportunism, and governmental propensities for propagandising are all enemies of artistic creativity; it is possible that the national governments will continue to ignore the use of the arts as instruments of political policy. Beyond this, nations may find ways of identifying talented individuals among their populations and of providing their development with the kind of "tender loving care" now reserved for the professions. On the consumption side, governments should be willing to back artistic institutions which work to make aesthetic resources available to the entire population. Indeed, Latin American governments may find a way to avoid the tyranny of the academy and the strangulation of bureaucracy in developing policy that will complement rather than impede the robust creativity of their societies.

While it is difficult to talk about the development of the arts in a policy context, it seems to us to be the only way in which the cultural dimensions of development and the incipient creativity of Latin American can be protected from the consequences of poorly calculated, if well-intentioned, policies toward the development of the arts. As opportunities emerge at the regional, international, or intranational levels someone or some group must be ready and able to move to exploit them. No region of nations has ever before deliberately set out to amplify and elaborate its style in the arts, to enrich its cultural roots, to stimulate and inspire through interchange of experience. Latin America's contribution to the world might well be the achievement of such purposes through a concordance of national and international policies designed with restraint and imagination.

4. THE POLITICAL AND THEORETICAL TASK OF THE PLANNER IN LATIN AMERICA

OSWALDO SUNKEL
Instituto Latinoamericano de Planificación Económico y Social [ILPES], Santiago

INTRODUCTION

In discussing America in the year 2000, one is always tempted to focus on the formal models to which planners are so attracted. They provide indispensable statistical projections in fields such as demography, urbanization, employment, margination, regional disequilibrium, external commerce and finance, and development; and these in turn perform valuable services, emphasizing the alarming dimensions and drifts of our problems, underscoring the need for bold, long term programs, and helping us evaluate different policies. But the models and their prognoses fail as practical guides to action. Consequently, the efforts of planners during the past decade have been unsatisfactory.

As uncertainty grows over the future of Latin America, the political climate becomes increasingly discouraging. Governments cling to antiquated policies, seeking greater foreign aid even as prospects for such contributions dim. Traditional political parties and middle and upper social groups fight among themselves, strengthening national dependency on foreign powers, and undermining their own democratic forms of government. Simultaneously, new political movements and revolutionary groups find support, or at least sympathy, among the young, the working class, the marginal urban and rural groups, and even the clergy, while they disrupt and discredit established leftist parties and organized labor.

These local trends, and international ones of equal importance are forcing Latin American social scientists to reexamine the interpretive schema upon which policies of national development, regional integration and international cooperation traditionally have been based. It is imperative that our scholars also study the profound crisis in which the theory and practice of development and planning now find themselves.

Of the many factors which influence the orientation and effectiveness of planning, I will discuss only those two which seem most fundamental and timely. The first is the social and political role of the planner; the second, the interpretation of the process of development in Latin America.

PLANNERS AND THE STRATEGY OF DEVELOPMENT

The recent experience of many countries illustrates the inadequacy of a strictly economic view of development, and a purely technical approach to planning.[1] We now understand that planners cannot ignore the history and foreign relations of their countries, and the numerous political, institutional, social and cultural factors which these denote.

In order to incorporate these additional elements into development policy, we must create a new strategy of development, according to which planners would examine the sociopolitical and cultural *objectives* of their communities, the social *agents* in the process of development, the initial social and economic *situation,* and the available *resources*. A program for development would consequently become a political plan for long term socioeconomic action, reflecting the aspirations and methodological preferences of each sector of a society. Each social group would be encouraged to develop its own plans, providing a nation with several different blueprints from which to choose. These programs would not be static: they would change along with the social structure.

The formulation of different plans for development would clearly help a society to organize its political options. Here, in my judgment, planners—each working within his own social groups—should play a major role. They must, however, encourage the active participation of people of all other occupations, for we can no longer see society as a mere recipient of decisions handed down from an invisible bureaucracy. All social groups, and particularly those which should benefit from development, are both subject and object in this process; only the ordering and administration of the different programs should be left to executives and technicians. We must, therefore, create new social and political mechanisms to stimulate and facilitate widespread participation. For this important work, we must again appeal to social scientists, and particularly to historians.

As I have said, the planner must assume greater responsibilities than he has usually been assigned. Conventional views of his role have limited his duties because they erroneously assume a well defined relationship between the politician and the expert. According to these views, the politician defines the objectives of a society and selects the means by which they are reached; the planner develops and offers the politician a variety of policies from which to choose. These definitions not only ignore certain crucial realities, but help to snarl the already subtle and complex relationship of the technical and the political. Why?

In the first place, it is unreasonable to expect a politician to choose intelligently from the alternatives offered by the planner. These are technical programs, and politicians lack the knowledge necessary to foresee their consequences. Similarly, planners generally lack the sociopolitical experience needed to understand the political implications of their plans.

Second, conventional views of the planner assume his scientific neutrality, disregarding his inevitable social conditioning. They reflect a nineteenth-century approach to scientific knowledge, in which the scientist is a dispassionate, unbiased instrument, more than human. He does not invent; he sees. He does not create order among natural and social phenomena; he only humbly verifies it. In this view, knowledge is passive, a large catalog which the scientist has merely to keep well-ordered and up-to-date. But this is the twentieth century, and scientists no longer believe that knowledge is so impersonal. Today, they see it as a constant activity, a dynamic process in which the means employed by the scientist inevitably affect his discoveries. The expert, furthermore, no longer indiscriminately provides facts for others to use as they please. He understands the implications of his discoveries, and therefore his own responsibility in communicating them to others.[2]

In the third place, conventional views of planning assume that means and ends are wholly unrelated; that when courses of action are chosen, the objectives are not affected. This is unacceptable, particularly since policies of development imply structural changes over long periods of time. In practice, the selection of means largely determines the ends, and conversely, the definition of certain goals demands the use of specific methods.

Suppose, for example, that one seeks to create an efficient, dynamic agriculture within a modern social structure (whether collectivized, capitalistic, or of any other system of ownership and organization). In choosing policies for this goal, one could not give equal weight to greater taxation, to expropriation (with or without indemnities), and to peasant seizure of the land. Each of these produces completely different institutional, economic, political and social situations.

For these reasons, among others, the fundamental responsibilities of development planning should not be divided among politicians and planners, so that the former define objectives and consider the political viability of programs, while the latter analyze situations and calculate the economic implications of different plans. Rather, politicians and experts should formulate policies together, so that each can benefit from the knowledge of the other. In the end, they will all be identified with the policies, and they will constitute the nucleus of the politico-technical organization which will put the programs into practice.

Thus in the future the planner should play two roles: one as an expert, the other as an intermediary between politics and technology. He should help politicians and citizens define their objectives, interpret the structure and behavior of their socioeconomic system, and evaluate their prospects. Simultaneously, he should explain to them the technical difficulties involved in the formulation of policy, and translate programs into language they can understand, so they can determine the sociopolitical implications and viability of different plans. But before he can perform these duties successfully, the planner must broaden his own sociopolitical, cultural and historical consciousness. Otherwise, he will not sufficiently understand and respect the crucial political sphere, and he will propose programs which are only technically optimal.

Different socioeconomic groups and their respective political organizations will formulate their own strategies, each according to its interpretation of the process of development. The social function of the planner will be to contribute his technical knowledge to the group of his choice. This work will not be easy, and it will be essential for the planner to maintain his scientific objectivity, for this is ultimately his greatest contribution to his social group.

The difficulty and complexity of relations between experts and politicians stems ultimately from a fundamental difference between science and politics. While scientific activity demands as much normative neutrality as possible, political activity is intrinsically normative. [3] This creates a very personal conflict for the planner, for his work is at once scientific and political. Unless we take into account this problematic duality, we cannot begin to understand the nature of the tasks which now fall to our experts.

THEORIES OF UNDERDEVELOPMENT AND STRATEGIES OF DEVELOPMENT

Thus the formulation of development strategies demands more than a merely technical view of the world. The complex, disordered reality of underdevelopment is defined in great part by institutions, traditions, social and political groups, modes of behavior, regional distributions, and international ties. And the order imposed on it by the planner depends substantially on his theoretical, methodological and ideological conditioning. [4] The Spanish poet was right to remind us that reality is colored by the crystal through which it is observed.

Planners have been looking through the crystal of conventional theories of growth and modernization. They have seen underdevelopment as a primitive stage in the growth of a nation toward the ideal of a mature capitalist society (represented in practice by the developed nations), and they have consequently missed the true structure and formative process of underdeveloped societies. We must replace their idealized, mechanistic notions with a new analytic scheme which will reveal the actual nature of underdevelopment, and serve as a scientific base in the formulation of development policy.

The characteristics of underdevelopment—low level and slow growth of income, regional imbalances, instability, unemployment, inequality, monoproductive dependency, and cultural, economic, social and political marginality—are not deviations from an ideal standard, or childhood illnesses which will be cured by modernization and growth. They are the normal results of the functioning of a determined system, and they will perpetuate themselves so long as development planning attacks the symptoms of underdevelopment, and not its basic structural elements. The results of a system are functions of its structure, and they will change only if that structure is changed.

In order to find the structural elements of underdevelopment, we must adopt an historical approach. Applying it to our countries, we immediately see the overwhelming influence of foreign powers on our socioeconomic systems. We cannot, however, allow external factors to obscure important internal conditioning structures, for structural transformation is a product of interaction between domestic and international elements.

A realistic analysis of Latin American development, then, stems from the assumption that a socioeconomic system is shaped by both external and internal factors. Among the external ones are all those institutions which determine the nature of the social, political, economic and cultural bonds between an underdeveloped society and the central nations. And among the internal factors, the most important are natural resources, population, political institutions, sociopolitical groups and their attitudes and ideologies, and the policies of the state.

We can now consider two crucial aspects of the socioeconomic process directly. The first is the behavior of the economic system; that is, the nature of the accumulation of capital, the utilization and mobilization of productive resources, the geographic distribution of economic activity, the extent of technological innovation, and the distribution of income. The second—and the one which is most interesting from the standpoint of development—is the process of structural transformation. A study of Latin American development suggests that structural change takes place in two different ways: first, as the economic system functions and grows over a period of time, giving way to the accumulation of capital, geographic and technological changes, and shifts in the distribution of income; and second, as external relations are altered by the evolution of the international socioeconomic system, and particularly by the actions of the predominant world power. Of the two, the latter has been the more common in Latin America. In fact, the periods of great change in the United States and Europe clearly mark the different stages of structural transformation in the Latin American countries.

Thus a useful analytic scheme for the study of underdevelopment and the formulation of development policy must rest on the concepts of process, structure and system. Underdevelopment is not a "moment" in the evolution of an isolated, autonomous society, but a part of the global historical process of development. Underdevelopment and development are interacting aspects of the same universal process, and they find expression in two great dualities: first, in the division of the world *between* the industrial, advanced, developed "centers" and the backward, poor, dependent nations; and second, in the division *within* countries between areas, social groups, and activities which are modern and ones which are primitive and marginal.

Underdevelopment and development, then, are interdependent structures which together form one system. The crucial difference between them is that *within* as well as *among* countries the developed structure, due to its endogenous capacity for growth, is dominant, while the underdeveloped structure is dependent. The fundamental problem for an underdeveloped structure is to overcome its state of dependency; to gain a greater autonomous capacity for growth and to reorient its economic, social, political and cultural system toward the satisfaction of its own needs. In other words, *development means growing effi-*

ciency and autonomy in the creative management of the natural, technological, social and cultural environment, and in the conduct of relations with other geographical and political entities. This definition implies a reorientation of development policy in both its domestic and its international aspects. In order for it to be effective, such a reformulation must be based on the active social, political and cultural participation, both in the definition of objectives and in the work which will attain them, of previously marginal groups. The "objects" of development must become "subjects" of the process.

In Latin America, only minorities have participated in and benefited from the efforts of development, while marginal groups have grown in absolute numbers, and often even in relation to other sectors. Although these efforts have occasionally been very important, they clearly have not involved the widespread participation so necessary to development. A nation's potential for social action is conditioned by the nature of external economic, political, technological and cultural ties, and consequently participation is directly related to the degree of the nation's dependency. Only when our countries gain greater control over those formidable external influences will they enjoy a greater amount of social and political participation.

Thus for our new approach to development to bear fruit, we must perform three vital tasks. First, we must change the very structures of political power, for these ultimately explain the nature of the internal and external social manipulation of culture, technology, productive resources and sociopolitical groups. Second, we must strengthen and enrich our national cultures, which largely determine the objectives our societies pursue. And finally, we must intensify scientific and technological investigations, for they, along with the power structure, are crucial to our capacity for action.

I will conclude with a few questions, which I hope will nag us during the following days. We know that the structural changes our countries have experienced are due mainly to external factors—particularly the actions of the United States—and to the work of domestic minorities which have used traditional development policies for their own benefit. Can we change this situation before the year 2000? Can we invert the dynamic of development so that structural change grows out of national interests, as defined by majorities within our countries and throughout our continent? Or will our dependency be consolidated? In our symposia we have excellent opportunities to elucidate these questions. If we fail, it will be difficult to define clearly our scientific and technical tasks, and impossible to determine our intellectual and political obligations to this Latin American society whose future we wish to affect.

NOTES

1. ILPES, *Discusiones sobre planificación.* (Mexico: Siglo XXI Editores and Santiago de Chile, Editorial Universitaria, 1966).
2. Bronowski, Y., "El pensamiento y sus repercusiones," in UNESCO. *Historia de la Humanidad.* Vol. VI, Part 1, Chap. 6.
3. Weber, Max, *El científico y el político.* (Madrid: Alianza Editoral, 1967).
4. Schumpeter, J.A., *History of Economic Analysis,* Part I. (New York: Oxford University Press, 1954).

5. CENTRALISM, NATIONALISM, AND INTEGRATION

CLAUDIO VÉLIZ
Instituto de Estudios Internacionales, Universidad de Chile

The situations in Germany, Italy, and North America seem to demonstrate a chronological correlation between certain modern processes of integration and a satisfactory rhythm of economic growth. However, closer examination reveals the drawbacks of these historical examples—each of them required recourse to military force or military threats. Even the creation of the European Economic Community would have been difficult without such critical political factors as fear of the Soviet Union and of German military resurgence.

Latin America's project for peaceful integration and economic development is by comparison very attractive. It remains debatable whether these countries can integrate without more adequate national economic development. But let us leave these considerations aside for the moment and examine instead the possible future implications of factors like nationalist resurgence and accentuated political centralism on the peaceful predisposition of integrationist forces.

Until very recently Latin American integration was unopposed; it seemed to threaten no one, and lacked any real political significance. There were no complaints as long as the proposal remained only rhetorical. But when concrete demands were made, opposition formed—opposition which has become well-defined and which now definitely threatens the process. Resistance is no surprise among some influential entrepreneurs, especially in Venezuela. But among the most important obstacles to integration, as it was conceived almost a decade ago, are political centralism and nationalism. Paradoxically, one could argue that whatever shape the integration process takes toward the end of the century, it will be successful only to the extent that it incorporates the forces associated with both centralism and resurgent nationalism.

For more than 150 years, Latin America has followed the lead of the northern hemisphere's more advanced nations. This era of borrowing (even of idologies, the full range of which derive from the European experience) is about to end. The domestic, political, and economic features of the so-called "western world" (in this sense including the Soviet Union) result primarily from the transformations wrought by the Industrial Revolution, which ran its course before reaching Latin America. Here industrialization has not sparked the great social transformations that accompanied it in the northern hemisphere. Latin America society, only recently a recipient of modern industrial technology, is also very different from the European society in which these processes originated.

Though it would be difficult to rank the cultural differences in order of their importance, I will at least suggest some principal determinants as a start toward a functional hypothesis. Three basic differences help explain why Latin America cannot continue to apply European ideological models, and also suggest the "political style" that will probably prevail in the region, domestically and internationally, around the year 2000. These are the lack of feudalism and religious nonconformity in Latin America's historical tradition, and of the peripheral development which characterized Europe's Industrial Revolution. At the same time, a key for understanding recent developments and the region's future is its deeply rooted and traditional centralism.

Although "feudalism" is often employed in pejorative descriptions of Latin America, the phenomenon never occurred here. The region was "discovered" 300 years after the death of European feudalism; more important, Spain had a strongly centralist administration under an absolute monarch.

Traditional centralism has survived to the present. All three of the region's real revolutions, which reconstructed national societies according to widely varying doctrines and ideologies, institutionalized single-party rule. Mexico's PRI has transformed itself into a centralist symbol in its own right; the Cuban regime, after some preliminary experiments, has also developed into a one-party system. I believe the explanation for this lies more in Cuba's Latin American status than in its Communism. The Bolivian revolution attempted to establish one-party rule under the MNR; its failure does not detract from the significance of the effort.[1] In any case, the present government is as much or more centralist than previous ones. The tendency of other Latin American countries—even excepting the absolute dictatorships—is clearly toward regimes where dominant parties are directly identified with the central government. This also applies to the continent's most democratic and sophisticated regimes.

Historical centralism is complemented by the universal trend toward greater state intervention in the main aspects of national life. This tendency clashes with pluralist and liberal conceptual models of political responsibility in countries like Great Britain, Sweden, and the United States; in Latin America, it reinforces the trend toward increased central control.

Thus the customary institutional compromise between alternative and coexisting political power centers is not part of Latin America's historical tradition. Europe's feudal experience, which obliged centralized and relatively weak monarchies to negotiate with peripheral power centers, is simply unknown in this region.

Both political and religious centralism have fared reasonably well during the last four centuries. There are strong dissensions within contemporary Latin American Catholicism, but these reflect uneasiness in the face of social and political issues, and are not likely to evolve into profound doctrinal problems or religious crises. Even the considerable recent growth of Protestantism still constitutes no real alternative, at least in the short run. Latin America's most significant non-Catholic minority, in Chile, constitutes only 10 percent of the population.

Both religious and political centralism are critical factors in our modern historical development. A third force is economic centralism, resulting from a long Iberian tradition, and strongly reinforced by the circumstances accompanying the region's industrialization. . . .

[The author goes on to contrast these basic forces with a synopsis of the industrial revolution in western Europe and the United States in which he stresses the interaction of economic behavior, especially capital accumulation, with dominant social and religious values; that industrialization was a lengthy process, owing little to government support; that the locus of industrial activity—geographically and politically—was separated from the nation's power center and often in conflict with the traditional classes; that industrial expansion accompanied urban growth, so that the incorporation of modern industry into the traditional social structure of Europe was the consequence of the existence of a new bourgeoisie, and produced a new industrial proletariat. (Ed.)]

None of these considerations really applies to Latin America. Our almost accidental industrialization by import substitution has been due primarily to external factors like the 1929 crisis and World War II. The necessary industrial technology was already essentially capital-intensive, requiring a relatively small and well-trained labor force which received high salaries. This technology was incorporated into a society which had long possessed a massive and complex preindustrial urban civilization. The decisions that brought rapid and large-scale industrialization to much of Latin America were not made by peripheral groups, but rather directly by the central power. These policies were firmly supported with subsidies, discriminatory tariffs, selective channeling of credit, and industrial development programs administered by state agencies. But hoped-for social changes, like those which accompanied European industrialization, have not come about. Many of the changes which have occurred were not anticipated by experts or politicians.

Rapid Latin American industrialization has neither followed the efforts of an industrial bourgeoisie, nor generated an industrial proletariat. Great Britain, the world's major industrial power in the 1870s, had at that time just reached the million-ton mark in steel production. This required a labor force of somewhat less than 400,000. Several Latin American countries have now surpassed this important threshold, and Brazilian production approaches four million tons. But a rough estimate indicates that barely 7000 workers are needed to produce a million tons. Peru is the world's greatest fish producer, but the labor force to catch and process nine million tons does not exceed 30,000. Comparable production a century ago would have required several hundred thousand workers. These examples illustrate the fundamental shift toward capital-intensive industrial technology. For this reason if no other, Latin America's industrial labor force does not compare with that spawned by Europe's industrial revolution, and cannot be characterized as a classical industrial proletariat. Complex and advanced technology demands fewer but better trained workers. For these reasons, and also because of social legislation and union activities nonexistent in nineteenth-century Europe, Latin America's skilled workers receive higher salaries than do other labor sectors. They form a kind of labor aristocracy, with incomes frequently higher than those of important groups in the tertiary sector. Industry's capacity to absorb workers is very limited; the hope that accelerated industrial growth could transform a significant part of the rural masses into an industrial urban mass has proven unfounded. With luck, the rural immigrant can find work in construction and other less demanding industries, though he more often gravitates to the service sector.

Modern industry sharply reduced the number of artisans and small shopkeepers, while increasing levels of tertiary employment. But this growth only underscored an interesting feature of our urban society. At the end of the nineteenth century, when Latin America had almost no modern industry, a very high percentage of the population lived in the capitals. Uruguay, Mexico, Argentina, and Chile did not industrialize before World War I, but their capitals ranked among the world's great urban centers. Uruguay remains an essentially agricultural country, but almost half its population lives in Montevideo. Latin American urbanization levels are extraordinary; while the region is obviously less industrialized than Europe, its proportion of urban population in cities of over 100,000 is higher.

Latin America's pre-industrial urbanization has weighed heavily on a vast tertiary sector which, during the last century, indirectly subsisted on raw material export earnings. The great cities grew rapidly during the second half of the nineteenth century, reflecting prosperity brought by nitrates, rubber, meat, wool, coffee, and other products with markets in the northern hemisphere. But rubber workers, miners, and cowboys did not live in the cities. These were peopled with huge members of white-collar workers, descendants of the army of notaries and bureaucrats needed to administer the Spanish Empire's vast foreign dominions. Professionals, public employees, domestic servants, merchants, and small artisans complemented this administrative sector. The middle sector, decisively urban, is equivalent to neither the British industrial bourgeoisie, nor the French and American middle classes. Its associations with industry are minimal. It is, moreover, directly or indirectly linked to the state, by employment or by dependence on social security or on secondary state organs. Possibly for this reason, its politics and organizations tend to be reformist, directed toward greater participation within the existing social structure rather than its destruction and replacement with a more egalitarian system.

This tertiary sector, so quintessentially Latin American, is the central axis and the main element of continental politics. The symbol of such politics would be neither a dispossessed *campesino* nor an exploited industrial worker, but rather an underpaid but aspiring bank clerk.

A reformist, anti-aristocratic, risk-taking, innovative, and creative industrial bourgeoisie simply does not exist. The dynamic functions of economic and social change have been assumed by state entities; private enterprise has rarely prospered without government protection. If subsidies, preferential treatment, credit, and similar state benefits were withdrawn from the region's so-called private enterprises, very few firms could survive. Moreover, the social group generally designated as the middle class (though it hardly fits the description) has been unable to create an autonomous cultural complex. Its wealth came from proximity to the government cornucopia in the 1940s and '50s, rather than personal effort or originality. Neither the middle class nor its commercial and political clientele are "industrial" in the accepted sense of the word; even when they own industries they are too ready to exchange the inherent risks and responsibilities of business for an agreement with a foreign company. Patents and production licenses shield them from local competitors, assure decorous living standards, and provide technical, financial, and advertising advice to cement their predominance in a limited market.

Docility and lack of imagination and dynamism have even kept this pseudoindustrial bourgeoisie from forming an important pressure group, except in a negative sense. For instance, associations of merchants and private industrialists resist plans for regional integration. The same groups, though, have never been able to formulate an ideology which could engender a viable political force to represent them. And thus there is no Latin American equivalent of Europe's industrial liberalism, except on a picturesque parochial level.

As Celso Furtado has noted, the extreme ease with which the most efficient and modern industrialists enter the external financial, technological, and economic world—to the detriment of an effective national development policy—is perhaps even more important.[2] In Europe and the United States, for various reasons, it was precisely these industrial groups that preponderated in planning and implementing national development policies. In Latin America they have intensified the processes leading to external dependency.

Similarly, they have not matched their European predecessors as social and cultural reformers. Social climbing and facile emulation of the upper class have been substituted for successful challenges to traditional groups. The middle sectors' greatest contribution to contemporary Latin America could almost be defined as the institutionalization of social climbing.

Nowhere does it appear that the historical tradition of centralism is being challenged from within. In Europe and the United States, pressure groups played an important role in promoting reforms demanded by modern industrial technology. In Latin America they are either incapable of, or lack interest in, assuming this responsibility. It is unclear which social sector can assume this function in the near future.

The concept of the state as instrument is generally accepted in Great Britain and the United States. On it are based premises and postulates which subtly signal the task of many sociologists and political scientists concerned with Latin American affairs. Eminent foreign students of Latin America have spent considerable time and effort identifying the pressure groups which compete to gain control of that presumably inert tool, the central state. Their studies share with classical European Marxism a liberal concept of the state; it is viewed as a passive instrument which one group or another inevitably uses to further its interests. The most recent literature on this subject, published in the northern hemisphere, reflects the feeling of some authors that diverse pressure groups are now favorably located to take charge of "modernization." Opinion differs as to which group will assume this leadership; some look to the rising middle sectors, and others to Nasserist groups in the armed forces. Some hope (or fear) that a peasant uprising will be the social and political motor for reforming the entire structure. And the student vanguard has recently been nominated for this leadership.

These speculations do not seem very useful. They derive from the mistaken notion that the state in Latin America is as instrumental as it was in Europe until a few decades ago—and just as sensitive to the pressures (orderly or not) of peripheral groups representing interests external to the state. This seems erroneous. The Latin American state is not at the mercy of the strongest faction, but rather is itself the most powerful pressure group, real or potential, within the social conglomerate. It exercises power through a highly centralized bureaucracy. Complex social security services and patronage systems have made an institutionalized clientele of almost the entire urban sector. The state controls the most important academic centers, and exercises almost absolute control over every aspect of economic life. Possibly the only institutions that could be considered alternative power centers, given their relative autonomy, are the Catholic Church and the armed forces. But, almost by definition, neither is pluralistic or peripheral. As long as their demands and basic principles are satisfied, these institutions tend to reinforce government centralism.[3] The armed forces have a conception of national responsibility which opposes any dispersion or attenuation of central power; traditional Church preoccupations, perhaps as a holdover from past control, are with increasing the state's social and economic role to solve the most urgent problems of poverty and of exploitation of the dispossessed. We will attempt at least one explanation of why the state, Latin America's basic and predominant pressure group, has not exercised a stronger influence before now. During the century preceding the crisis of 1929, conditions in most of Latin America made significant state intervention unnecessary. Ruling groups prospered, and Europe's intellectual vanguard remained closely committed to the postulates of economic liberalism. With the same assiduousness and enthusiasm with which they imported English fashions, French architecture, and Italian opera, Latin America's rulers also imported British liberalism to fill the doctrinal void. Growing European demand for Latin America's raw materials made laissez-faire not only socially and intellectually advantageous, but also extremely attractive from a commercial and financial point of view. The apparent passivity of the central state was less an external imposition than an internal decision— or, perhaps more accurately, an omission—founded in the ruling group's objective prosperity. Sarmiento was not alone in arguing that Latin America would become civilized to the extent that it could effectively imitate all things European.

The 1929 crisis terminated this long prosperity. The veil of pluralist and peripheral liberalism imported from Europe began unraveling, and traditional political centralism revived. This coincided with massive incorporation of modern industrial technology by means of indiscriminate import substitution. The external pressures generated by the Second World War postponed nationalist resurgence for several decades; otherwise it would have coincided with these two other phenomena.

The wartime hiatus in Latin American nationalism had one primary cause. Our continent fell into the Allied sphere of influence. Apart from the support many of our countries lent the democratic cause, there were strong pressures for their active participation in the conflict. One result was a political moratorium on both domestic and international levels.

Since unchecked nationalism was regarded as one of the war's main causes, it was generally rejected afterward. This phenomenon undermined nationalist politics throughout the western world. The victorious allies enthusiastically formed the United Nations, in some ways a symbolic repudiation of traditional nationalism. This organization represented a new and sincere commitment to internationalist ideals, with which it hoped to prevent a recurrence of war.

Latin American nationalism could hardly have prospered at this moment—the new religion was internationalism, and the new ethic, cooperation across national boundaries.

But the world soon faced a new division. In his famous doctrinal declaration of 1947, President Truman divided the world between democracies and totalitarian dictarorships. The dawn of the Cold War thus posed Latin America a formidable, though false, dilemma. Truman's division contained an obvious fallacy; the many dictatorships in the supposedly "democratic" world were apparent to the least astute. It was also evident that Latin American communist parties did not really espouse the revolutionary politics attributed to them by the postulates with which the conflict was defined. On only two occasions in recent history—El Salvador in 1932 and Brazil in 1935,—did Latin American Communists directly participate in violent attempts to seize power. As a rule, they have reflected the Soviet Union's pragmatic acceptance of Latin America's location within the North American sphere of influence. Though this circumstance was abundantly clear to the area's political leaders, Cold War pressures forced anticommunism to become dogma. The supposed subversive threat was widely publicized. Even sensible politicians fulminated against the Red menace, all the while perfectly aware that their actions were only a rather frivolous means of assuring United States friendship and material aid.

Almost inevitably, Latin America's internal politics were determined by world politics, in which Washington censured all deviations from the status quo. Though both the United States and the Soviet Union sponsored "international" organizations throughout the world, subordination of national interests to the

Cold War brought fears of greater political dependency. As nominally "aligned" countries like China, Yugoslavia, and France manifest increasing independence, and as it becomes clear that all-out war will not occur, relations between the superpowers have mellowed. The resurgence of Latin American nationalism comes at a time when more and more politicians and intellectuals are convinced that models of economic and social change based on the northern hemisphere's experiences simply do not apply to this part of the world. It is also widely felt that one of Latin America's main problems is increasing external dependence—economic, cultural, and political.

For want of a complex ideological framework, social conglomerates tend to accept the imposition of basic political loyalties with surprising docility. Elsewhere these may be as simple as loyalty to tribe or family; the Latin American equivalent is nationalism. This sentiment makes no intellectual demands. It diffuses with a minimum of effort and facilities, and overcomes all internal frontiers, social or political.

Nationalism thus constitutes a formidable social and political force which cannot be ignored. Its dynamic power, however, does not necessarily reflect a content capable of stimulating positive achievements. While it may bridge an uncertain present and a satisfactory future, the transition is not without dangers. By definition, nationalism looks beyond national boundaries, and tends to exaggerate external influences on the domestic situation. Even when this feeling is founded on a reasoned understanding of national problems, it tends to create international frictions. These become ever more serious with a successful policy of national affirmation. Such a phenomenon, simultaneously affecting all major Latin American countries, could have serious repercussions on integration. For example, it is no secret that phantoms of balance of power politics, which many believed dead with the nineteenth century, have returned to haunt numerous Latin American chancellories. The current armament policies of some area countries highlight the risks on our political horizon.

A main objective of Latin American nationalism is, of course, lessening dependency on the United States. North American

policy statements often support this view, while including corollary exhortations for our countries to work harder at national
development. North American financial difficulties may make
this position obligatory rather than optional. In any case, limiting
autonomous management of national affairs is a tricky business; a
country trying to plan and execute its economic development will
naturally tend toward independence in foreign policy.

Latin American attitudes toward the United States may be on
the verge of a major change. This does not imply returning to the
extreme left's furious Cold War antiyankeeism; but rather a subtle
but generalized divergence, parallelling nationalist resurgence,
and with no particular political affiliation.

For instance, until recently the Latin American military
unconditionally supported all of Washington's suggestions. But a
more critical attitude is appearing. In some cases, United States
refusals to contribute to Latin America's arms race have provoked
severe comments in high military circles and affected dispositions
toward collaboration. But change has also reflected genuine
national sentiments, which find excessive American interference
an obstacle to development. Finally, some military sectors feel
that plans for integration simply echo Washington's directives,
and are unrelated to Latin America's best interests.

Recent student movements in many of our countries, despite
their diverse origins, objectives, and political affiliations, share a
preoccupation with research as the only effective way to counter
North American cultural penetration and end scientific and
technological dependence. These aspirations, common to groups
of middle-and upper-class background, are divorced from party
politics.

Moreover, the remains of the Alliance for Progress, after its
tranquil dissolution, include various social-democratic movements which believe, with or without justification, that the
United States has not fulfilled the promises it made at Punta del
Este. These groups feel that while they made every effort to
implement requested structural reforms, the North American
government failed to come through with expected moral and
material support. But this frustration is insignificant compared to
that of the traditional groups to the right of the political spec-

trum. After loyally supporting almost all United States political initiatives during the last two decades, even in the face of strong domestic opposition to measures like the Bay of Pigs invasion and the overthrow of the Guatemalan government, these parties felt totally betrayed when the Kennedy administration proposed a reform program whose success would have undermined their economic and political bases.

Concern over the nature of Latin American integration focuses on its close ties with North American initiatives, financing, and support. Three main international organs are concerned with integration: the InterAmerican Development Bank, the InterAmerican Committee of the Alliance for Progress, and the Latin American Free Trade Association. The first two (and the strongest) are Washington-based and primarily financed by nonregional resources. Only the third is essentially Latin American, but its success has hardly been overwhelming. The need for a genuinely Latin American integration has frequently been noted at high level academic meetings and in other contexts. The current process is disturbingly interAmerican; one way or another, North American influence in guiding change is likely to remain excessive.

Assuming an accentuation of traditional political centralism, and that our continent will reflect the worldwide nationalist resurgence (one of the most important and subtle aspirations of which is to diminish cultural, economic, and political dependency), the following problems could materialize in the next three decades. It is altogether possible that interAmerican relations will cool. Latin America's challenge will not necessarily originate in the extreme left. The state, whatever its political color, will define new terms; these will be especially difficult to appreciate in terms of the traditional right–left spectrum, since governments will be characterized by a pragmatism defying classification. The United States may prove vulnerable to this centralist and nationalist challenge, since its enormous political and military arsenal is geared to possible attack from the extreme left. For example, Washington would have trouble neutralizing a Latin American deGaullism.

Second, nationalist resurgence may obstruct integration. This will become more evident as the link between integration and United States support and initiatives grows closer and clearer. One solution would be a genuinely Latin American integration program. To satisfy the demands of both nationalism and integration, though, a coalition would have to be formed. Rather than accepting political and economic proximity to the United States, this body would search for decorous but effective ways to terminate the external dependence which determines and limits Latin American development.

Third, restored fluidity in international politics, combined with nationalist upswing (which is certain to continue for some time), will create growing government responsibilities which require even greater state intervention in all aspects of national life. The role of both foreign and domestic private enterprise will be substantially altered. For instance, multinational state enterprise, not private corporations, may be the main vehicle for integration development—if integration changes character and receives new impetus.

Finally, present tendencies may generate a Latin American political style firmly rooted in an autochthonous centralist tradition. The intelligentsia might then successfully define a development model based on the area's real situation.

Recent Latin American literary and artistic production has been abundant and of high quality. Perhaps the best contemporary novels have been written by Peruvians, Argentines, and Colombians during the last ten years. But political and scientific achievements are less impressive. Our intellectuals have assiduously imitated supposedly exemplary models from Europe and the United States over a long period. Worse, they have looked abroad not only for answers, but for questions as well. This has cemented a grave cultural dependency. It is quite possible that the only escape from this unacceptable historical situation will involve the dangerous spur of nationalist resurgence.

NOTES

1. The failure refers to the MNR's inability to consolidate its power as well as to its continuing schismatic tendencies. Since Paz Estenssoro was ousted in 1964 different factions of the military have run the government. (Ed.)

2. Celso Furtado, "La concentracion del poder economico en los Estados Unidos y sus proyecciones en América Latina," *Estudios Internacionales* (Santiago), Octubre, 1967, pp. 323–336.

3. With the notable exception of controversies over patronage during the nineteenth century; but, as is well known, these were resolved before World War I.

6. MULTINATIONAL PUBLIC CORPORATIONS IN LATIN AMERICAN SUB-REGIONAL INTEGRATION

Marcos Kaplan

Consejo Latino Americano de Ciencias Sociales, Buenos Aires

This study will attempt to evaluate continental integration via the Latin American Free Trade Association (LAFTA), and will propose multinational public corporations as agents of the process.

I. A CRISIS MODEL OF INTEGRATION: LAFTA

The integration of Latin America involves a huge area composed of many nations, each with its own socioeconomic, institutional, political, and cultural systems. It is a process in which various aspects interact, interpenetrate, and condition one another. [1] Neither of the ongoing integration experiments—the Latin American Free Trade Association and the Central American Common Market—has been dynamic enough to guarantee uninterrupted progress.

LAFTA, the region's largest and most ambitious integration project, neither originated in nor has evolved according to a conscious model. It is instead the largely accidental byproduct of empirical reactions to the continent's grave structural crises. A precarious syncretism of abstract theory and short range pragmatism handicapped LAFTA from the outset, as demonstrated in its real motives and in the arguments used to justify it.

Real Motivations and Doctrinal Bases

1. Outward-oriented, superficial changes in the determinants and conditioners of the traditional dependent growth model, including declining export prices and demand, deteriorating terms of trade, a weakened and differently oriented international flow of private capital, and mounting indebtedness.
2. The need for mechanisms to solve balance of payment problems (scarcity, control, and nonconvertibility of exchange), to compensate favorable bilateral monetary balances by multilateralizing their use, and to increase intrazone commerce.
3. The limitations of import-substitution industrialization, which is neither integrated nor supported by structural changes, demands heavy imports in the face of decreasing exports and growing debts, and must be maintained with a greater self-supply of raw materials, intermediate products, and capital goods. Difficulties in achieving integrated industrialization and continuous, self-sustained development with physically and demographically inadequate markets, further complicated by existing socioeconomic, occupational, and income structures, and by external instability.
4. In consequence, integration is more and more being conceptualized in terms of a general model allowing:

   a) Enlarged and permanent new markets for primary and industrial production, which will encourage large-scale operations and heavy investments with long term and medium range returns.
   b) Advance beyond the binomial: "redundant production in inadequate markets"–"wasted installed capacity."
   c) Reciprocal benefits from complementary activities.
   d) New undertakings, enterprises, and technology, which individual countries could not sustain alone.
   e) Optimum factor use, economies of scale, localization of new investments, technological and scientific development, mobilization of cadres, specialization of tasks, and rationalization of human effort without higher unemployment.

f) Continuing import substitution.

g) Increased investments, productivity, and consumption.

5. The current integration model has been a response to various factors, including fear of disruptions caused by economic stagnation in a context of explosive population growth; the impact of the "demonstration effect" and rising expectations; and related social, ideological, and political conflicts and tensions. The Cuban challenge is perceived as a revolutionary danger which cannot be combatted by repression alone. As these characteristics indicate, the integration model was born in a context of modernizing conservatism.

6. Integration is not presented as an option which excludes national development or greater participation in the world market, but as a prerequisite for new possibilites. It must encourage and facilitate more rapid and diversified internal growth, modernization, national integration, and the mobilization of dynamic social groups. It can afford members the advantages of combined national markets, and facilitate access to those of the advanced countries. Participation in a large regional market would offer the benefits traditionally attributed to an international division of labor. At the same time it would eliminate the difficulties underdeveloped countries have encountered from the unrestricted application of this doctrine, particularly in activities involving industrial competition with the advanced countries.

7. Regional integration is both necessary and feasible for countries in close geographic proximity or which have similar origins and histories, ethnic compositions, socioeconomic, political, and cultural structures, and external obstacles to progress—for countries separated by the vicissitudes of history and the manipulations of foreign powers, but which aspire to be autonomous subjects, not passive objects, in their own histories and in world politics. Integration will create a single powerful bloc that will strengthen Latin America's international position, negotiating capacity, and effective autonomy. These conditions are generated and reinforced by circumstances and tendencies like the following.

8. The international system has recently tended to organize large economic spaces. The United States and Russia, the European Common Market, COMECON, and China are both examples and challenges for Latin America. Large communities and continental and subcontinental areas are the contemporary form of supra-national economic organization, and will persist over an indefinite period. It is apparent, by contrast, that no single Latin American state can boast the resources or the sociopolitical and institutional basis for adequate development. Consolidation of a regional macrosociety, parallelled by a neo- or supra-nationalism of continental scope, are essential in the near future.

9. The North American government and its large private enterprises are becoming more interested in Latin American integration.[2] Though initially wary and hostile, they are now willing to adapt to and benefit from LAFTA. This model offers vast possibilities for North American private investment and could lead to the definitive consolidation of hegemonic control. Eliminating intraregional barriers while establishing common external tariff levels,would create a unified market of hundreds of millions. This is tempting for North American marco-units now operating at peak efficiency or capable of creating highly capitalized and dynamic enterprises of optimum size. Such activities could profit from enlarged and stabilized markets, economies of scale, and reduced costs, and thus more easily eliminate or subordinate local and European competition; they could function on a continental scale, according to new divisions and specializations of labor by branches and regions. Integration tends to stimulate corporate growth and concentration, and thus encourages monopolies and oligopolies in key sectors. It aids in creating, multiplying, and strengthening international power centers— veritable superpowers external to the region. These units will make ever more basic and far-reaching decisions for each country's structure and direction, as well as for Latin America as a whole, in areas including investments, localization, technology, production and employment, income, foreign

trade, the extent of the national economies' internal integration, types of specialization, and patterns of equilibrium and disequilibrium among countries, areas, and social groups.

The hegemony of North American macro-enterprises implies a development and integration model in which they would play the fundamental role and reap most of the benefits. Their overwhelming power, the unlimited support they receive from their governments, and the equation of the Latin American status quo with North American security, all lead to strict external control and rigorous supervision of Latin American development, economic policies, power structures, and social processes. The Alliance for Progress, regional integration, and military mechanisms for repressing subversion are viewed as inseparable elements in a unified strategy. Latin American states could lose many of their political functions, especially those for orienting socioeconomic change. The nation could become less and less important as a substantial and operative reality, and nationalism itself might become obsolete.

These are possible implications of the proposed integration scheme. To the extent this model describes the present process, these results are now apparent. The risks and dangers for Latin America are reasons for support by North America's government and industrial consortiums.

Progress

LAFTA, created by the Montevideo Treaty in February 1960, has achieved much in spite of its original limitations and subsequent shortcomings. It is the first step in a new and risky experiment at uniting countries dissimilar in structure and development, in particularly difficult world and regional conditions. An accord—though limited and controversial—has been reached despite these obstacles and widespread pessimism, and the Association has survived for more than eight years.

LAFTA, through an institutional mechanism designed to overcome national barriers, has created a framework for negotiating commercial liberation. Intrazone trade has increased significantly. Two accords concerning complementary industries have been put into effect. The Brussels Customs Nomenclature has been adopted as a common base for statistics, analysis, and negotiation. Criteria have been established for determining the real origin of merchandise involved in regional commerce, to correctly apply tariff concessions and to reduce fraud via re-export machinations. Many sectoral meetings have been held, and special commissions and work groups formed, to consider different aspects of integration. A uniform statistical system has been elaborated to analyze intrazone commerce. Infrastructure has not been ignored: LAFTA encourages regional entrepreneurs to meet and participate in the integration process, and ideas and problems are publicized throughout member countries.

Obstacles and Shortcomings

Our portrayal of integration's positive aspects must be balanced by a summary of obstacles and shortcomings.[3] We will begin with LAFTA's original capabilities and mechanisms.

National Diversity. In contrast to the European Common Market, Latin America attempted integration only after a long time-lag in which its position was worsening even as the process began, and which paralyzed attempts to overcome it. Historical lateness and the consequent underdevelopment were both motivations for and obstacles to integration.

There is a basic conflict between the region to be integrated and the nations that compose it. Latin American countries are quite heterogeneous, and fall into at least three categories: "the Big Three," an intermediate group, and the less developed countries. They are separated by enormous geographic and historical differences, and highly diverse developmental stages, socio-economic structures, levels of industrialization, salary scales, living standards, market situations, and policies and available instruments (tax, customs, monetary, exchange, and credit policies). In terms of integration, these variations generate demands for special treatment by the participating countries.

The situation is further complicated by the centrifugal character of Latin American economies, which have closer links to Europe and the United States than with each other. They are competitive rather than complementary, separated by great distances and imposing geographic obstacles, and lacking the infrastructure which would facilitate contact. Varying political regimes, foreign policies, cultural patterns, and ideological orientations aggravate the problems. The continent lacks both traditions and instruments of multilateral economic cooperation. Regional solidarity is not strong enough to overcome individual nationalisms. No one state is sufficiently endowed and motivated to direct the project on its own, the "Big Three" (Argentina, Brazil, and Mexico) have not agreed to assume joint leadership.

Groups opposed to integration.   These circumstances strengthen resistance to change in groups linked to the traditional socioeconomic structure, who oppose any alteration of the status quo, fear how integration might affect their personal interests, and see no potential benefits. Though forces both for and against integration operate at national, regional, and international levels, the sectors that must eventually spur the process are relatively weak.

Factors actively or passively opposing integration include:

a) those linked to the traditional structure or to stagnant and unprofitable activities, especially agriculturalists, exporters, importers, and middle men;

b) those tied to small and medium industries which have remained static behind protective tariff barriers;

c) old-style public and private bureaucracies;

d) the armed forces, who see integration as a possible threat to traditional national sovereignty and thus to their own predominance;

e) political parties linked to traditional groups or inspired by some variant of developmentalism (Argentina's Frondizi-ism for example), and the Old Left. (The New Left seems to recognize the need for integration, though it seeks a revolutionary-socializing form.);

f) foreign enterprises with primary-sector investments and which are not participating in internal industrialization;

g) the smallest or relatively less developed countries, which fear the possible lack of reciprocity in integration and the danger of greater inequality or absorption. These states have taken a marginal, wait-and-see position. Also, those large countries which consider integration unnecessary for and incompatible with their own presumed potentials for independent development (Argentina, for example).

Groups in favor of integration. Sectors and groups that favor—or at least do not completely oppose—integration include:

a) intellectuals, university students, technicians, and national and international bureaucrats;
b) parties and governments inspired by certain developmentalist ideals (Chile's Christian Democracy, Mexico's PRI);
c) international technical and financial institutions (ECLA, IDB);
d) sectors linked to the production of goods and services for the internal market and "nontraditional" exports (metallurgy, machinery, durable consumption goods);
e) some of the larger and better developed countries (Mexico, Brazil);
f) some major powers and their international consortiums, interested in a specific type of Latin American growth and industrialization (especially the United States, for the reasons and with the qualifications mentioned above).

These forces vary considerably in content, implication, and intensity. Those opposing integration seem to outnumber those in favor, actually or potentially. Particularly noteworthy is the widespread ignorance, indifference, and passivity of industrial entrepreneurs, the middle sectors, and labor unions.

The nonexistence or weakness of social forces favoring integration makes the process a kind of abstract drama without specific actors. This is apparent in the actions of political parties and the state, collective attitudes toward integration, and the features of the proposed model.

Contemporary Latin American development is characterized by a superposition of socioeconomic, political, ideological, and cultural forms and forces corresponding to different historical stages; the area's social structures are heterogeneous and conflicting. Politically, this wide variation has delayed and confused the formulation of objectives and rational plans for action. It is thus difficult to obtain a clear consensus on the nature of major national tasks and goals, and on how to implement them. The wide range of conflicting phases, social structures, and regional bases aggravates antagonisms, irreducible options, and incongruent alliances; incoherence and impasse result. This impedes clear formulation of problems and really effective solutions, especially for the basic issues of economic development and social change. Political parties cannot unite the diverse interests or offer coherent and representative programs. Almost none are actively concerned with integration, or include it as one of their emotional and intellectual bases. At best, support is only rhetorical. The project is not a really compelling priority reflected in systematic political activities; nor is it part of a general model for internal transformation.

Class and party indifference to integration detract from its popular appeal and retard formation of a favorable consensus; they also affect the attitude and conduct of area nations.[4]

The role of state governments. The Latin American state inherited and perpetuates antiquated administrative machinery and a tradition of laissez-faire liberalism that have left it unprepared for the growing number of new and complex tasks, and made state intervention seem abnormal and transitory. This situation—unequal and combined development which decays before it has a chance to mature—is typical of dependent capitalism. Usually only national and foreign ruling class interests are represented, though some cases include pressures corresponding to relatively complex and diversified societies as well.

State enterprises and economic interventions, both susceptible to penetration by private groups, are distorted or obstructed in contexts resistant to development, social change, modernization, and rationality. This negative conditioning is manifested in several ways: external aid and dependency replace national initiative; private property, enterprise and gain, backed by an almost mythological dogma, reign supreme; social stratification systems and the power structure are rigid and conservative. The crisis of hegemony in Latin America means that no single class or faction dominates the state or can utilize it to further a defined and coherent strategy. Each class and group exerts pressure for its own sectoral interests, and state policies often seem no more than an unstable product of this play of forces. Monopolistic consortiums and foreign governments (especially the United States) and their local allies are hostile to state intervention and regulation. But these groups simultaneously use the state for their own ends, penetrating it with their representatives, influence, control, and ideology. The national industrial bourgeoisie has failed to provide skilled cadres, a strategy, entrepreneurial experience, or models of rationality and efficiency. It has tried to penetrate and influence the state only for its own immediate and limited goals. One example of false consciousness is its consistent opposition to government intervention, without which it could not have arisen and prospered. The middle and popular strata have usually exerted pressure either mechanically and externally, without direct and active participation in the state, or through vicarious and subordinated populist and bureaucratic participation. Divergent or antagonistic social and political pressures have made government action weak and irrational, when it has not been paralyzed altogether.

The combination of economic liberalization with political absolutism has aggravated conditions. Latin American societies increasingly tend toward stagnation and rigidity, regressive income redistribution, concentration of power in small groups, and frustration of middle sector and popular aspirations; greater imbalances, tensions, and conflicts are the consequence. This process is reflected in a double phenomenon. A movement for economic liberalization has advocated weakening the state apparatus, and disabling or suppressing or rendering inoperative its powers of regulation, orientation, promotion, entrepreneurial activity, and intervention in socioeconomic life. Economic decision-making power would be transferred from the state to market forces, or rather to the private national and foreign corporate structures which dominate the market. The traditional structure would thus be reinforced, and the way cleared for colonialist penetration, reinforced dependency, and stagnation. But, at the same time, political absolutism is being affirmed: movements for social change are declared illegal, repressive methods are perfected and capabilities enlarged, and such elements of the liberal political-judicial system as the rule of law, popular sovereignty, universal suffrage, public liberties, and democratic controls, are degraded and suppressed. Economic liberalization, combined with political absolutism, will either introduce or reinforce the stasis, crisis, and irrationality of state activities.

Other aspects of government action are better understood within this general perspective. The Latin American state has neither valid precedents nor a unified, up-to-date, and efficient philosophy to define the character, extent, and methods of its intervention and control. These do not presently result from a deliberate intention to plan and transform; they are usually improvised, and persist as unsystematic responses to the unforeseen pressures of events. Though most are more lasting than initially anticipated, they also reflect a "bad conscience" and a paralyzing ambiguity which lead to nonemployment or poor use of both economic policy instruments and the enterprise's powers. Interventions are unplanned, inorganic, uncoordinated, contradictory, and disorganizing. They create unforeseen difficulties, generate all manner of conflicts—including with other state policies and goals—and feed irrationality and anarchy. The repercussions are apparent in the indiscriminate, erratic, and ineffective activities of the public sector and its enterprises. These are utilized indiscriminately, erratically, and to limited effect.

Latin America's public sector and its enterprises could be powerful tools for development; at present they are either misused or ignored. The state begins with a limited, ambiguous view of both its agencies and its own role. It generally denies the right of the public sector to direct the economy. With few exceptions, the state and its enterprises have expanded no faster than private entities, and only survive from historical inertia and the stalemate of social forces. State action usually neither expands nor favors the public sector; nor is it used to pioneer development. Governments exalt the power and role of large private enterprise while reducing their own functions to minimal regulation, and to filling economic and social gaps left by the free market.

The state can neither initiate nor impose regression to a pure liberal economy. But it has not openly committed itself to maintaining a mixed economy either; while this has been taking place, the state has left undefined both the terms of the process and its own function within it. Criteria are rarely specified, nor are general norms fixed to delineate the type of coexistence between public and private sectors, which will prevail, and where they will compete or where one will have exclusive control. When the state does retain powers to intervene or monopolizes some activity, it still may either concentrate on directly productive tasks or settle for technical and financial assistance to private entities. The situation is ambiguous and unstable. Such ill-defined coexistence of the public and private sectors can never become mechanical or lasting; it involves mutual relations and influences, reciprocal modifications, contradictions and conflicts, and political and institutional repercussions. One or the other must ultimately prevail. The combination persists nonetheless, though it tends to fortify private enterprises at the expense of the public sector's importance and efficiency.

All this helps explain the Latin American state's limitations as an effective agent for development and integration. Unrepresentative governments generally reject or postpone the daring, dynamic, and long term actions which integration requires. These governments lack either the support of socioeconomic and political forces actively committed to development and integration or, in many cases, even the strength deriving from national unity. Minority pressures, a precarious political base, and absorption in difficulties of the moment obstruct clear vision and sure, rapid decisions. State adhesion to a laissez-faire system and ideology, and its persistent interventions to support them, signify its renunciation of the power to control and transform the economy. And so, in the face of multiple alternatives, plans, and programs, the state is incapable of synthesizing an ideology, values, or clear options for a viable integration and development strategy. The process remains subject to market dynamics and to the most organized and powerful private interests, which are either not concerned with such matters, or recognize them only in terms of their own desires and goals. Integrationist activities are usually relegated to second-echelon bureaucrats with little or no decision-making power.

LAFTA represents but one of several integration models. The initial exclusion of many alternatives covered a basic ideological stance with the appearance of technocratic neutrality. The LAFTA model, under the guise of conservative reformism, was presented as a response to revolutionary danger. It appears as a sort of panacea which, automatically and independently, will generate development, modernization, and autonomy. Since it requires only certain predetermined changes, it will maintain social stability and class and power structures, and perpetuate the region's historical position under North American hegemony. Integration is conceptualized as necessary and sufficient for development, or as a basic element in a particular and noteworthy vision of the process. This image of development is, paradoxically, shared by both supporters and opponents of integration.[5]

Its starting point is superficial and mechanistic, and presumes that the classical model of western capitalistic development can be imitated. But this supposition ignores the profound differences between the historical context of capitalism in Western Europe and North America, and that in which Latin America's would develop. Radical differences in international circumstances, and particularly the decisive role of Latin American dependency, are also overlooked—and thus the consequent external obstacles to economic development, social change, political autonomy, and democratization.

Second, the model's conception of development and underdevelopment is banal, fragmented, and purely economic. Underdevelopment is apparently limited to problems like external strangulation, disproportionately high production, and industrial backwardness. Development plans and perspectives stress economics while ignoring social, ideological, and psychological features, and their correlations and interactions in this complex and all-enveloping process. These limitations are particularly apparent in the analysis of integration, which is expected to unleash economic and technological development. These, as autonomous and exogenous agents, would in turn transform, modernize, and rationalize society, while guaranteeing full sovereignty and internal democracy.

The presentation of only one model for development and integration ignores other possibilities. The significance and content of integration are not precisely defined; nor are the value system to be adopted or the range of alternatives and options, objectives and means, internal and external requisites, actors and obstacles, or instruments and consequences.

Social, ideological, and political aspects are either overlooked or played down. Opponents are not clearly defined, and the strategies for bypassing them are unclear. The role of hegemonic power and the dominant classes is merely attributed to backwardness, and expected to disappear along with it. The need to overcome Latin America's external dependency and subordination to the United States is never mentioned; it is assumed that relations with the superpower obey a preestablished harmony of interests.[6]

Virtually no attempt has been made to specify which classes and sectors could promote total, uninterrupted development and integration. There have been no suggestions for how these groups would be structured, would recruit leadership, or formulate and express motivations, attitudes, and ideologies; their potential contribution to change and to the creation of a massive consensus favoring the proposed objectives remains vague. Nor has it been determined how costs, sacrifices, and benefits might be shared.

A large gap divides the binomial "development-integration" and "sociopolitical change." Significant modifications in the social and power structures which sustain the dominant classes seem to be feared rather than encouraged. These structures are not questioned; either they are considered normal and innocuous, or democratization is expected automatically to accompany progress toward economic development and integration. No real political strategy, including alternatives, mobilizing ideologies, and successive forms and phases, has been elaborated. The implications of an uninterrupted development and integration process are not discussed; nor is the image of the society that would emerge from it and which is sought as a historical project. The underlying or explicit ideology is inadequate to mobilize likely protagonists intellectually or emotionally. The disruptions and violence which always occur in this kind of process are rejected as pathological manifestations to be prevented *a priori* and at any cost. Suggested institutional schemes are abstract and formal, unrelated to the overall context, and either inoperative or lacking a basis for implementation. The proposed model is utopian and achronistic. Its advantages are not readily apparent, and the dangers that could result from nonimplementation are not specified. It has roots in neither the ruling elite nor the masses; it does not provide for mobilizing support within the countries. The model's present day functioning demonstrates these failings.

Economic factors.   In this play of forces, each country tends to consider its own economic development as an exclusively national and autarchic undertaking. Each indiscriminately protects its own enterprises, with no thought for efficiency or future possibilities. Several states have attempted to create key industries (metallurgy, automobiles), but these have proved uneconomical; scarce resources have been wasted, and economies of scale are not well understood. Most important, this policy has created powerful interests which may block progress toward integration. The "nation-region" dilemma has also been aggravated, maintaining national industrialization possibilities rather than creating economic spaces necessary for increased planned production. Some countries do not believe that their economic space is inadequate. Others fear that regional economic cooperation, functioning according to criteria of profitability set by the play of market forces, would either destroy their own industries (to the benefit of the region's large countries) or lock them into their status quo as nonindustrial states.

Regional integration has only been accepted when circumstances demanded it, and even then with intellectual and practical reservations. The focus is confining and progress ever less satisfactory; overall outlines have simply never been sketched. The basis for the scheme, a Free Trade Zone, limits action to the mercantile field. Commerce is stimulated through periodic negotiations both to lower or suspend tariffs and restrictions on reciprocal trade and to create commercial preferences between members. Only limited obligations have been imposed, and only minimal subsidiary planning is intended; progress is entrusted to competition in the enlarged market. Members have not advanced beyond simple cooperation through small-scale agreements. National sovereignties remain intact, and there has been no real modification in loose, restricted, and undynamic relations. No one urges or imposes the changes in economic, social, and political structures that would lead to sustained and autonomous development. All this has hampered solutions to the growing problems of imbalance and stagnation.

Tariffs.   Tariffs are reduced only gradually and selectively, with separate negotiations on each product and minimum annual reductions according to average duties throughout the zone. The system is at once too rigid and too flexible. Every country dickers in the same way over thousands of products, one by one, after which they all haggle together. But then each is free to fix how, when, and by how much duties will be reduced for each item. Conflicts generated by the confrontation of vested interests must also be solved, which further limits any advance toward integration. Even small groups can frustrate integrationist measures. Each member state constantly fears it will yield too much, and that costs will outweigh benefits—which usually appear remote, abstract, and controversial. There are always hopes that integration will afford unilateral profits. No one is sure how long or extensively preferential rates will continue. Thus it is difficult to assess the situation facing some products; uncertainty delays both exploitation of concessions and effective programming of public and private investments.

Difficulties are exacerbated by recent economic stagnation in almost all LAFTA countries. Their structures have become more rigid, while capacities for adjusting to change have diminished. LAFTA is increasingly viewed as an outlet for the national surpluses resulting from economic stagnation. Existing economies of scale are not used to best advantage, and new ones are not created; trade in industrial products is more and more difficult. This reaffirms the following circular relationship: while integration is to advance development, its progress is impaired by the absence of rapid and effective development.

Organizations and institutions. There is at present no adequate institutional structure to support integration. Treaty-linked organizations haven't the power to implement efficiently the enlarged tasks of a new stage of integration. Existing organizations represent and defend each country's interests, expressed through governments which are seldom representative, so continuing support for integration is discourage. Community institutions capable of formulating and executing policies of regional integration and development do not yet exist.

LAFTA itself is showing signs of stagnation. Progress was rapid in early negotiations, but affected only traditionally commercialized products, and those already covered by bilateral agreements for special discounts, and which required only renegotiation or consolidation. Some tariff concessions have only reduced theoretically high rates that were never actually applied. Countries with high duties have been in an advantageous position for reducing them, without this implying any real curtailment of protection.

Initial progress in negotiations involved traditionally important products from third countries, or commodities like raw materials and agricultural goods in which every nation feels efficient and competitive. Difficulties arose over articles with significant current production or good prospects for it in the supplier country, or which could be imported at international prices. This applied especially to industrial products: final consumption goods, light metallurgy, uncomplicated machinery, and vehicles. Controlling or barring certain imports to protect the balance of payments has also caused problems. It is thus more and more difficult to negotiate tariff reductions on most dutiable goods, especially those that could stimulate and diversify regional trade.

Other obstacles include structural and rate differences in customs schedules, monetary and credit systems, and other instruments of economic policy; and varying productivity levels, salary rates, and social welfare systems. "The distinct composition of each Latin American country's imports from within the zone, and each nation's right to choose the products for negotiation, as well as the level of tariff reductions, means that not all negotiate on the same articles; furthermore, customs reductions and preferences are seldom uniform. Until 1973, when the Common List goes into effect, there is no way to ensure that the products included in the liberation program receive uniform customs treatment." And so there is no guarantee of equal preference margins or similar policies for all items. "Hardly any of the products included in this program has a regional market. Few opportunities, of varying real effectiveness, have opened in the presumably importing countries."[7] Difficulties in weighting taxes and duties to have similar effects, and in confirming whether minimum agreements have been fulfilled, have led to negotiations based primarily "on the a priori establishment of a certain balance of opportunities." As a result, countries minimize their concessions.

The heterogeneity of LAFTA members' monetary, customs, exchange, credit, and financing policies hinders integration. Problems of differing customs rates are compounded by the rarely negotiable systems of licenses, prior deposits, and fiscal charges, for which the Treaty has left various loopholes. There has been little progress toward a common external tariff structure.

Strangulation of their external sectors, permanent instability in gold and exchange reserves, and almost uninterrupted inflation plague nearly all the LAFTA nations. Inflation in particular hampers growth by thwarting efforts at public and private savings. It causes violent fluctuations in costs and productivity, and often results in the coexistence of formal stabilization policies with effective devaluation. Internal monetary anarchy is then reflected in the integration process. Inflation, compounded by anarchic and heterogeneous monetary systems hinders growth in intrazonal commerce and especially impairs the incorporation of industrial goods. Fluctuating costs and productivity make policies even more contradictory and unstable. They multiply over- and under-valuations and all manner of exchange artifices. The principle of reciprocity, essential in Treaty mechanics, is affected at its base; the many negative repercussions of monetary and exchange disparities limit the effectiveness of both tariff reductions and agreements for complementarity.

Opposition from the International Monetary Fund, the World Bank, and the United States, has obstructed the creation of financing systems for regional industrial planning and for integrative enterprises, and blocked instruments which would compensate for bilateral or multilateral trade surpluses or deficits, either among LAFTA members or between them and the rest of the world. These are essential to put an end to constant crises and to prepare a system of full convertibility and a monetary union.

Nonstandardized credit policies give competitive advantages to countries which grant special facilities for their exports. Similarly, countries with low pay scales and less ample social welfare systems can expect eventual amelioration of their competitive position.

Public and private savings are inadequate, while productive activities and integration lack sufficient resources. There is limited communication between the zone's financial and capital markets, and almost no framework for negotiating with wealthier countries and credit-supplying international organs.

LAFTA's crisis and stagnation are intensifying under the combined impact of these circumstances. Ever fewer products are negotiated in successive rounds of tariff reductions. Intrazonal commerce is expanding slowly. Only two agreements on industrial complementarity are being discussed between international enterprises, and the results are negligible. Trade in manufactured goods is growing slowly, and integration has barely affected industrial expansion. Multilateral enterprises and investments, as well as specific projects for strategic activities and regional development poles, are urgently needed. As yet there is no common policy toward foreign investments. Plans to intensify regional trade and to coordinate agricultural policies have not been implemented.

II. AN AGENT FOR A NEW STRATEGY: THE MULTINATIONAL PUBLIC CORPORATION

The Montevideo Treaty represented the absolute minimum starting point for Latin American integration. LAFTA's achievements are indisputable, as demonstrated by its experimental and catalytic function and its many accomplishments (which include the revelation of its own inadequacies).

But its serious limitations signal a phase of seemingly insoluble crisis and stagnation. LAFTA must advance beyond its present form and attempt, simultaneously or in succession, a customs union, a common market, and full integration and economic community. The accomplishments of the first phase of integration must be maintained, and increased flexibility and comprehensiveness introduced. An initial step would be brief or medium term transitional measures, but only as elements in a totally new program for development and integration. We shall expand on this later.

A global strategy for Latin American integration must be complemented by more specific partial measures, which supplement and enrich the general program.[8] These measures should focus on limited multinational projects to create and maintain centers of integrationist activity. These centers would stimulate integration at all levels, concentrating on formation of effective solidarity movements with a strong multiplier effect and maximum participation from various spaces, systems, groups, and individuals. These new interests would encourage new integration projects, and thus reinforce the general dynamic of the process. By providing a conceptual, analytical, and operative instrument, their activity would accentuate the necessity and viability of integration. It would guarantee sectoral unity, create economies of scale, and allow better use of material, financial, and human resources; by helping to equalize LAFTA members' development levels, it could promote greater relative equilibrium among them.

Such results demand prior determination of the varieties of current and future relationships which this subintegrative potential may incorporate. Structuring these relationships within general systems and specific projects with a major multiplier effect must be considered, along with economic, social, institutional, political, and cultural preconditions. A few types of subcontinental groupings can be mentioned for illustration: subregional groupings (Gran Colombia, the "Southern Cone," the La Plata basin, the Andean Group); sectoral integrations (basic or dynamic industries, infrastructures); united frontiers; and specific multinational projects and programs. We will discuss the structural possibilities and the problems of multinational public corporations as agents and foci of development and integration.

Integrating the Public Sectors

The state, state enterprise, and the public sector of the economy must play a decisive role in Latin American development and integration. The problem of state economic activity has intensified with Latin America's recent tendency toward increased state intervention, more numerous state enterprises, and growth of the public economic sector. Since 1930, especially, the process has intensified in response to:

—weakened traditional mechanisms of superficial growth by external stimuli and strictly private activity;
—accelerated urbanization and industrialization;
—the emergence of new, upward-aspiring social groups (the middle sectors, the industrial proletariat);
—substantial changes in the international economic and political structure;
—new models for obtaining and exercising political power;
—the affirmation of a nationalism that emphasizes internal factors and the need for instruments to promote rational organization and expansion of an independent economy;
—resistance to change by traditional structures and groups;
—the disunity, weakness, and directionlessness of sectors theoretically interested in modernization and structural change (industrial entrepreneurs and the labor movement).

All these have affected the state's willingness to intervene to compensate or substitute for weak traditional growth factors and to promote the urgent development demanded by stagnation and the crisis of traditional structures.[9]

Latin America's major countries have thus increased both the range and the quantity of state interventions and agencies. A mixed economy has emerged, with expanding public control and a plurality of decision-making centers. Clear examples are the growing number and scope of public development and finance corporations, departments of the central administration, state commercial societies, pure public enterprises, and mixed entities. Though we lack space to list them, data abound on high public sector participation in: total spending and investment; the formation and distribution of gross national product and income;

national capital; infrastructure and basic industrial development; transactions of goods and services; absorption of the growing labor force; subsidies to individual consumers and producers through price and fee reductions; and maintenance of the market's acquisitive capacity and regulation of its structure and functions. In sum, public sector participation is high in national economic development by means of internal stimuli and mechanisms.

We must consider some additional points to fully understand how important the state's economic sector and enterprises can become in the integration process. These include the role of government initiative in the creation and growth of the European Common Market. The state has a natural aptitude for overcoming regional or sectoral particularisms. All supranational power must originate in and filter through existing national states.

Integration also demands that Latin American public sectors unify their economic policies. Their contributions can include often-exclusive participation in such important activities as transportation, communications, electricity, petroleum, and basic industries; some of the main forms of international cooperation have emanated from the public sector. It should also balance or compensate private efforts to establish monopolies, and should match private enterprise in forgoing irreversible socioeconomic ties. Public sector cooperation would encompass such essential tasks as infrastructure integration, the creation or consolidation of key industries, technological progress, and regional planning (frontiers, international river basins). Finally, public sectors can help harmonize members' economic (monetary, credit, and banking) and social policies (employment and work conditions; a common statute for state workers, which could become a model for the private sector); and move toward unified legislation. [10]

Regional investment plans must prescribe the operational convergence of the public sectors' main economic activities. By extending and harmonizing national plans, as well as through tangible benefits for participants, these activities will help generate common goals. This will probably foster lasting solidarity of interests among states, within each one, and with the region as a whole. More specifically, regional investment planning would encourage common economic activities and the persistent interchange needed for balanced growth. It would also contribute to a new socioeconomic and political geography, deliberately fostered by scientific and technological advance; specialization and multilateral intraregional exchange; overcoming disequilibria and distortions; stimulating national interdependence; creating habits of cooperation; and adapting national boundaries to socioeconomic realities.

Such public-sector collaboration might correspond to recent experiments in "coproduction." The international model would include these characteristics:[11]

1. Contractual association between public decision making and productive centers from different countries, requiring specialized contributions under predetermined conditions to reach objectives through common efforts.

2. Durable institutionalized links of interests and of production and exchange among decision-making centers representing the general interest (the state, decentralized public entities).

3. Installation of coproductive units via international accords. These may only set general conditions, or they may specifically commit states to certain activities.

4. Definition of conditions for creating such associations, which might include the method of selecting plans, programs, and projects; financing; contributions; location vis-a-vis markets; distribution of profits and losses; modes of reinvestment.

Each participant would retain independent objectives and rationales without affecting the common goal of the two or more participants. Public sector coproduction must remain a field of competition and conflict for an indeterminate period. Mutually reinforcing groups may appear, while confrontations between opposed powers could generate new tensions. On the other hand, coproduction also affirms a commitment between different levels and types of state interests, economies, and societies. Thus the endeavor must always respect its members' goals, and never contradict them. Its structure and functions and the developmental sequence to generate or reinforce it, must be adjusted to the participants' overall development conditions.

An immediate problem is to construct units that can within set limits undertake development and regional integration as organic and functionally autonomous common enterprises. Participation in such units could be private, public, or a combination. We will focus on multinational enterprises exclusive to Latin American states, which now seem the most convenient and viable model for integrative cooperation.[12]

A Range of Possibilities

This general form allows many variations. Member governments might limit the number of independent cooperative entities and thus avoid financial, juridical, and administrative burdens and complications. A preexisting international organization could then assume the new activity or enterprise, provide the necessary facilities, and administer it as a "special program" or "special accord." Participants might also create a national department—not a new juridical person—charged with executing the common project as a collective agent of the member states, and on their account ("agency contract").

A juridical person (corporation) could be created to give permanence and formal autonomy to interstate cooperation. The task or project would largely determine the organization's type and structure. If activities ultimately reduced to preparing texts (studies, reports, resolutions, proposals), an apparatus like that of any national administration would suffice (permanent secretariat, council of representatives from participating states). More complex organization would be required, however, for a large-scale enterprise or installation involving a wide range of activities (and thus various laws of many states), considerable income and expenses, and multiple relations with individuals, private enterprises, and collectivities.

Multinational enterprises have recently expanded in scope and number. They include multinational public enterprises, international companies and corporations, joint undertakings, and international public establishments. These structures are predominantly economic, rather than political; they involve creation, construction, and/or sponsorship and operation of infrastructure, productive installations, and public services. Specific activities might include air, land, river, and maritime transport; roads and communications; other public services; industry (steel, petrochemicals, heavy machinery); energy and fuel programs; hydraulic works; education; scientific and technological research; health; expansion and diversification of agricultural and mining production to supply the regional market; and agrarian reform and colonization. Most of these activities demand extensive human, material, and financial resources and expanded markets. They involve long term public plans, programs, and projects, and require a permanent multigovernment organization, with powers and instruments for action. [13]

These agencies thus require territorial authority coextensive with projected activities. Organic and functional autonomy are essential, and governmental powers must be combined with a high degree of freedom, flexibility, and initiative. Rigidity, caution, and typical administrative routine should be discouraged. Multinational public enterprises must be supported against merely national, political, or private pressures. They will thus be able to attract and retain an innovative managerial elite and capable personnel committed to development and regional integration. Autonomy is also needed to foster multistate participation, balancing individual interests and objectives while preventing special advantages for one member at the expense of the others. A unified directorate and the guarantee of participating states would facilitate international financing for these enterprises, as well as simplifying loan administration and project supervision.

Institutional and Juridical Structures

Multinational public enterprises originate in an agreement between two or more member states. (They might, alternatively, incorporate autonomous public entities.) This accord allows a special international regime, which can reflect various situations and act under different institutional and juridical structures. The agreement must be formalized in a treaty, convention, or accord, drawn up in conformity with each state's procedures (with or without legislative approval). This becomes the multinational public enterprise's constituent instrument. It must determine whether to locate the body's main activities and tasks in one state or several, consider the dangers of excessive member influence, and so on. In very general terms, the constituent instrument should define the enterprise, the law which will govern it, its juridical personality and capacity, and its nationality. Both pure forms and variants are possible:

1. The Treaty only delineates objectives and range of operations of the common enterprise and obligations and rights of the participating governments. Establishing the enterprise, determining its structure and functions and law governing them, and granting juridical personality, capacity, and nationality, can be included as detailed statutes in an additional Protocol, or in subsequent Conventions.

2. The Treaty creates the enterprise, establishing the pertinent law, juridical personality and capacity, nationality, structure, and the modes of functioning. This variant opens several possibilities, especially:

   a) The type of enterprise derives from the juridical system of a single member state. The new body establishes its seat in that country, where it is treated as a national enterprise. Juridical personality is recognized by other members, and the enterprise's status and internal affairs are regulated by the national laws applicable to all other public enterprises.

   b) The constituent instrument submits the new enterprise to an international regime, determines its type and category, becomes its law (overriding contradictory national legislation), and grants international juridical personality and capacity within participants' territories. Nationality is of all and each of the member states. There are many possible combinations and variations. Some points can be resolved with a separate instrument or protocol, or with an annex to the Treaty. The constituent instrument can provide that certain future modifications will not require ratification by national parliaments. Objective circumstances (the functional arrangements necessary to meet goals, the exigencies of operating with many participants) may substitute for formal clauses to establish international juridical personality and capacity. Each member might grant independent juridical personality, as might one or several states; the multinational public enterprise would then be governed by a national law, as limited by the Treaty. The law in force may be a single state's, modified or restricted by treaty, or the constituent instrument can establish its own preferential status, and the subsidiary jurisdiction of some national law.

Most multinational public enterprises combine features of private and public national enterprises. Nonetheless, modifications are inevitable given the inclusion of both intrastate and international elements and the corporation's creation by treaty. The assigned function, in particular, determines the range of jurisdiction and the extent of the powers needed to meet objectives.

The prototype of the public corporation, appropriately modified, seems most useful. William A. Robson describes this as "the twentieth century's most important invention in the realm of public institutions. . . destined to play a role in this century's nationalized industry as important as private enterprise in the capitalist organization of the nineteenth century." Its characteristics adapted to specific regional mandates and to potential difficulties, are set for it below.

Characteristics and Problems of The Public Corporation

The basic charter. The constituent Treaty should create the multinational public corporation, determine its type and objective, the law governing it, its juridical personality and capacity, and its nationality. It should also at least set forth the body's general structure, functions, and operative modalities; its rights and obligations and those of participating states; its partimony and privileges; and its relations with governments and with other public and private enterprises. Detailed regulation of structure and function can be included in protocols and annexes to the original Treaty, subsequent conventions, and statutes. The Treaty should establish procedures for regulations and for complementary agreements, including the possibility of not requiring diplomatic accords of the same level as the Treaty. It should also establish means to resolve possible conflicts between the constituent instrument and subsidiary national laws.

All these dispositions involve primarily the juridical personality and capacity of multinational public corporations within member states. Juridical personality and capacity are otherwise determined by the extent to which the corporation's international personality is recognized, and by the faculties derived from its original status. Third countries may not recognize an international personality; or other states and their public entities and private enterprises may accept juridical relations (purchases and sales, location of installations and services, loans). Problems also arise from the responsibility of participating states for acts of the multinational public corporation outside their territories, and the corporation's possible right to diplomatic protection. The situation is further complicated because neither constituent instruments nor International Public Law can, at present, anticipate all possible situations and contingencies which might arise from the activity of a multinational public corporation. Moreover, no international tribunal has obligatory jurisdiction over such cases. For relations between the multinational public corporation and third countries and their citizens, the principles of International Private Law applying to conflicting legislation must necessarily be applied.

Multinational public corporations, common instruments inserted in the public economic sector of participating states, have public ends. They combine activities, tasks, and entities already included in the member states' public sectors, or incorporated within them specifically for the integration experiment. Various mechanisms can provide this incorporation: expropriation, nationalization with or without redefinition as a state enterprise, confiscation (as a penalty or through revolution), and socialization. Decisions on incorporation, as on participation in creating the multinational public corporation, are made by each state in accord with its own norms and procedures.

Creation of a multinational public corporation does not necessarily imply transfer of sovereignty, but rather creation of a common authority and policy for some sector, program, or project. The corporation should, however, be an independent entity with its own personality and capacity, administrative autonomy, responsibility, and right to petition in lawsuits. It requires ample authority over economic and financial activities, accounting, partimony, acquisition and disposition of goods and services, personnel, and general contractual arrangements. The extent of its competence is determined in part by its functions and goals. Powers can be delegated in either the constituent instrument or its complements and regulations, or they can be inferred from these and from the corporation's means and ends. Participating states can also agree on legal, financial, fiscal, customs, and partimonial measures to facilitate corporation activities.

The multinational public corporation is independent of the states which constitute it, boasting its own personality and relative autonomy. Nonetheless, it remains organically tied to the creator nations, is subject to their control, and is responsible before them. Links to and control by participant states originate at the corporation's birth. They include the elaboration and amendment of constituent instruments and their complements; and participation via shareholding, votes in stockholders' assemblies, and naming and renewing directorates. Control should be centralized in a supranational agency which represents all members.

Control by the executive branches of associated states should be exercised in only the most important matters, such as those affecting general policy or special problems; and always in areas precisely determined by the Treaty and/or the pertinent law. Limitations on or interference in normal activities is ill-advised.

Control by national executives is complemented by that of parliamentary, judicial, financial, and planning organs, and by the criterion of efficiency. Some aspects of operations can be encharged to an external body, preexisting or created for the purpose, which represents member states. As a general rule, control mechanisms should be regulated precisely and thoroughly.

The multinational public corporation should have independent directive and executive organs. These can include: an assembly which unites shareholders (states, autonomous public entities) or their equivalents, an external supervisory junta like that mentioned above, a president, a board of directors or an administrative council functioning permanently in the home city, and a general manager or administrative director. The president and members of the board or council should have fixed terms and be appointed by agreements between governments. The general manager or administrative director can be chosen the same way, or by the shareholders and/or the board or council.

Constituent instruments, their complements, and procedural regulations, should specify the functions and powers of these organs, the relations between them, and their relations with participating states. This aspect is particularly important since the multinational public corporation is at once relatively autonomous with respect to nations, provinces, and local organs yet inserted in the respective public sectors. The corporation must maintain a wide range of relations with all of these, as well as with the political-administrative systems.

In any case, it is essential that directive and executive organs be independent and be protected from political viscissitudes and private pressure groups. They require limited freedom in specifically enumerated areas, and guaranteed rights of self defense.

The multinational public corporation must have wide powers to determine its personnel statute, which may differ from that affecting the public employees of member states. At no level will corporation staff be public agents in a traditional sense. Governments should theoretically be voiceless in matters of salaries, hiring and firing, work conditions, and discipline.

All personnel should be qualified and devoted to public goals, the corporation's success, and unity. Staff should be recruited from member states and with some balance in national origin, though the latter criterion should not become absolute or exclusive. Capable personnel and high operating standards could be extremely important in fostering Latin American development and integration.

The constituent instrument and its complements should specify general corporation functions. However, the corporation needs wide independence in economic, patrimonial, and financial activities. Complex problems result. The creating instrument must outline: the mode of establishing plans, programs, and projects; financing; distribution of contributions, markets, and benfits; and modes of investment. Serious difficulties can arise when the multinational public corporation is formed by unequally-developed states with dissimilar economic potentials. Though the common enterprise absorbs resources from all participating states, its activities may favor one nation, region, or group. Operating procedures must assure roughly balanced sacrifices and benefits among all participants.

Members can contribute: natural resources and materials, land and buildings, infrastructure, labor, financing, science and technology, information, and markets. Financing, especially, can come from the multinational public corporation's own sources (income from the goods and services it provides), or from external sources, including government contributions and loans, reservation of certain tax revenues for the common enterprise, loans or credits from other public corporations, emission of shares on the public market, recourse to the monetary market and bank credits, authorization to contract debts via overdrafts or other means, and funds from international institutions or foreign governments.

There are two alternatives for distributing profits: The multinational public corporation may be obliged to transfer all its returns to the member states; or, after paying its debts (including advances from governments or other bodies, taxes, etc.), it might freely disburse returns according to its own priorities (reinvestment, wage increases and bonuses). On the other hand, participating governments may fix mechanisms for distributing profits; these could include revenue sharing, participation in goods and services produced, participation in markets, or some combination of these three.

The corporation should control its own patrimony. By a restrictive conception, which I consider ill-advised, the patrimony available to the multinational public corporation would not belong to it as a distinct juridical person, but rather to participating states in proportion to their contributions. The members would thus be the actual titleholders, and the corporation would only have use and usufruct of the estate. Its other resources would be limited to circulating and operating funds. Member states would authorize the disposition of goods, and fix conditions for using the partimony. They could unilaterally enlarge, reduce, or eliminate this estate at any moment. It is preferable that the corporation dispose of patrimony within the general terms set by its constituent instrument, in the largest and freest possible sense.

The patrimony and finances of the multinational public corporation should be autonomous; both income and benefits should theoretically be distinguished from ordinary national budgets. If a self-sufficient industrial, commercial, or service corporation is created, its public end should preclude the type of profit orientation which motivates private enterprises. It must rather embody and cultivate the larger interests of participating nations and the region. It should generate income equalling or surpassing expenses; any surplus should be reinvested, saved, applied to price reductions, or used to improve efficiency, work conditions, or salaries. The corporation should administer its reserves without prejudice to general directives of either governments or the common organ of supervision and control.

In any case, the multinational public enterprise should strive for self-sufficiency, meeting both current expenses and investment costs out of revenues. As noted, it could also appeal to credits and subsidies from governments or international organisms, and public loans. If shares are issued in the general capital market, their owners will have neither voice nor vote in corporate operations. The central questions concerning such an entity's structure and dynamic include the reconciliation of socioeconomic and political ends with profitability and financial self-sufficiency; and the options between deficit, balance, or profitable operations.

Problems.   Various special problems should also be mentioned, though detailed analysis is beyond the scope of this study.

1. The multinational public corporation should have privileges and immunities related to its goals, operational necessities, and level of autonomy, and to the need for balance between participating states and their interests. These privileges and immunities could include:

— full or partial tax exemptions;

— exoneration from customs duties and other restrictions on raw materials, capital goods, and equipment, on operations and installations; and on goods and services produced, traded, and supplied by the multinational public corporation;

— suppression of obstacles to buying, holding, and using shares and to transferring funds;

— guarantees for the enterprise's property, particularly protection against requisitions, expropriations, and confiscations;

— delineation of responsibility toward states and other public and private entities, inside as well as outside the corporation's territorial limits.

2. Submission to or exemption from norms regulating free competition or repressing monopolies.

3. Procedures and powers to interpret and resolve controversies between member states, between these and the multinational public corporation, between it and public and private enterprises, and with governments and individuals of third countries. Possibilities include a conciliatory tribunal; a pre-existing or newly created independent court; a special arbitral entity; or an emergency mediator granted decisive powers.

4. Full implementation of the constituent instrument; termination and liquidation of the multinational public corporation.

5. The corporation can operate in various areas. If it is a general development corporation, its most important functions would include studying aspects of members' national economies or of the region in which it would act; coordinating development efforts; mobilizing capital to finance plans, programs and projects; achieving goals directly, through secondary public enterprises, mixed societies, or promotion of private enterprise with various types of support (capital, credit, technical and administrative assistance); and buying and selling materials and production and service units.

In other cases the corporation might promote and finance certain industrial, agricultural, and service activities; or administration for the integral development of river basins. Another possibility is multinational public corporations operating throughout member states in a integration experiment like the Andean Corporation created by the Bogotá Accord, or only in specified activities or regions. There are, finally, two types of distortion to which this type of enterprise is susceptible. One is bureaucratizing overcentralization from excessive interference by participating governments, or from their rivalries and conflicts for control of the corporation. The other is excessive autonomy, which generates dispersion, irresponsibility, and anarchy. Experiences of many countries demonstrate the difficulties in giving real operational content to the letter and intent of legislation, and to finding the path midway between autonomy and control, initiative and uniformity. These goals are challenging, but not impossible: the general considerations of our conclusions elaborate on this theme.

III. CONCLUSIONS: EVALUATION AND PERSPECTIVES

The multinational public corporation is an agent, instrument, and mechanism which can participate in, promote, and reinforce a combined process of development and integration. The probability that such corporations will fulfill these functions is, in turn, conditioned by the course of development and integration. Possible interactions between the two are easily imagined. Though corporations can aid development, they have to contend with the limitations of Latin American states and their public sectors mentioned in Section I, paragraph 4. These, combined with the resistance of traditional forces and structures, can prevent effectively functioning multinational public corporations, or convert them into mere modernizing transplants in realities which they cannot modify and which will ultimately cause their failure. But the present and immediate future allow alternative models. At the risk of oversimplification we will present two of these.[14]

The Existing Model

Recent patterns may persist for an indefinite period. These assume continued unrestricted functioning of a system of private property, initiative, and gain; free play of market forces; and external dependency. These conditions might allow a specific type of development and integration. But the process would conform to the interests, initiative, and control of great international corporations, financed by North American capital and supported by the United States government. These entities will institute a new international division of labor elaborated in the metropolis for the good of the metropolis and benefiting only certain Latin American social classes, economic activities, and regions. North American consortiums and the United States government will more and more control key economic sectors, including the most important mechanisms of production, commercialization, and financing; populations and markets; and the selections, elaboration, and use of science and technology. Should this process freeze or retard profound social change, a wide range of tensions and conflicts will result. And thus North American hegemony will require absolute control of political and military systems; totalitarian repression will become an almost exclusive model for social organization and equilibrium. Decision making will increasingly center in the metropolis. Latin America will finally have to incorporate itself definitively into a satellizing interAmericanism—area countries will lose not only what remnants of real autonomy they still enjoy, but also the minimum requisites of national viability (even though they will retain some atavistic and external forms of nominal independence). The resultant integration will be achieved, echoing Antonio García's felicitous phrase, from without and from above. With it will come dependent and distorted development which will multiply imbalances between countries, regions, economic sectors, and social classes.

An Alternative Model

If we assume that integration is in any case inevitable and irreversible, and that achieving it from without and from above must be avoided, another possibility arises. This presupposes a strategy corresponding to a concrete model based on a global conception of development and integration. It would embrace economic, social, political, ideological, and cultural aspects, and stress the interaction between development and integration as elements in a single process generated from within and from below. National structural transformations and regional integration must reciprocally suppose and support one another. The following aspects must be determined precisely and realistically:

1. The value system, on the basis of which alternatives are to be chosen, goals and priorities fixed, the past model rejected, and new approaches formulated.
2. An ideology supplying the guiding criteria and rationale for intellectual and sociopolitical mobilization of renovating groups and national majorities, and for transforming political parties and institutions.
3. The interests, forces, beneficiaries and agents—real and potential—of the desired development and integration; their relative importance; possible modes of articulation, alliance, and leadership. The enemies, and how they can be neutralized or eliminated.
4. Goals, conditions, methods, instruments, and phases of development and integration. Requirements and consequences. Desired types of economy, society, culture, political system, institutional structure, and location in the international system.

Regional development and integration from within and below requires critical and creative analyses and original solutions adjusted to specific local conditions, rather than servile imitation of foreign models. It implies a plan and thus a strategy, a more or less coherent set of decisions concerning a series of economic, social, political, ideological, and cultural options.

A unified Latin American policy must ensure an immediate and large-scale impulse toward development; simultaneous promotion of structural transformations and increased productivity in agriculture and mining, and post-import industrialization; progressive income redistribution; national economic independence, which does not exclude but rather enhances the possibility of regional integration; priority of national capital accumulation, with subordinated and controlled external support; and better intraregional balance. Economic development must be accompanied by significant changes in social structure; more equitable socioeconomic relations and distributions of efforts, sacrifices, benefits, status, and power; awakened and active masses; and democratization of economy, society, state, and culture. Erratic economic growth in more or less liberal regimes must be replaced by planned, total development, fostered by the state and by other respresentative organizations. If sociopolitical contents and administrative structures are profoundly modified, Latin American states can be valuable agents of their own development and integration. The ultimate objective of and justification for this strategy is the creation of economic, sociopolitical, and cultural structures which satisfy the population's growing needs as much as possible, and guarantee members full individual development.

To the extent that these processes can be implemented, the conditions for integration will be met. These include:

1. Increasing control over power and decision-making systems by dynamic groups which neither fear nor resist integration, but rather require and promote it.
2. Growing internal articulation and consensus in favor of development and integration, upon which a representative, consolidated, and efficient state can base its activity.
3. Reciprocal adjustment of internal and continental structures and mechanisms. Effective national policies and plans, increasingly coordinated with those of regional scope.
4. Creation of supranational or regional authorities for political decisions, planning, and diplomatic action.
5. Termination of external dependence on the United States and recovery of political and diplomatic autonomy. Elaboration and execution of a foreign policy which allows a unified front before international blocs and the great powers.

In a still wider perspective, the model presupposes the convergence of three orders of elements:

1. An operational alliance of relatively dynamic groups and classes: the industrial proletariat; urban and rural working masses; intellectuals; professionals; technicians; and small and medium national capitalists. Hegemony within this constellation must fall to the sectors most disposed to a profound and continuous development and integration process.

2. The appearance and affirmation of a political and administrative vanguard with a clear vision of ends, priorities, and means; ideologically and politically lucid and technically efficient; devoted to the interests of society, nation, and region; committed to executing necessary tasks; and aware of the dangers of becoming a privileged elite alienated from the nation, or of promoting a bureaucratic state capitalism which would distort the desired ends and frustrate their achievement.

3. Large-scale and intense consciousness, interest, and participation in change, and in the search for and imposition of changes, and in restructuring and managing the state.

This roughly outlined alternative model can be achieved only if its proponents understand that development and integration imply rapid, profound, and disruptive changes in all aspects of national society and in the region as a whole, as part of an uninterrupted process over an indeterminate period. Conflicts both internal and external, convulsions, sociopolitical cataclysms, and violence are likely. The model can theoretically maintain a mixed economy for some time. But, due to its inherent dynamism, this structure will become increasingly incompatible with a system of private property, enterprise, and profit. Two sets of options will ultimately result: reform or revolution, capitalism or socialism.

Neither of these basic models can be assured longevity or success. In modern Latin America, as always and everywhere, history lacks inevitability or predetermined goals. Alternatives and actual sequences result from the activities of living groups and individuals in a nexus of determinisms, conscious efforts, and chance. The confrontation between the models, and a definitive choice between them, is a central element in Latin America's profound crisis. Overcoming this dilemma will be the necessary goal of the collective praxis increasingly demanded of the continent's inhabitants in the present and the coming historical stage.

NOTES

1. The vast bibliography concerning Latin American integration includes Miguel S. Wionczek, ed., *Integración de América Latina— Experiencias y perspectivas* (Buenos Aires: Fondo de Cultura Económica, 1964); *Hacia la Integración Acelerada de América Latina* (Buenos Aires: Fondo de Cultura Económica, 1965); Banco Interamericano de Desarrollo, ed., *Factores para la Integración Latinoamericana* (Buenos Aires: Fondo de Cultura Económica, 1966); Instituto para la Integración Latinoamericana, *La Integración Latinoamericana—Situación y Perspectivas* (Buenos Aires, INTAL 1965); Sidney Dell, *Experiencias de la Integración Económica en América Latina* (Mexico: C.E.M.L.A., 1966); and Sociedad Interamericana de Planificación, *Hacia una Política de Integración para el Desarrollo de la América Latina* (San Juan, Puerto Rico: np, 1967).

2. For attitudes and policies of North American private enterprise and the United States government see Marcos Kaplan, *Problemas del Desarrollo y de la Integración de América Latina* (Valparaíso: EDEVAL, 1967); Víctor Urquidi, *Viabilidad Económica de América Latina* (Fondo de Cultura Económica, 1962); Helio Jaguaribe, "Inversiones extranjeras y desarrollo nacional," *Desarrollo Económico* (Buenos Aires), Vol. 6, Nos. 22–23; Oswaldo Sunkel, "Política nacional de desarrollo y dependencia externa, "*Estudios Internacionales* (Santiago de Chile), Año I, No. 1 (abril de 1967), [also available in English, "National Development and External Dependence in Latin America, " Journal of Development Studies, VI, No. 1. (Ed.)]

3. See Marcos Kaplan, op. cit. (*Problemas del Desarrollo.* . .); Jorge Graciarena, *Poder y clases sociales en el desarrollo de América Latina* (Buenos Aires: Paidós, l967), p. 213 et seq. and the works cited in Note 1: This theme was discussed at length in the Arica Seminar of January l968, organized by the Instituto de Estudios Internacionales of the University of Chile. See *Estudios Internacionales,* No. 5.

4. The nature and the structural weaknesses of the Latin American state are treated in Marcos Kaplan, *op. cit.* (*Problemas del Desarrollo.* . .); Marcos Kaplan and Raúl O. Basaldúa, *Problemas Estructurales de América Latina y Planificación para el Desarrollo* (Buenos Aires: Omeba, 1968); Jacques Lambert, *Amérique Latine— Structures Sociales et Institutions Politiques* (Paris: Presses Universitaires de France, 1963) [also available in English as *Latin*

America: Social Structure and Political Institutions (Berkeley: University of California Press, 1967] Frederico G. Gil, *Instituciones y Desarrollo Político de América Latina* (Buenos Aires: INTAL, 1966); and Jorge Graciarena, *op. cit.* (Poder y clases . . .).

5. For a solid criticism of certain contemporary notions on development see Sergio Bagú, "Necesidad de adaptar el desarrollo económico a la realidad social y política," *La Gaceta* (publicación del Fondo de Cultura Económica, Mexico), junio de 1963, p. 5.

6. See James Petras, " 'La armonía de intereses,' ideología de las naciones dominantes," *Desarrollo Económico* (Buenos Aires), Vol. 6, Nos. 22–23 (julio-diciembre, 1966).

7. *Hacia la Integración Acelerada de América Latina, op. cit.,* pp. 84–85.

8. See "Hacia una estrategia de los polos de integración," in INTAL, *Boletín de la Integración* (Buenos Aires), marzo de 1966.

9. See the bibliography cited in Note 4.

10. See André Marchal, *L'Europe Solidaire* (Paris: Editions Cujas, 1964), and his *L'Intégration Territoriale* (Paris: Presses Universitaires de France, 1965).

11. Maurice Byé, "Cooperación en la producción y convergencia en los sistemas económicos," in INTAL, *Boletín de la Integración*, julio de 1966; and R. Demonts, "La coproducción," in INTAL, *Boletín de la Integración,* marzo de 1967.

12. See Paul Reuter, *Organisations Européennes* (Paris: Presses Universitaires de France, 1965); Louis Cartou, *Organisations Europeennes* (Paris: Dalloz, 1965); Claude-Albert Colliard, *Institutions Internationales* (Paris: Dalloz, 1966); Carlos Fligler, *Multinational Public Enterprises* (International Bank for Reconstruction and Development, June, 1967; mimeo); and "Creación de empresas multinacionales," in INTAL, *Boletín de la Integración*, agosto de 1966.

13. See Konstantin Katzarov, *Teoría de la Nacionalización (El Estado y la Propiedad)* (Mexico: Instituto de Derecho Comparado, 1963); William A. Robson, *L'Industria Nazionalizzata e la Propietá Pubblica* (Milan: Edizioni di Comunitá, 1962); A.H. Hanson, ed., *Nationalization—A Book of Readings* (London: George Allen and Unwin Ltd., 1963); *Le Fonctionnement des Entreprises Nationalisées en France—Traveaux du 3e. Colloque des facultés de Droit* (Paris: Dalloz, 1956); Pierre Bauchet, *Propriété Publique et Planification (Enterprises Publiques Non Financières)* (Paris: Editions Cujas, 1962); A.H.

Hanson, *Public Enterprise and Economic Development* (London: Routledge & Kegan Paul, Ltd., 1959); Ignacy Sachs, *Patterns of Public Sector Spending in Underdeveloped Economies* (New York: Asia Publishing House, 1964); and Marcos Kaplan, *Países en Desarrollo y Empresas Públicas* (Buenos Aires: Editorial Macchi, 1965).

14. Within the abundant literature on development and integration models, see Claudio Véliz, ed., *Obstacles to Change in Latin America* (London: Oxford University Press, 1965); Claudio Véliz, ed., *The Politics of Conformity in Latin America* (London: Oxford University Press, 1967); James Petras and Maurice Zeitlin, eds., *Latin America, Reform or Revolution* (Greenwich: Fawcett Publications, Inc., 1968); and works cited in Note 1.

THE FUTURE OF POLITICS AND SOCIETY

7. THE ORGANIZATION OF LATIN AMERICAN GOVERNMENTS

Luis Escobar Cerda
International Bank for Reconstruction and Development

THE NEED FOR A NATIONAL INTERPRETATION OF POLITICAL DEVELOPMENT

Conceptions and definitions of political development are highly diverse. Nonetheless, Martin Needler notes the following area of consensus:[1]

> In the present era, at least, political development can be regarded as having two aspects, which we call the quantitative and the qualitative. "Quantitative" development has as its distinctive characteristic the increase in the proportion of the population that participates, in some sense, in political life . . . .
>
> In the "qualitative" sense, political development can be regarded as the increasing tendency for government to function in accordance with its own formal norms; that is for administrative and judicial organs to administer the law fairly and equitably, for public officials to be honest, for elections to be fairly conducted, for governments to succeed each other in office in the manner prescribed by the country's constitution, for military officers to subordinate themselves to the decisions of their civilian superiors and so on.

The "development phenomenon" is a complex of interdependent political, social, and economic variables. One could argue that any topic treats some aspect of development. If we talked of education or politics, sociological themes, or any of the many aspects of contemporary economics, we would be touching on some facet of the problem.

Economic policy in all countries and at all times has been inspired by some theoretical interpretation of the functioning of communities and of the laws that regulate social change. Contemporary Latin America is no exception.

However, there are no documents which present government interpretations of social functions and the change process. As far as I know, the Latin American countries lack either an explicit national development theory or a statement from which social scientists could sketch the theoretical framework for government decisions. Inconsistencies abound in the absence of a clear development theory—policies can be antagonistic, or at least incompatible. The lack of a theory of economic development, of how national economies function, is a basic cause of our weakness.

Why does such a theory remain unformulated? Perhaps because we economists have conditioned ourselves to universal laws, applicable in all circumstances. But each region has its own development problems, which must be interpreted in the light of political, social, historical, cultural, and economic variables. Even the same country shows different development problems at different times. This principle implies that no valid development theory can fit every case. Each situation demands a separate interpretation; some may be similar, while others will have nothing in common. Of course a higher level of abstraction—a larger number of "suppositions"—affords greater possibilities of generalization. These may take the form of general theories, and in some cases may describe basic relations which are applicable in most instances.

This is different from arguing that each level of development shows similar "external" characteristics or results. Moreover, one cannot conclude that external similarities result from identical "internal" features—that would confuse definition with explanation. The task for each country's social scientists is to discover its fundamentally national, "interior" characteristics in order to explain society's functioning and the laws governing its change.

Though it gives me no satisfaction, it is pertinent that, at least in Latin America, economists have predominated in diagnosing development problems and recommending original policies. As a general rule, economists have worked in closer contact with the reality of Latin American life than have other social scientists. They have also been more active in controversies over public and private interests. Other social scientists have only occasionally participated in such debates, though some sociologists have played prominent roles. There are both methodological factors related to more intensive use of quanitative techniques, and historical reasons for the special role of economics among the social sciences. Though much work remains, Latin American economics appears to have developed further than the other social sciences.

But, for the reasons explained above, economists have become convinced that they must work more closely with other social scientists, especially sociologists and political scientists. This seems the only way eventually to formulate a national interpretation of development. Social science has shown, for example, that "propensity to change" is not so much a characteristic inherent in human nature as the result of social conditioning, and thus influenced by numerous factors. Economic development is shaped by the social and political climate. Progress toward an interdisciplinary focus for studying development seems inevitable in the next decades. Perhaps by 2000 a new kind of social scientist, who fits none of the current specializations (economist, sociologist, political scientist), will have emerged. And widespread use of computers will allow simultaneous consideration of many more variables than at present. Though I have emphasized only the economist's concerns and limitations, these also apply to social scientists in other disciplines, including political science.

Economic models are usually foreign-inspired as far as Latin America is concerned; so are the theory of the nation and the state, administrative organization, and most concepts used in political science. All these originated in the industrialized regions of Europe and the United States. Similarly, most criticisms of the system were inspired by eastern Europe, the Soviet Union, and

China. Latin America lacks national interpretations of political, economic, and social development. Finally, though Latin American forms of political organization are those prevalent in more advanced countries, these have proved inadequate for promoting development.

On such uncertain ground—weak analytical instruments, inadequate information, and uncertainty as to how our leaders should deal with these dilemmas—the future looks even more problematic. But this is the task at hand; it is an interesting intellectual exercise, and may produce some new ideas to orient our work in the next thirty years.

I shall not propose a development theory and strategy for attaining democratic wellbeing, but will limit myself to suggesting what such a theory's objectives might be. I will urge social scientists to undertake the crucial task of theory-building in the next few decades, since this is the only way that a rational sequence of events can be ensured.

Political reform is essential both to accelerate development and to prevent violent and unpredictable situations. There are two clear alternatives: a) dictatorship, which eliminates or severely restricts individual liberties to maintain order; and b) democratic reform that, by increasing popular participation in decision making, can spark responsive mass action while limiting aspirations to the possibilities of an equitable economic system. The grand task of today's social scientist is to outline this system.

Predicting how different forms of government will evolve by 2000 is difficult, since more than one may achieve the same objectives. To provide "legitimacy," each country's great majorities must support the path chosen. Collective discontent may arise from the incompatibility of growing expectations with possibilities of satisfying them; if this discontent is the main cause of instability, then legitimacy is crucial for stability. Community members must feel they are participating in the system, and there must be consensus in favor of the so-called rules of the game, or constitutional principles. But expressions of discontent will not disappear. Some groups will always want to change the system. Others will be dissatisfied with those in power, or want to alter income distribution or national priorities in resource allocation (more education and less military spending, for example), but seek such modifications within the system.

The future political order must ensure popular participation and the opportunity for communication and dialogue among all sectors (students, unions, regional organisms, political parties). Its organization must allow the rapid decisions demanded in the modern world. Technology in 2000 will make this easier; speed and efficiency will not have to be sacrificed for popular participation and collective dialogue. Greater national solidarity will allow more efficient execution of government tasks.

State efficiency and productivity imply the ability to present clear alternatives to the public and to make quick decisions requiring popular support, even if these demand present sacrifices for the future good. Not only must the system proclaim fundamental human rights; it must also guarantee their exercise. A permanent state of full employment must thus substantiate professions of concern for the right to work. Education must in fact be made available according to ability rather than financial position, in conformity with proclamations of universal rights to knowledge. In short, a legitimate system must actually guarantee the rights it professes.

Recognizing the need for a national interpretation of development is of course easier than suggesting how to reach it. We could conclude this chapter by citing some Latin American countries with a degree of political stability and socioeconomic development success, and varying levels of democracy and popular participation. We could try to see if they have or will soon produce an adequate national interpretation of development, which would allow autochthonous policies supported by masses who consider the system legitimate. These people can look optimistically to 2000; they expect improvements within the system, without revolutionary change. The scope of our study precludes this exercise; I shall mention just one country to illustrate the type of analysis.

Mexico has developed as a one-party system where, nevertheless, public liberties seem firm. The mixed economy includes a strong private sector and a public sector that guides development. Foreign investment, while important, is carefully controlled by legitimate national interests. Workers and capitalists are in a stable equilibrium. This pragmatic outlook has allowed Mexico to attain a relatively high growth rate. The political stability that permitted this advance has in turn been fostered by it. However, as Needler notes:[2]

> The path followed was the expensive one of trial and error, expensive in terms of human lives and suffering. But one may hope that the Mexican demonstration of how the goals of developing countries can be reached may make it possible for other countries in similar situations to achieve what Mexico has accomplished, but at a lower cost in terms of human values.

PLANNING

By 2000, Latin American governments will certainly be planning to achieve economic development with political and financial stability.

There is no need to explain the concept of planning to rationalize government policy before members of the InterAmerican Planning Society. In a world in which expectations are growing faster than resources, social discipline and a sense of public responsibility by all groups will be mandatory for stable development.

Discipline and responsibility are essential if different sectors are to postpone some demands until necessary resources become available. But the population must be convinced that their voluntary sacrifices are justified in national terms. The relative importance of future and present needs must be clearly understood—the people have to realize that denial today will bring faster development. Planning is the best instrument for illustrating this relationship.

A socially equitable political order is also essential, with sacrifices shared by all.[3] This will eliminate an absurd situation common to many of our countries. Abstract discussion of certain problems brings apparent agreement on diagnosis and solution. But practical measures are impossible; everyone hopes someone else will make the sacrifices, and no one accepts change where his own interests are involved. Thus planning's political dimension: economic development planning must be realized within a democratic society.

For reasons already cited, accelerated economic development and democracy often seem incompatible in contemporary Latin America. Campaigning politicians offer more than the country can provide. Governments announce impossible goals, either for demagogic effect, from ignorance or gaps in technical analysis, or because this seems a way to spark imaginations and stimulate development efforts. Frustration is too often the result. People note that the promised manna is not falling from the sky. The government can't even make artificial rain, but certainly won't blame its demagogic promises or miscalculations. Rather, the opposition will be charged with obstructing progress; the predictable retort is that the government is incapable of reaching its goals. But the opposition will not call the goals excessive. On the contrary; if elected, they—by definition much more capable than the incumbents—will produce the rain of manna. But their victory only sparks another cycle of collective frustration.

A group from the military, the oligarchy, or occasionally some other stratum, may plan a coup d' état to rid the country of incompetence, corruption, and discontent. It predicts order, progress, and wellbeing and, doubtless, makes more unrealistic promises. New frustration follows, until this group is in turn replaced, with or without elections. The cycle of hope, dissatisfaction, and rebellion begins anew.

Problems of an international order impinge on all countries. Latin America's biggest challenge is integration. The world in 2000 should be more united—or at least less disunited—than it is today. Regional economic blocs will probably be stronger, and interbloc cooperation will increase. To stimulate growth and take full advantage of scientific and technological advances, Latin America's only alternative is union. Governments willing to move against current anti-integration interests are essential for future progress. As an instrument for diagnosis and prognosis, planning can help rally collective support for certain economic policies. While a tool for persuasion, it also helps strengthen government authority. This is absolutely necessary, not only to give the community needed leadership, but also to allow reactions with the speed and efficiency demanded by the computer world.

It is important that governments be more authoritative and efficient by 2000, and it is inevitable that each country will elect them. The breach between rich and poor nations will almost certainly widen, largely because of disproportionately high population growth in underdeveloped countries.

All this strengthens my conviction that planning is necessary to order resource use according to strict priorities, and to give intellectuals and the people alike a sense of participating in nation building, without which stable governments cannot exist. This is a political planning task both for liberty and democracy and for government organization. The state must promote economic and political development. Mechanisms are needed to ensure adequate utilization of productive resources as well as popular responsibility and participation in development benefits. They must also allow flexibility in adapting to rapid technological and scientific progress, and encourage the institutionalization of change.

Form and content are important considerations for an adequate government structure. I will only treat the latter, though illustrations—limited to democratic governments—will also involve form.

Both national and international ruling circles are skeptical about the usefulness of planning. In this regard, my own opinions coincide with recent statements by World Bank experts. Medium-term plans have been under critical examination in recent years, as has their relevance to decisions on development and aid to development. For example, Albert Waterston of the World Bank staff has directed an interesting study during the last seven years. Evidence from more than 100 countries strongly suggests that plans too often have very little effect on development. There are various reasons. Some plans extrapolate beyond their basic data. Others are methodologically weak or too abstract —made by Don Quixotes in a world of Sancho Panzas. Planners and their plans often operate in an administrative and budgetary vacuum. Very few of the plans examined were, or could have been, coherently and effectively executed.

The planning systems we envision for 2000, with the aid of computers and technological advances in communication, transportation, and so on, must signify substantial progress in terms of Latin America's accumulated experience.

CENTRALIZATION AND DECENTRALIZATION

In theory, centralization allows decisions where "global" interests ("national" considerations) override those of the parts—localities, cities, or regions. But this approach can limit both popular participation and the government's sensitivity and capacity for responding to collective aspirations, especially on the regional level. Instead of national interests taking precedence over those of the regions, a few political pressure groups may dictate to the inadequately represented masses.

This failure of one sector to participate, and of the other to respond, can hinder or prevent the government from implementing economic and financial plans. People feel no responsibility for something in which they are not involved. In a democracy, structural change requires full participation.

For economic, political, and administrative reasons, most developing countries are overcentralized. Where governments have not consciously and continuously encouraged development, economic activities have tended to concentrate in a relatively small geographic area. Different activities can thus reinforce one another, as well as benefitting from the larger market. Most such networks of mutually coinciding interest have formed around capital cities, which are also centers of state administration, political power, and university and technical education.

The main exceptions have involved natural resources, which must be exploited where they are found. But these centers lack the multiplier effect that exists in the capitals due to their concentration of industrial, commercial, educational, administrative, and recreational activities. The capital is also reinforced by its tremendous attraction for the rest of the population. Interestingly, this phenomenon is common to both federal and unitary government systems.

If a Latin American development policy is to meet the requisites discussed thus far, governments in 2000 will have to decentralize more than ever before. There must be major changes in government organization and operation, as well as a solid program of regional planning. Meeting this goal will not necessarily demand replacement of traditionally unitary governments by federal systems. Well organized planning could promote mass participation on a regional scale. We lack space to expand on this theme. A decentralized system could be based on the political and administrative patterns of federal governments. Though this would not guarantee success, such structures could simplify the task. New mechanisms must stimulate local and regional participation in political and administrative authority, decisions on production and distribution, and ordering national priorities.

Overcoming technical obstacles like inefficient transportation and communications would facilitate decentralization. The world will be much smaller by 2000, and to adapt, state administrations must become more agile.

Decentralization, a *sine qua non* for political development, will also foster more rapid, balanced, and equitable economic development. A fairer income distribution will be encouraged when all groups can participate in national dialogues.

Though it may seem superfluous so far into the presentation, I should point out that merely formal political and administrative decentralization alone cannot resolve the problem of popular participation. Economic power must also be effectively decentralized to foster better distributions of property and income. Some cases demand agrarian reform; in others, education must be both improved and made more accessible. This is of course a process, and cannot come about overnight. Optimum utilization of scanty economic resources requires determination of specific objectives and deadlines, with a clear delineation of priorities.

The danger is that scientific and technological advances in 2000 will be employed for excessive centralization. Computers, increased information, and better transportation and communication will also simplify the centralized exercise of power, and make political development much more difficult.

BUREAUCRACY

Bureaucracy is another important aspect of political organization. A key issue is whether it should be an independent force with its own ends, or a neutral instrument to carry out directives of the political system. In other words, should it be autonomous or dependent?

If, by 2000, the state incorporates the characteristics previously described, it will have both clearly delineated goals and methods to achieve them. Public officials will know exactly what is expected of them. Tasks must be executed efficiently to implement policies on which there is national consensus. This is but one likely consequence if popular participation and government legitimacy are to reach satisfactory levels by 2000.

Bureaucracy must manifest a sense of "belonging," of willingness and commitment to advance the national task. But political leadership will not lose its role in promoting, maintaining, perfecting and directing the system; the last, especially, instills a sense of mission. Political control must also ensure that the bureaucracy acts as a modernizing force rather than a guardian of the status quo.

The administration must be flexible enough to adjust to the policy innovations of new leadership. With greater continuity in politics itself, shifts in running the government will not imply fundamental systemic changes. Profound modifications before 2000 should generate relatively long lasting political systems throughout Latin America. Area states will have formulated models of national development and adopted appropriate policies.

Most of our countries are at an early stage of political development. Bureaucracies are relatively stronger than underdeveloped political institutions. The scarcity of qualified personnel means that governments cannot renew stale administrative frameworks. Bureaucracy will remain very influential in 2000, since the state must reinforce rather than renounce the technical nature of its functions. Bolstering the prestige of administrators will benefit the political leadership insofar as technical judgments can influence public opinion. Leaders can thus reinforce their own proposals and inspire confidence in, for example, a financial stabilization strategy, citing studies by the Central Bank, the Ministry of Finance, and the state's technical organs. On the other hand, political power must restrain bureaucracy from exceeding its administrative role, and, due to incompetent political direction, assuming directive functions that the people have not granted it.

Both the state of 2000 and its administrative cadres must emphasize "research and development." Attention to present affairs must be reconciled with concern for the future. Ideally, the state structure will include groups which only deal with the future. These would investigate and criticize the present, propose innovations and alternatives, experiment, and study the application of technical and scientific advances for the common good. Institutionalizing change is essential for economic progress and political stability. We will return to this point later.

Confidence in the bureaucracy requires that recruitment and promotion be based on technical preparation and efficiency. This will simplify communication with all groups and help stabilize political direction, which can be crucial for attaining long term national development goals.

Our countries were precariously equipped for the first steps toward integration in the Latin American Free Trade Association (LAFTA). Better preparation for conceptualizing its implications would have allowed much faster progress. We might now be concerned with a Latin American political union including all, or at least the major countries. But at this point, who is even thinking of that? And how could we possibly achieve it?

ORGANIZATION OF THE EXECUTIVE BRANCH

We have noted that the executive branch must institutionalize research and development activities. These are necessary for two reasons:

1. In a world of rapid scientific and technological advance, political and administrative structures should neither lag behind nor hinder change. They should rather adapt to and promote it.
2. It is extremely difficult for governments to balance energies expended for the present and for the future. Short term needs

almost always receive priority. Election- and support-conscious leaders are sensitive to political pressures which encourage this response. An official is often accused of lacking "political criteria" if he favors an action geared to the future rather than the present. Members of congress, in closest contact with the electorate, are particularly susceptible to these attitudes.

It is common for experienced administrators to come to resist discussions of all but immediate problems. Any issue which doesn't seem urgent is shelved—even though it may not just affect government policy or national destinies, but also better performance of their own duties. Everyone has heard such administrators contemptuously refer to "those dreamers" concerned with the future, particularly when they do not understand the issue. If they direct a successful organization, resistance is even greater. What reason for concern, if things have gone well up to the present? These officials do not seem to realize that, at any moment, modernization may create new possibilities.

The executive, then, must be organized so that particular visions do not obstruct the general interest—"particular" and "general" also corresponding to "present" and "future."

The highly specialized functions of the administration in 2000 must be coordinated to permit an overview of the whole situation which is as accurate as the perspectives on specific aspects. Anyone acquainted with our administrations will recall situations where a need is recognized, and all agree on how to resolve it—but no decisions are made because the matter does not precisely fall into anyone's domain. Various ministries and public offices have partial jurisdiction, but none can assume complete responsibility. Neither is the nation's presidency organized to convoke a special committee to handle the problem. These mechanisms should exist, and should be based on groups dedicated to investigation and to evaluating diverse propositions, with a future perspective and an eye toward development. This topic could lead to a general discussion of how to organize planning, though I will pursue it no further here.

Harvey Perloff in his article "Government Organization for Stable Development," refers to "development as a key task of government," and discusses two basic organizational requisites: a relatively strong executive power, and its ability to design and execute a medium or long term development strategy. But he warns that not every strong executive is an aid to national development:[4]

> However, it does not necessarily follow that *any* strong executive is invariably an asset to national development. The many dictators and "strong men," as well as autocratic regimes of the past decades have amply proved this.

The government of 2000 must also be prepared to solve conflicts of interest, and specifically to achieve an equitable income distribution that will stimulate the community's developmental spirit. Strikes have high social costs. Interrupting some corporations' operations can seriously damage a country's economy. This is especially true of one-product countries, or nations where one export predominates over the rest, as in Latin America. We have already discussed the importance of social discipline for development: the former can only exist when all sectors are incorporated in community decisions. A feeling of solidarity and participation in the national effort is then inspired, motivating an attitude of public responsibility which is essential for the stable resolution of conflicts of interest. As with several topics we have touched on, there are many ways to attain objectives in a democratic system. Latin America must choose its own paths from the respective interpretations of national development.

We lack space to more than mention other important areas in which government structure must alter to meet the needs of 2000, needs which will really be exaggerations of present requirements. For example:

1. Our chancelleries must acquire the information and means to help resolve such vital problems as: export promotion, regional integration, import and export negotiations, external financing, policies of international organs, and so on.
2. National education. Governments will have to resolve both the quantitative problem of educating the masses and the qualitative one of preparing them for development.
3. Exploration and exploitation of natural resources, at national and multinational levels.

POLITICAL PARTIES

The pluralist society I envision for 2000 will display basic consensus on common goals and a framework of democratic coexistence for pursuing them. But there will still be disagreements over methods, policies to follow, and instruments to use. Different social groups will coexist, and their interests may conflict. Objectives of the industrial sector will frequently compete with those of agriculture and commerce; the interests of exporters and importers will clash, as will those of intellectuals and specialized vocational workers, and youths and adults. Despite basic consensus, some dissidents will inevitably believe the system itself inadequate, and seek its replacement. In a democracy, these minorities must be guaranteed representation and free expression; all viewpoints will be reflected in political parties and other organizations.

Some countries may have only one party. This would have to be structured to afford all groups expression, without affecting the activities of other organizations (not necessarily parties) which serve as vehicles for opinion.

Other states may be bipartisan. Most will probably have multiparty systems, however, since agreement on goals does not imply consensus on how to attain them. Neither will agreement on courses of action necessarily signal consensus on final objectives.

A multiparty system must not lead to the inactive, unproductive equilibrium of an inoperative democracy. Our constitutions must consider formulas which will ensure formation of a governing alliance after an election, thus guaranteeing a stable parliamentary majority to allow a positive program.

Before elections, then, parties must declare how they would associate if there were no absolute majority, and how they would modify their programs if they had to govern in a coalition. This would require more communication and clear definitions of differences in goals and means; only in this way would the people understand, in advance, the compromises necessary to form a government. Parties must be conscious of the responsibility they contract with the votes they receive.

Without such arrangements, many of our countries will continue to experience violent and unconstitutional changes in governments which, for this very reason, contain within them the germ of instability. But appropriate solutions seem likely within the next thirty years.

Coalitions obviously do not imply that the government embrace all parties. Only those which can reach a compromise on goals and means will participate. The rest will form the opposition, a vital element if democracy is to prosper.

EXECUTIVE-CONGRESSIONAL RELATIONS

A multiparty political system presents problems which are especially relevant in terms of executive–congressional relations. Difficulties persist even when a government adopts the measures outlined in the previous chapter, to force coalitions and a parliamentary majority which allows government operations. The changing conditions of modernization magnify disagreements over means and ends. In the face of constant adjustments to a changing reality, political alliances built on formerly viable bases are rendered obsolete. Executive action thus requires a wide range of flexibility.

Some parliaments in effect function independently of the state, and legislate by drawing up and enforcing regulations. Instead of limiting themselves to general principles to guide government actions, they elaborate detailed legislation which presumes to foresee all future alternatives. The inevitable consequences are extremely slow legislative progress and drastically limited executive operation.

The democratic structure of 2000 requires an independent, efficient, and prestigious parliament. It will have to fulfill two basic functions: first, it must accurately interpret national opinion. Policy debates will eventually generate laws to define executive action, but these must not take the form of detailed regulations. The other congressional function is control: constant scrutiny of the executive will assure its constitutional activity. We will only touch on the topic of desirable congressional characteristics. To reiterate, the legislature must limit itself to controlling and fixing policy guidelines. In an issue about social security, for example, congress would discuss the system's bases and generally define its goals and means, but not in any operational detail. Parliament should grant the executive special privileges to modify existing arrangements and adapt them to newly established principles once these have been adopted. The same applies to an issue like wages. Parliament will approve general principles, but refrain from statements about specific adjustments for the public or private sector, or any components thereof. Relatively little opportunity will thus exist for community interests to sway congressmen. Legislative acquiescence to either workers or owners raises the danger that private visions will prevail over the national perspective. Legislators, elected locally and representing an economic or geographic constituency, fear unpopularity; the chief executive, on the other hand, has a national responsibility. (It would thus be advisable for one branch of congress to be elected nationally, though we will not now pursue this topic.)

It would also be valuable for congress to clarify, as far as possible, the essential nature of questions under debate to provide background information for national opinion and to stimulate participation. In discussing an initiative, congressmen must be forbidden from presenting material unrelated to the matter at hand. Nonenforcement of this norm may bring excesses which impede the legislative process and damage parliamentary prestige.

Congress should also stay aware of long and medium range programs, regional development schemes, and the national budgets accompanying each year's fiscal budget. Foreign policy in 2000 will be an even more important factor in development strategy. Though this may be a presidential responsibility, congress must understand and analyze it.

The executive and congress will always differ on some fundamental themes; their positions may even be irreconcilable. But this should not prevent the government from adopting programs desired by the people. Conversely, the executive should not attempt to impose policies if these have been rejected by both congress and the people. A plebiscite—direct popular consultation—is one way to resolve conflicts. While usurping neither congressional nor executive functions, this democratic mechanism can settle major disagreements. As a supreme and sovereign form of democratic arbitration, plebiscites should be reserved for only the most critical problems. Perhaps an illustration will best summarize this chapter. One example, which we will neither criticize nor qualify, is presented by the objectives of the constitutional reform which Chile's government presented to its Congress in November, 1964:

1. Expedite the legislative process. Delays damage both the nation and congressional prestige.
2. Authorize the Congress to allow the President to dictate norms in specified areas and within prescribed limits, and thus regularize existing practice.
3. Allow direct expression of popular opinion on fundamental problems, by plebiscite.
4. Facilitate effective social and economic policy planning by empowering the Executive to legislate on matters which might interfere with plans.
5. Safeguard the moral prestige of public servants by declaring the incompatibility between exercise of public duties and representation of economic interests.
6. Harmonize Chile's Constitution with other national charters, as well as international instruments to which Chile has subscribed, by recognizing the working class's fundamental social rights.
7. Encourage the social function of property rights. Empower the state to undertake, following legislative authorization, basic reforms to make property accessible to most Chileans.
8. Organize and decentralize public administration, to speed its operations, and to satisfy old regional and provincial aspirations for greater autonomy.
9. Empower the Chilean State to collaborate in and commit itself to supranational organs working for Latin American integration.

NOTES

1. Martin C. Needler, "Mexico as a Case Study in Political Development," *International Development Review* (March, 1968) X, No. 1, p. 9.
2. *Ibid.*, p. 13.
3. Many aspirations of the poorest sectors of the community relate to satisfying basic necessities; postponing action on such demands is almost impossible without a development mystique, which can only arise in regimes with high national solidarity.
4. Harvey Perloff, "Government Organization for Growth and Stability," in Werner Baer and Isaac Kerstenetsky, eds., *Inflation and Growth in Latin America* (New Haven: Yale University Press, 1964), p. 165.

8. THE POPULAR CLASSES AND THE POLITICS OF CHANGE IN LATIN AMERICA

ATILIO ALBERTO BORÓN
Research Associate, Latin American School of Political Science and Public Administration of FLACSO

Though the "development decade" is nearing its end, the goals proposed at Punta del Este in 1960 remain unfulfilled. Pessimism abounds, and not without good cause. Though the growth rate of GNP per capita was maintained during the two postwar decades, it never exceeded the 3.2 percent registered in 1945–50, despite considerable increase in export volume. Unfavorable trade relations persisted, and there was no apparent income redistribution program. Job opportunities, in Oswaldo Sunkel's authoritative opinion, are "frankly abysmal."[1] Celso Furtado shares this feeling; while annual growth of industrial output reached 6.2 percent in the fifties, industrial employment only grew at a rate of 1.6 percent.[2] Relatively advanced technology augments worker productivity and aggravates the unemployment problem, constantly renewed by the annual addition of more than two million people to the labor force, mostly in the less productive sectors.[3] Signs of stagnation are also visible in other sectors; rather than strengthening vis-a-vis the outside world, the region's economy is becoming increasingly vulnerable. Imports and exports, their destination and origin, international prices,, external financing, foreign investments, and so on, all reflect this deterioration.

Latin America is in a period of economic stagnation; the accompanying political crisis even affects countries quite stable until recently. In relative terms, the region is deteriorating.[4]

Students of Latin America argue that the principle cause is the continent's dependency, peripheral position, and subordination to activities of a hegemonic center. Numerous works on dependency have thrown light on the problems of underdevelopment, particularly the economic aspects. In this study we hope to characterize the political facets of the dependency situation, consider the possibility that it will stabilize, and outline the type of political order necessary to overcome it. Instead of considering all variables, concepts, and categories, we will focus only on some which help relate political regimes, the system of international stratification, and dependency itself. Any discussion of Latin America's political perspectives must necessarily contemplate this central problem. Attempting to characterize them without considering dependency and the continent's role in the international system is both historically invalid and inadequate for dealing with the uniqueness of Latin America's situation.

TOWARD A CHARACTERIZATION OF THE LATIN AMERICAN POLITICAL PROCESS

Though Latin American politics have not been investigated extensively, many theories have sought to explain and predict political behavior. As might be expected, results are not very satisfactory. They reveal serious gaps and conceptual distortions, and mechanical application of categories and theories abstracted from very different contexts. There has been almost no empirical political investigation that would allow a theory of Latin American politics based on the region's concrete problems. It is not a question of expanding the range of theories elaborated to explain other situations, a favorite practice of social scientists, but rather of developing hypotheses to explain the area's political processes. These hypotheses should derive from a core of basic categories relevant to the peculiarities of continental politics. We will not discuss the details of choosing such categories, the concrete strategy of theory building, or the role of investigation. But awareness of such needs is necessary, since social scientists usually just characterize our political systems and their social structures as "backward" in relation to the more developed nations.[5] Apart from the ethnocentricity underlying this theoretical current, it is too deterministic, dogmatic, and unilineal to convince any critical student of Latin America. It assumes an "ideology of development," by which progress should automatically result from the same institutions and structures as brought it to presently developed countries. We will not waste time on the notion of a single, "necessary road" to development. The multiple alternatives which have appeared in history show that this approach is fallacious. Moreover, this kind of analysis ignores Latin America's position in the international hierarchy and its links with the hegemonic center. Could development strategies possibly be similar in countries starting from such widely varying structural contexts? A simple comparison of some features of the process in the central countries and in Latin America demonstrates that theories of social, economic, and political development appropriate for the former just do not apply:

1. *The international economic, social, and political context.* The central countries were never underdeveloped; they never filled a dependent, passive, and subordinate role in the international market. On the contrary, they organized international trade for their own interests and predominance. Latin America's situation is quite distinct: it participates in the market as a supplier of food and raw materials and consumer of manufactured goods. This position puts structural limitations on its development possibilities.

2. *Characteristics of social mobilization.* Urbanization, occupational mobility, access to education, and the extension of political, civil, and social rights required centuries in Europe; in Latin America they came about in a few decades.

3. *Europe's political system had an efficient escape valve.* More than sixty million people, mostly unemployed or without industrial skills, emigrated throughout the world in less than one hundred years. (In Latin America they concentrated on Argentina and Brazil.) But Latin America cannot "export" its unemployed and marginal population. These people aggregate in the major cities, where industrial development is negligible. One reason for the peculiar quality of the process of working class acculturation in Latin America is its politics and its corresponding political parties.

4. *European industrialization necessarily employed labor-intensive technology.* In Latin America, industrial technology is more highly advanced than is its socioeconomic context. Most technology is not the most recent, but it is relatively modern. Because it is capital-intensive it immediately reduces absorption of labor in the manufacturing sector. Other *consequences* of growing unemployment and increased demand for jobs on working class progress include salary reductions, weakened union negotiating power, and delayed development of class consciousness and its political expression.

5. *Finally, Europe's industrializing powers supplemented funds to finance development and income redistribution with returns from African and Asian colonies.* Europe's working class received a share in the colonial enterprise. Latin America lacks colonial empires; however, as González Casanova has suggested, internal colonialism is helping finance "development" in the "modern" regions.[6] And thus a sharp contrast: Europe's external colonialism integrated and enriched the working class; the Latin American variant is internal, fragments the nation, and hinders the growth of working class consciousness.

Some American political scientists are convinced that Latin America cannot be adequately interpreted with criteria derived from the European experience. They propose using the Afro-Asian model (nonwestern political process) to examine area politics. Fully analyzing this new orientation, which represents a backward step in constructing a theory of Latin American politics, would be a lengthy process; only an abbreviated discussion of its implications can be presented here.[7]

Horacio Godoy and Carlos Fortín recently began elaborating a model for Latin American political analysis, in which they emphasized the need for structural characterizations referring to both internal and external variables.[8] The latter are frequently ignored by sociologists and political scientists. Variables include:

1. *National integration.* The proportion of the population conscious of the nation as a political entity and recognizing the national community as an instrument for resolving con-

flicts. The group manifests a minimum of loyalty to the political community and would be incorporated in every type of national transaction.

2. *Legitimacy of the political and governmental order.* The number of people accepting the political system's most general features: values and norms, the rules of the game, the authority structure, and the government constituted in accord with all these.

3. *Differentiation of the social structure.* How far a society has progressed beyond an "elite–mass" dichotomy.

4. *Political participation.* The intensity with which different strata integrate themselves into the political process and are able to influence decisions.

5. *External dependency.* The ability of a political system to make autonomous decisions on vital issues.

David Apter has developed a typology of political systems in terms of their capacity to generate and absorb change, distinguishing three models. The *mobilization type* emphasizes acceleration of the national revolution and systematic opposition to all elements of backwardness and underdevelopment. The *reconciliation type* is preoccupied with maintaining a compromise between distinct but equally powerful social groups; it ignores transformation policies. Finally, *modernizing autocracy* modernizes the traditional without questioning the power structure. The sociologist Jorge Graciarena has reworked Apter's hypotheses and typology with reference to Latin America. [9]

According to Graciarena, political systems divide between two basic orientations. One, the *development orientation*, stresses utilizing all resources and radically altering the political order to promote social, economic, and political change. This system combines great development potential with low maintenance costs.

The second type, the *compromise orientation*, concentrates on maintaining stability. Authorities mediate differences between antagonistic groups which would otherwise end up in stalemate. Such systems show little promise for development, and their maintenance costs are high. According to Graciarena, the politics of compromise predominates in Latin America. He and Apter agree that Cuba is the only country which fits the oriented mobilization model of development.

How does Latin America manifest the compromise model? Our discussion must be limited to some common trends, with few illustrations. Though countries in the area are mainly compromise-oriented, they show important internal variations. Chile's political process is different from that of the Honduras, as is Argentina's from Ecuador's. A one-dimensional categorization (compromise, development or rupture) does not exclude other considerations for better understanding area political systems. For example, if countries within the compromise model were classified according to socioeconomic development, substantially different subtypes would result. A typology, a group of theoretical propositions, is never more than a starting point for fruitful investigation, and it makes no pretense of depicting all the complexities of reality. Having made this caveat, we will identify some salient characteristics of the Latin American political process.

1. The system is limited; few social and economic interests ever enter the political arena.
2. Political participation, the effort of individuals, groups, sectors, and social classes to influence decisions, is minimal. Low participation levels might result from the traditional character of the political system, which has not yet generated political mobilization and the consequent demands of formerly excluded masses for greater participation. They could also result from "demobilizing" the popular sectors, whose participation in different activities has been drastically reduced, and whose organizing structures have been dismantled. This possibility will be more fully examined later.
3. The party system is based on the norms of "pluralistic, representative democracy": two or more parties compete electorally to gain majority support; the people choose leaders by universal secret ballot. The kind of party compatible with the democratic-representative institutional type is very different from that which would apply in another context. In the case under consideration, contact between party leaders and constituents is ephemeral, and most intense during campaigns.

Party organization, based on committees, is directed and financed by influential individuals and permanent professional cadres enjoying extensive autonomy from the electorate. This situation facilitates "oligarchization" of the party (in Michels' sense). These systems have not brought the political socialization proposed in the classical model; they have not spread the norms, attitudes, values, ideologies, and knowledge that could generate a more rational political process and furnish the best leaders for the political community.

4. The central authority in the compromise model is primarily coordinative, carrying on a minimum of functions necessary for the political community to survive. Its basic concern is to keep any participant groups from becoming too powerful, since this could cause grave crisis. Authority in a compromise model operates to protect the socio-economic structure from alterations that would affect the system's "normalcy." As we shall see, the state must eliminate structures of internal domination as a first step in overcoming dependency and underdevelopment. But such a state would not just coordinate the oligarchy's factional interests. This new state, based on a new political system, will be described shortly.

A PERSPECTIVE ON LATIN AMERICAN POLITICS

Short- and medium-range prospects will be summarized in a few general propositions concerning the type of political order necessary for overcoming dependency.

In the last decade, Latin America has experienced political mobilization which has been accelerated in some cases (Chile since 1962), and less so in others (Colombia). Variations are marked. Argentina and Uruguay mobilized very early, at the beginning of this century. But in most countries the process only began around 1930, or even later, with the Second World War. The phenomenon is analogous to Mannheim's "fundamental democratization," and to the extension of civil, political, and social rights which T.H. Marshall has analyzed for England, and Bendix and Rokkan for Europe. One of many indices is growing political participation, at least as measured by voting. Other aspects of political mobilization may not show similar transformations, since the process is not simultaneous. How does rapid mobilization, understood as the incorporation of sectors formerly excluded by the rules of the political game, affect the political system? [10]

No matter how traditional and elitist the system, at least one mobilized group requires—and achieves—political participation. The circle may include only a small dominant elite. But socioeconomic changes affecting the entire social structure generate demands for wider participation. New sectors integrate themselves into the political structure and gain rights once reserved for the participant minority. This process has a multiplier effect, and influences both different groups and social classes and different areas of activity, all at different rates. Political mobilization is thus expansive, embracing ever more formerly isolated and excluded groups, and affecting a wide range of attitudes, behavior, and norms. The process is ultimately irreversible; regression to former patterns is virtually impossible. As formerly excluded sectors and social classes gain access to the political arena, an institutionalized means of at least electoral participation in politics (by universal suffrage, for example) becomes available. Legal recourse alone, however, does not confirm a mobilization process; this is not a sufficient condition, and it may not even be necessary. The only real proof of political mobilization is concrete exercise of rights and powers through support of a party representing the interests of newly mobilized groups. Even when existing parties or structures are channels for integration, there is a time lag between political mobilization and formation of a party to capture the new electorate. Interim political behavior of the recently mobilized clearly indicates their entry into active politics.

New groups have formed the base of European socialist parties and of Latin American populism. Access to the ballot is one measure of progress; in the European "core" countries, suffrage was gradually extended during more than a century. In Latin America the process has required a maximum of thirty years.

The assertion that political mobility is irreversible could be attacked *prima facie* in light of serious recent setbacks in many

Latin American countries (Argentina and Brazil, for example). In other cases, instability and latent political crisis do not support our statement. Some military governments have suspended working class political rights, liquidated organizing structures, lowered real wages, and reduced participation. Though we cannot deny the gravity of these "demobilizing" attempts, it could be argued that they are only temporary.[11] Regression to former levels of political (and socioeconomic) participation is notoriously unstable, and incurs extremely high tensions and maintenance costs. Some "soft" sectors reject the "hard line" and eventually negotiate a status quo more acceptable to part of the opposition. A cyclical phenomenon of alternating demobilizing military coups and liberal civilian governments can result. The latter, obliged to extend some guarantees to popular sectors, fall victim to the dynamics of mobilization; the military intervenes, in the face of resurgent popular political participation, and all continuity is destroyed. Recent Latin American politics have only repeated this vicious cycle, which effectively bars recently mobilized masses from the political game.

The politics of compromise does not guarantee social and political conditions that will overcome dependency. Demobilization perpetuates the status quo. New political alternatives are thus needed to overcome the compromise model's limitations. Perhaps we are questioning not only the political model, but also the viability of Latin American economic development in a liberal capitalist mode. An adequate response would far exceed the scope of this work. But in the opinion of many authorities, economic crisis and political and social stagnation indicates deeper crisis in the system of social organization. As Sunkel affirms, "The fundamental question raised by a national development policy is not, however, making the traditional core-periphery model successful, but rather *definitively overcoming it.*"[12] (italics added) Furtado states, "The North American government's plan for Latin American development, based on the activities of huge North American enterprises and on preventing 'subversion,' only seems a means of freezing the status quo." And from a political viewpoint, ". . . North American hegemony, unduly reinforcing anachronistic power structures, is a serious obstacle to development for most Latin American countries."[13]

Sunkel's and Furtado's conclusions pose a fundamental theoretical dilemma for social scientists: does not surpassing a capitalist development model, necessarily dependent in countries that initiated their industrialization late, also imply the obsolescence of corresponding political development models? The answer is obviously affirmative; the functional autonomy of a political system is very limited in terms of given economic and social patterns. When an economic model has outlived its usefulness, political crisis must eventually ensue. Latin America has experienced this sequence several times. Political systems changed drastically in those countries entering the international market in the mid-nineteenth century. Isolationist regionalism disappeared and nations expanded to enlarge their export base. An "enlightened" Europeanizing elite appeared, eager to imitate Britain's historical path. This group was able to organize the countries to meet the center's increasing demand for export commodities, and readily guaranteed British businesses and investments. The 1929 crisis bankrupted the externally oriented growth model. In the more advanced countries it provoked profound political change; specific cases varied widely, but all fell under the general category "populism." Exhaustion of the import–substitution cycle, apparent around 1955, sparked present crises. As in past cases it is likely that the current predominant political model—compromise—will have to be abandoned. Asserting the permanence of this model would reflect an antihistorical prejudice; there is no logical foundation for stating that the political system characterizing most of Latin America is definitive. Today's profound crisis, affecting some countries more than others, signals imminent and significant change in the character of area politics.

THE NEW POLITICAL ORDER

Briefly, the new political order will include these features:

1. Latin American societies can only be reorganized when popular class interests are legitimized and become predominant over those of other groups and classes in the political arena. The interests of the old ruling class, which controlled the nation's productive apparatus, must be excluded or subordi-

nated to those of the masses. Since the two groups conflict, their coexistence would obstruct an accelerated development policy. The working class will express its interests through its own very diverse structures.

2. The new political order presupposes a marked increase in popular participation. Jorge Ahumada stressed this requirement of the revolutionary order: "Revolution does not occur unless the people are organized and mobilized to win and then defend power. Real solidarity is lacking when the people accept an externally imposed revolution, and any enemy could destroy it."[14] Richard Fagen recently described mass mobilization in the Cuban revolution. Organization centered around Revolutionary Defense Committees; there were also less important counterparts, such as the armed militia, party militants, and schools of revolutionary instruction.[15] Together, the many channels for political participation ensure active popular support for the new political order and its authorities.

3. The electoral system is based on a single party or some other noncompetitive variant: hegemonic parties coexisting with minor, noncompetitive groupings; or dominant parties with a small but also noncompetitive opposition.[16] The party in power monopolizes legitimate political activity and strategic state positions, and controls the access of new groups. Opposition, particularly from outside the party, remains uninstitutionalized. But the absence of opposition does not imply a lack of control; opposition is neither necessary nor sufficient for effective control.[17]

Checks in this political order work from within the governing party, which is almost pluralistic due to its wide representation of sectoral interests. Relative controls also are exercised from outside the governing party by sometimes autonomous bodies such as the army, unions, and popular juntas.

The first of two final observations on one-party regimes concerns modes of access to power, recently a subject of heated debate in the continent's radical circles. Can electoral politics alone create a social movement like the one considered here?

Isn't guerrilla warfare the only workable strategy? Since the societal basis for political conflict varies widely between countries, no formula can be universal. Moreover, a nonelectoral path is not monolithic, but implies a series of distinct options with a whole range of effects on the political system. General insurrection, for example, is quite different from a war developing from a revolutionary "foco." An elected governing coalition might quickly radicalize, under certain internal or external conditions. While too complex for further discussion here, the issue merits extended analysis.[18]

The second observation involves the relationship between one-party systems and democracy. As Duverger has noted, "Linking the terms 'one party' and 'democracy' would seem sacrilegious to many. No matter—the real problem is to see if this association is sometimes valid. Every science begins with sacrilege."[19] Does democracy demand two or more parties? Obviously not, at least if democracy is seen as the oligarchic domination which, since ancient Greece, has been considered a degeneration of the pure form. Democracy implies no particular method of access to the political system—various structural equivalents can fill this function. And isn't democracy a constantly changing concept? For the Greeks, democracy did not exclude slavery; today the two are incompatible. In eighteenth and nineteenth century Europe, democratic ideology restricted participation to the educated and landed classes, a concept now anachronistic. We will not pursue this controversy, but the tendency to automatically associate single-party with totalitarianism and formal pluralism with democracy must be challenged. It represents an attitude which would hinder, rather than enhance, analysis of these concepts with regard to Latin America's current historical development.

In this political model, power must be concentrated in the central executive, which must have full authority for internal and international negotiations, and should be closely linked to all associations and organizations. Finally, the central authority should be strongly interventionist, and assume control over almost all productive and administrative tasks.

The state thus becomes the supreme authority, the only national body able to negotiate with and impose its will on the economic and political superpowers. It must then become an autonomous decision-making center, inspired by national rather than sectoral interests and based on a popular political movement.

Gabriel Almond's categories, devised to explain the effects of authority in the compromise model, help clarify the differences between both types. In one-party systems, the central authority's capacity to mobilize material and human resources is very great. Since the primary concern is not to neutralize resources excluded from arrangements within the dominant group, the state can draw on all available resources. A typical compromise model situation, for example, is fertile lands left fallow to maintain high crop prices. Class bias throughout the educational system has similar negative effects for society as a whole. Resources are underemployed in one instance, but amply utilized in the other.

The central authority in a one-party system no longer just coordinates activities for the real power holders. It is a monolithic structure which can regulate both internal and external actors. Its distributive capacity is released from particular interests and interference, allowing free allocation of punishments and rewards.

Authority in this model originates in a wide range of social interests which are actively integrated by various structures. Legitimacy is accentuated, along with effective political power and response capacity.

This brief preliminary characterization has sketched some general patterns relevant for development-oriented political systems (to use J. Graciarena's felicitous expression). Our list has not exhausted the details, but such an effort would be pointless.

Postulating the model for sociopolitical development would be as fatuous as insisting on a single path for economic development. Various political forms have accompanied development— one need only recall the contrasts between Japan and France, England and Germany, Russia and the United States, China and Sweden. Further specification of the model, beyond indicating other general features, would thus be byzantine. Among other reasons, differences between Latin American countries are just too great. Could any sociopolitical model have the same force in

Honduras and Brazil, Argentina and Bolivia, or Chile and Haiti? The answer is obviously no.

FINAL COMMENTS: THE POLITICAL ROLE OF THE MIDDLE CLASSES AND THE "EXTERNAL FACTOR"

Two basic and omnipresent factors in discussions of Latin American politics must be considered, though we will only advance some reflections which elaborate on the preceding commentary. Changing class structure has been cited repeatedly as an indicator of Latin American social development. Traditional dichotomy has ceded to numerous classes, though divisions may not always be clear. Emergent groups, including the industrial bourgeoisie, the urban proletariat, and the middle classes, have begun to transform Latin America. Our discussion will concentrate on the last group.[20]

Many received the rise of the middle classes optimistically, considering them the messianic agent which could "implant" modern society. Such optimism was based on the reformist and egalitarian orientations of these middle classes several decades ago and, especially, on the example of the middle class in some Anglo-Saxon countries. European middle class fidelity to the Puritan ethic, its work discipline, capacity for saving and for postponing gratification, freedom from seigneurial traditions, and constant innovation, sparked these perhaps exaggerated hopes. But Latin America's middle classes have not mimicked their European analogues, and never will. Economic and social class conditions, as well as society's structural characteristics, were and are completely distinct from those of the central countries in the early stages of classic capitalism. The "unilineal" development theory cannot satisfactorily explain this anomolous "deviation" from the ideal model; nevertheless, analysis has advanced as Latin Americans begin to study their middle classes.

Di Tella and Ratinoff, working separately, have reached similar conclusions: in early stages of economic and social development, the main line of class conflict runs between oligarchic sectors on one hand, and middle and popular sectors on the other. At this point, economic and social circumstances enlarge and strengthen the middle classes. These groups then try to obtain civil, political, and social rights, including universal secret ballot; freedom of association in parties and unions; and access to education, some types of economic activities, and positions within the state bureaucracy. As Nun correctly observed, such demands do not imply basic change in the oligarchic system, but rather legitimate participation within it. During this phase the middle classes manifest a certain aggressiveness toward the status quo, and do succeed in many of their "democratizing" objectives. Afterwards, though, coalition with the popular sectors can no longer exist; the middle classes, now integrated into the system, enthusiastically support the "establishment." The new division falls between the oligarchy–middle class alliance and the popular sectors.

Could the middle classes, then, possibly be the catalysts for social change? Historical experience, especially in the continent's most advanced countries, belies the notion of dynamic and progressive middle classes. Not only have they sustained the bases of oligarchic domination, but they have been principal supporters of demobilizing regimes. Military coups to maintain the status quo have counted on the active support, or at least the acquiescence, of the middle classes. There are neither historical nor theoretical bases for attributing leadership in Latin America's great transformation to these groups—their conformism and propensity toward demobilization cannot be reconciled with the economic and technical rationality needed to direct development.

There is great controversy concerning the veto power that the hegemonic center, the United States, can exercise over any Latin American country attempting structural reform. The Santo Domingo intervention, North American policy toward Cuba, and participation in the Brazilian and Argentine coups, and growing United States military counseling in antiguerrilla tactics, are only a few salient examples. Clearly, any major social changes in Latin America will run the risk of active intervention. Generalized fatalism is the result; given the finality of the external vote, it is felt that Latin America must just accept the current international stratification, dependency, and relative backwardness. Though we shall refrain from polemics, this fatalistic notion doesn't seem very serious, and is ideologically tainted with conservatism and immobilism. A development-oriented political coalition such as we have described can certainly resist the hegemonic center's pressure and achieve its own social reconstruction. Each country's specific response will naturally be affected by national and international variables, but none of these by itself can explain the changes.

NOTES

1. Oswaldo Sunkel, "El trasfondo estructural de los problemas del desarrollo latinoamericano," *El Trimestre Económico*, No. 133 (enero–marzo, 1967).
2. Celso Furtado, *Subdesarrollo y estancamiento en América Latina* (Buenos Aires: Eudeba, 1966), p. 19.
3. Esteban Lederman, *Los recursos humanos y el desarrollo en América Latina* (CEPAL, 1967).
4. Gustavo Lagos, *International Stratification and Underdeveloped Countries* (Chapel Hill: University of North Carolina Press, 1966).
5. The distinction between developed and underdeveloped nations is often discussed in terms of a center of world economic and political power and a dependent periphery. The nations of the Third World are on the periphery. The super powers and industrialized nations of Europe are spoken of as "central countries" in this context. (Ed.)
6. Pablo González Casanova, "Sociedad plural, colonialismo interno y desarrollo," *América Latina*, No. 3 (julio-setiembre, 1963).
7. John Martz, "The Place of Latin America in the Study of Comparative Politics," *Journal of Politics*, Vol. 28.
8. Horacio Godoy and Carlos Fortín, *Some Suggestions for a Typology of Latin American Political Systems* (Brussels: Seventh Congress of the International Political Science Association, September, 1967).
9. Jorge Graciarena, *Poder y clases sociales en el desarrollo de América Latina* (Buenos Aires: Paidós, 1967); David Apter, "System, process and politics of economic development," *Industrialization and Society* (UNESCO, Mouton, 1963).
10. Adam Przeworski, *Toward a Theory of Political Mobilization* (St. Louis: Washington University, 1966); Gino Germani, *Política y sociedad en una época de transición* (Buenos Aires: Paidós, 1962).
11. José Nun, "América Latina; la crisis hegemónica y el golpe militar," *Desarrollo Económico*, No. 22–23; Gino Germani, "Hacia una teoría del fascismo," *Revista Mexicana de Sociología*, No. 1 (1968).
12. Oswaldo Sunkel, "Política nacional de desarrollo y dependencia externa," *Revista de Estudios Internacionales* (Santiago), No. 1.
13. Celso Furtado, *op. cit.*

14. Carlos Neey, *Cambios políticos para el desarrollo* (Santiago: Editorial Universitaria, 1968).
15. Richard Fagen, "Mass Mobilization in Cuba," *Journal of Interamerican Affairs,* No. 2 (1966).
16. Jerzy Wiatr, "The One Party System," in Allardt y Littunen, eds., *Cleavages, Ideologies and Party System* (Helsinki: The Academic Bookstore, 1964).
17. Jerzy Wiatr and A. Przeworsky, "Control Without Opposition," *Government and Opposition,* Vol. 1, No. 2.
18. The appearance of Regis Debray's *Revolution in the Revolution* sparked an important polemic around this issue.
19. Maurice Duverger, *Los partidos políticos* (México: Fondo de Cultura Económica, 1957).
20. See, above all, Torcuato Di Tella, *La teoría del primer impacto del crecimiento económico* (Rosario: Univ. del Litoral, 1966); "The New Urban Groups: The Middle Classes," in Seymour Martin Lipset and Aldo Solari, eds., *Elites in Latin America* (N.Y.: Oxford University Press, 1967).

9. SOCIAL MARGINALITY

BETTY CABEZAS DE GONZALES
DESAL, Santiago
AND
EDMUR FONSECA

Latin America's most pressing problems are economic, political, and demographic. But little information is available; attempted solutions have been partial and ineffective, and predictions for 2000 are problematic. Despite methodological controversies, longterm projections taking into account variations between countries must be attempted as a first step toward formulating development policies.

THE SPECIAL CHARACTER OF LATIN AMERICAN SOCIAL REALITY

The continent's problems are unique. Except in the extent of its economic lag behind the United States and Europe, the region cannot merely be categorized as "underdeveloped," since it is quite distinct from other economically underdeveloped zones like Africa and Asia.

It is also inaccurate to assign our countries to the western pole of an east–west dichotomy. Iberian conquest and colonization, followed by other European models, imbued Latin America with many elements of western culture, but our continent was not just a passive recipient. Initial conditions and subsequent events in each country have given a special cast to its European cultural inheritance. Despite strong European influence throughout Latin

American history, cultural kinship is not as close as might be imagined. Classifying Latin America according to such vague categories as "western" or "underdeveloped" can only be justified in certain specific cases. For the most part analysis in such general terms is worthless.

The area's social situation and problems are so unique that methods used in other regions would never work. There have been no systematic expositions of Latin America's distinctive features, although an understanding of them has been apparent in some measures to promote area development.

Cultural Superposition

Perhaps Latin American society's most distinctive characteristic is the predominant cultural dualism initiated with Luso-Hispanic colonization. Superposition of cultures and civilizations is manifested chiefly in the dichotomy of values, social structure, life styles, customs, and politics and administration.[1]

The nature of this superposition has made Latin America unique in the modern world. From it derive the basic features distinguishing the continent from Europe in the Industrial Revolution, and from the English speaking North American society which grew out of European expansion. Cultural fusion has been minimal; the superposition has weakened through the centuries, but the basic features engendered by dualism have not been overcome.

Our countries show neither the marked homogeneity of nineteenth century Europe nor the new forms of expression—before a new ecological fact—of a mature cultural fusion, projected *in toto* in the United States. The Iberian confrontation with important and vital American cultures (nonexistent in North America) resulted in the forced inferiority of indigenous populations. As stated in the Desarrollo Económico y Social de América Latina (DESAL) study already cited:

> The Conquest initiated and cemented the rupture between invaders and invaded, conquerors and conquered. Three centuries of colonialsim only ratified the original system, fruit of a still-per-

sisting cultural superposition rather than of fusion. This contrasts with the European case, where invaders were culturally subjugated. Latin America's distinct cultures have remained almost intact, at least in extreme cases, and excepting atypical osmosis and ethnic *mestizaje*. The "white" of Lima and the "Indian" of Cuzco or Puno have almost nothing in common; they are separated by the same gap as four centuries ago.[2]

Such special cases as Uruguay, Argentina, and sections of some other countries (southern and southwestern Brazil, for example), do not invalidate the thesis. Cultural superposition in these instances tends to be the opposite of that in countries where suppression of local civilizations precluded economic and social fusion of the upper indigenous strata with the conquerors. In countries like Argentina, immigration from Paraguay, Bolivia, and Chile is creating ethnocultural and/or ethnosocial differentiation. The process resembles the development of cultural bipolarity in much of Latin America; it also reflects the "transitional phenomenon, representing a kind of sociological crystallization or processes like anthropological 'cholification,' by which an intermediate group is being created."[3]

This case falls between that of countries which have attained higher levels of linguistic or racial homogeneity, where superposition is manifested in clearcut distinctions between rural and urban culture; and those like Bolivia, Peru, Ecuador, Paraguay, Honduras, and Guatemala, where anthropophysical differences are most pronounced. Only Latin America shows this sharp superposition of cultures, embracing both important population sectors. Superposition has made each country's social reality unique; European cultural elements reflect its effect.

The largest population sectors' nonparticipation in economic, social, and cultural development is probably the clearest indicator of the continent's strict separation into two different worlds. González Casanova notes that nonparticipation and cultural, economic, and political heterogeneity are intimately connected with the much more profound phenomenon of internal colonialism—the domination and exploitation of some cultural groups by others. "Nonparticipation in economic, social, and cultural development by the large group of the dispossessed indicates a very unequal distribution of income, culture, and technology. It also frequently reveals two sociocultural conglomerates, as in Mexico: one super-participant and one super-marginal; one dominant, 'criollo' or 'ladino'; the other dominated, 'native' or 'Indian.' "[4] The novelty of Latin American society lies largely in the peculiarities produced by this four hundred year old dichotomy. Change is unlikely in this century without modification of the social structures which are based in ethnic heterogeneity. As González Casanova notes, certain ethnic groups dominate and others are dominated.

Metropolitan Concentration and Accelerated Demographic Growth

Two aspects of Latin America's demographic situation—accelerated population growth and concentration in major urban centers—also attest to the region's uniqueness.

World population is growing faster than ever before, especially in the poorest areas; Latin America's growth is by far the most rapid. The continent covers 16 percent of all inhabited land (22 million square kilometers); its population grew from 156 million in 1950 to 237 million in 1965. According to Latin America Demography Center (CELADE) statistics, confirmed by the Economic Commission for Latin America (ECLA), this figure will grow to 365 million in 1980, and 619 million by 2000.[5]

Carmen Miró summarizes the problem thus: "Although Latin America's population has been gaining in relative importance (from 4.7 percent of the world total in 1920, to 6.9 percent in 1960), it is still among the smallest; in 1960 it exceeded only North America's and Oceania's. However, according to a median growth projection, area population in 2000 will also surpass that of Europe and Russia. If these predictions are fulfilled, the figure will represent 10.3 percent of world population—estimated at 5.965 billion people.[6]

Other important features are rapid urbanization and concentration of urban population in the main cities. A larger percentage of Latin America's population resides in its capital cities than in any other region. Fifteen percent of its inhabitants live in these metropolitan zones; the figure never exceeds 10 percent in Europe, or 5 percent in other areas. Specialists refuse to speculate on urbanization's course in the next thirty-two years, maintaining that the pattern will depend on diverse and very complex economic, sociological, political, and demographic factors. This is Carmen Miró's position. But she agrees that, given potential growth and current tendencies, between 204 and 220 million people will reside in centers of 20,000 or more by the year 2000. The Latin American Center for Social Scientific Investigation (of Rio de Janeiro) observes: "In 1950 about 61 million people lived in centers of more than 2000. Ten years later, the figure was slightly over 95 million, representing a 55 percent increase. In this same period, the number of rural inhabitants grew from 95 to 111 million, an increase of only about 12 percent."[7] By our estimates, in the year 2000 about 70 percent of the population—slightly over 433 million people—will be living in towns of more than 2000 people. Countries like Uruguay, Chile, Mexico, and Venezuela will have passed 80 percent; Argentina and Colombia will be just behind, with a little more than 75 percent. The figure will be under 50 percent in only three of the area's twenty countries: El Salvador (46.5 percent), Haiti (41.5 percent), and Paraguay (35 percent).

Latin America's demographic symbol, rural–urban migration, will also affect metropolitan concentrations. Another DESAL study considered urban and rural growth rates and noted that although rural fecundity is greater, urban age structures favor high birth rates.[8] Since the final difference is insignificant, rapid urban growth reflects the importance of migration from rural zones and small towns to the large cities.

Industrial Stagnation

The same DESAL study indicates that Latin America's accelerated urbanization has been paralleled by neither significant industrial growth nor any decisive change in traditional economic structures.[9]

Latin America's development model differs from the European, where agricultural technology and industrial expansion stimulated rural–urban migration. Rapid agricultural progress generated a superfluous rural labor force, which was then absorbed by a growing industrial labor market.

According to some authors, "Latin America's situation is exactly the opposite. Our urbanization is proceeding much faster than nineteenth century England's, though growth of GNP per capita remains one of the world's lowest."[10] According to others,

> The productive system's inability to create enough jobs to absorb the region's growing population is proof of the lack of dynamism in economic development. Consequently, when either urbanization or industrialization accelerates, typical conditions of underdevelopment are immediately manifest. These are not so apparent in agrarian economies, even though in these cases they may be all the more vigorous. Industrialization and urbanization highlight the situation's precariousness. Formation of *favelas, barriadas, callampas*—whatever name is given these miserable shanty towns—brings the same conditions of inadequate health, housing, education, etc., to the cities, in which lives a large part of the population.[11]

Agriculture remains the main source of employment in most of our countries. Land tenure and rural production relations resist technological change, perpetuate domination by key elements of traditional societies, and impede effective economic, political, and social incorporation of men and women subjugated for centuries. Migration to urban centers does not alleviate the problem:

> In Latin America, as distinct from Europe and North America, urbanization has preceded industrialization, and in recent decades has grown relatively faster. Since cities cannot even meet the needs of the original urban population, they certainly cannot provide immigrants with jobs, incomes, and the goods and services necessary to satisfy either basic needs or growing aspirations. These new groups can only swell the poorest and most miserable social strata. With few job opportunities, very low earnings, almost no professional training, and an ineffective system of social services, the immigrant masses remain permanently marginal to urban life. As a culmination of lifelong marginality, begun in the countryside, immigrants are packed into sordid center-city tenements or the huge barriadas located in the least urbanized zones.[12]

Industry cannot absorb these rural migrants, and they establish themselves in the tertiary sector, above all in "badly paid and unstable commercial and service jobs with many characteristics of traditional occupations."[13] Compared to services, industry's growth is neglibible. Celso Furtado dwells on this in his discussion of political obstacles to Brazilian economic development: "While total population grew by 3.2 percent a year between 1950 and 1960, and urban population by almost 6 percent, agricultural production grew by 4.5 percent and manufacturing by 9 percent. But, while urban population grew by nearly 6 percent, annual expansion in manufacturing employment was less than 3 percent. The masses accumulating in the cities had to find work in service occupations, or join the underemployed in the miserable conditions which characterize Brazil's urban agglomerations.[14]

This tendency is even more pronounced in Latin America as a whole. Between 1925 and 1960, while active population in nonagricultural occupations grew from 38.7 percent to 52.7 percent of the total, labor absorption in the manufacturing sector remained nearly stationary. The proportion of manufacturing workers only advanced from 13.7 percent to 14.3 percent during the same period; in the tertiary sector (excluding government employment) the figure rose from 20.8 percent to 28.8 percent.[15]

According to ECLA,

Extremes of income and productivity per inhabitant are probably diverging in all types of employment. One hypothesis states that less than 5 percent of the agriculturally active population is highly productive, and fewer than 40 percent are of medium productivity; the rest show low productivity. In manufacturing, construction, and basic services, the respective proportions are 20 percent, 60 percent, and 20 percent; in other services 15 percent, 50 percent, 35 percent. Overall, productivity of 11 percent of the active population, which generates 40 percent of the regional product, is comparable to Western Europe's. At the other extreme, 40 percent of the population shows productivity on a level with the poorest countries of Asia.[16]

The less productive occupations, which barely afford subsistence to the population flooding into the great cities, may well become saturated, in which case unemployment will become critical. This tendency, and consequently poverty and marginality, are expected to intensify by 2000. Manufacturing will represent no more than 17.2 percent of nonagricultural employment, and construction 8 percent, as opposed to 43.6 percent in services. Government will employ barely 5 percent. Sectoral contributions to national product will be: 42 percent for services in general, commerce and finances; 25 percent for industry; and 15 percent for agriculture (a considerable drop from 1960's 22.6 percent). Mining's contribution will also drop sharply. While area GNP per capita in 2000 will barely reach $643, the proportion employed in the tertiary sector will approach present levels for the United States (47.1 percent) and other developed countries. But there will be neither the technological nor the industrial base existing in these nations.[17] Per capita product will be less than half of Europe's in 1965, a third of Oceania's, and considerably less than a quarter of North America's. It thus appears that the same dangerous internal imbalances will persist, with very negative implications for sustained, harmonious, integrated development.

An Intermediate Situation in Economic and Socioeconomic Conditions

Latin America could be classified as a "middle class continent" among world regions. This term has nothing to do with having a larger or better organized middle class, but rather to the fact that, economically and socioeconomically, it lies between the extremes of highly developed and very poor regions. Empirical data reflect this continental stratification. Conditions are most favorable in North America, Europe, and Oceania, and most unfavorable in Africa and Asia; Latin America, clearly intermediate, can be classified with neither extreme.

In 1965, Latin American GNP per capita was $371, much lower than Europe's (including the Soviet Union) $1369, or North America's (the United States and Canada) $3010; but far above Africa's $141 and Asia's $152. Estimates for 2000 are: Latin America, $643; North America, $8615; Europe, $5055; Africa, $277; and Asia, $577.[18]

Distribution of active population by productive sectors is also relevant. In industrialized countries, active population in the primary sector fluctuates between 8 percent and 34 percent; the figure oscillates between 65 percent and 69 percent in the boundary cases of underdevelopment. Latin America's is 54 percent.

Conversely, Latin America's active population in the secondary and tertiary sectors—16 percent and 27 percent—respectively is below levels in North America and Europe (where the secondary sector includes over 33 percent); but much greater than those of Africa and Asia, with, respectively, 10 percent and 13 percent in the secondary sector, and 18 percent and 21 percent in services. Projecting these data thirty-two years hence suggests that participation in Latin America's primary sector will have diminished to 16 percent, while rising to 25 percent in the secondary, and to 58 percent in the tertiary (including government). These levels will be roughly comparable to those in advanced countries.

Latin America is also intermediate in terms of natural resources. One of many indicators is installed capacity and electric energy consumption. In Europe and North America, comparative per capita indices are five and thirteen times larger than in Latin America, while installed capacity in Asia and Africa is less than a third of Latin America's. Though absolute gaps will probably increase, current relative positions will persist.

These strictly economic principles also apply to socioeconomic features. We cannot enumerate figures and projections for every tendency, but they reaffirm that Latin America, more than just a well-defined geographic area, is a complex totality, profoundly differentiated from all others, and with a unique set of problems.

LATIN AMERICA'S INTERNAL DIFFERENCES

The similarity of the social problems confronting Latin American countries by no means reflects regional homogeneity—each nation has many unique features. Specific social situations have been determined by natural resources, geographic position, relative area, population size and composition, the rigidity of social stratification systems, levels of economic development, history, the nature of foreign influences, and the degree of political maturity.

The differences are easily illustrated. Demographically, for example, the combined population of Brazil and Mexico is more than half the region's total. Of the 619 million inhabitants estimated for Latin America in 2000, 347 million will live in these two countries, perpetuating the current disproportion. Urban population ranges from 15 percent in Haiti to 83 percent in Uruguay—both growth rates and levels of urban concentration vary widely. By 2000, only three countries will have less than half their population concentrated in cities; in ten the proportion will range between 50 percent and 70 percent and in seven, between 70 percent and 88 percent.

A good example of economic differences is the proportion of each country's main export relative to its total exports. This figure varies from Argentina's 25 percent to as high as 70 percent in some others. Shifts in export composition follow general economic tendencies; significant change in basic structures is not likely in the next three decades.

THE MULTIDIMENSIONALITY OF THE TOTAL SOCIAL PHENOMENON

DESAL has made the first detailed studies of Latin America's basic dichotomy.[19] With the concept of "total social phenomenon," defined by Gurvitoh as the interrelation of the many dimensions of social reality within one irreducible unity, the groundwork has been laid for a new interpretation of Latin America. While it treats the region as a unit, it allows for distinguishing specific dimensions.

In this context development appears a unitary process including economic, demographic, social, political, and psychosocial dimensions—collectively referred to as "social development." Reflecting the concrete forms of social phenomena and specific geographic and temporal contexts, this concept corresponds to all the nuances of a given social situation.

A GLOBAL APPROACH TO LATIN AMERICAN SOCIAL REALITY

Different models can be applied to interpret a country's most characteristic social features. Regional problems are too often diagnosed from a single viewpoint—economic, political, or sociocultural. Each theoretically approximates reality, but without a unifying theoretical or methodological orientation.[20] Reports on "Latin America's social situation" adopt a highly restricted definition of "social." The same problem characterizes studies on "social sectors," which traditionally have dealt with such factors as housing, health, and education.[21]

While lacking a unified theoretical orientation, another kind of study attempts to rise above the unidimensionality of each specialized social science by using descriptive analysis. A global focus is achieved, but only in a methodological plane.[22]

Neither approach is adequate for a complete understanding of a social system. One based on a unitary theoretical orientation and going beyond description is needed to allow a multidimensional focus; it must not only aggregate static descriptions, but also conserve an accurate image of phenomena.

Existing attempts vary in the breadth and dynamism of their focus. However, adapting one theoretical underpinning to another does not necessarily imply divergent interpretations. Two approaches have been most popular: the first analyzes key groups throughout the social structure (social classes, student and corporate organizations, political groups, and so on);[23] the second studies sub-societies, or segments of the total society. The latter approach has stressed urban and rural areas, which are considered as two different worlds—one transitional or modern, the other predominantly traditional. Other studies have differentiated sociocultural systems or subcultures, segments distinguished a priori as the product of significant discontinuity within society.[24]

Both methods of fusing are useful for scientifically approximating reality; but neither the former's dynamism, nor the latter's perception of society's internal discontinuities, adequately encompasses the magnitude and complexity of the problem.

DESAL, using a different approach, has concentrated on the points where continuity breaks and a new delineation arises. This requires a transverse cut through societies, which are then considered not in terms of different levels of the social structure, but rather in terms of some generalized key phenomenon which reflects the widest possible range of elements. Social marginality could thus play the role of key variable. As a phenomenon typical of Latin America, it lends coherence to the diversity of information on area societies—not because marginality is their only characteristic, but rather because it provides a basis for the overall vision we seek.

In an exhaustive analysis, DESAL is attacking the difficulties of specifying the elements which constitute the phenomenon. At present, only general conclusions can be advanced concerning the problem's magnitude and promising lines of investigation.

The Theory of Social Marginality

Marginality is a unique and very real social problem. While susceptible to analysis, it also urgently demands a solution. As they discover the more or less grave social imbalances existing in different societies, specialists are treating it more and more seriously.

The first marginality studies were stimulated in the United States by conflicts between racial and religious minorities and the dominant majority, and by the difficulties rural migrants experienced in adapting to the cities. Similar problems in Latin America have sparked local interest. Though adjustment problems are regarded as manifestations of marginality in both cases, conceptualizations differ.

Attempts to explain marginality have taken one of three approaches: one seeks a theory of the marginal personality; the second, a theory of the marginal culture; and the third, a theory of social marginality. We will focus on the last approach. The first two concentrate on individual personality traits and on the conditions in which a marginal subculture can be produced, while neglecting the structural conditions within which such situations arise. These approaches do not consider structural modifications of society as a means to overcome marginality. Using an integrated society as a reference point, in which marginality would be exceptional and anomalous, they search instead for causes within the subgroup itself. Not surprisingly, such a restrictive approach has proved inadequate for conceptualizing Latin America's problems. Integration has not even begun in most of our countries; marginality cannot just be considered an accidental occurrence of little import to society as a whole. Marginal segments correspond to structural characteristics of each total society, and marginality cannot be overcome without profound transformation. These facts have stimulated a new theoretical current which seeks to interpret the Latin American phenomenon ad hoc, without drawing on analytical efforts from other regions. Roger Vekemans, individually and through participation in DESAL's investigations, developed this position in its most typical form. Simultaneously, Pablo González Casanova employed a similar approach to study the Mexican social system, replicated by Jorge Graciarena in a third original effort.[25]

The Concept of Social Integration

For Vekemans, the theory is based on the concept of social integration.[26] Like Jacques Leclercq, he believes, "Each person participates in the totality of the social life only to the extent that society is integrated." A core of shared values, satisfying certain needs and oriented toward developing harmoniously balanced communities, is the basic analytical category.[27]

The extent of societal integration is reflected in the degree of consensus, the more or less harmonious combination of social functions and activities. Integration is always understood as a process, a measure of society's dynamic internal equilibrium. All societies could theoretically be fixed on a continuum extending from complete integration to total disintegration, although the extreme cases do not actually exist.

Two forces operate simultaneously in all societies: one tends to unify the centrifugal social grouping; the other is centripetal and pluralistic. The resulting equilibrium signals each society's degree of integration. When plurality dominates, integration is presumably low; conversely, greater integration is indicated when unity prevails. Lack of coordination between diverse social elements, signaling a weakly integrated society, is closely related to marginality—which results from multiple societal deficiencies, and appears when continued equilibrium can only be assured by splitting society into two or more segments. Each segment then tends to form a separate social world, and many links which should unite the parts are severed. Independent cultural patterns and establishments develop and reinforce the rift; relations may even become combative. But the most serious is the institutionalization of deficiencies and subsequent rupture of the social body.

Integration and Social Marginality

Segments in this kind of torn society can be viewed as dominant and dominated. The first forms the core of society, holding decision-making positions and enjoying greater access to social benefits. The dominated sectors, on the other hand, form society's periphery and depend completely on the power centers. Suffering the consequences of decisions in which they did not participate obliterates their destinies as individuals and as a group. This is social marginality in essence. Indigenous groups, most *campesinos*, and the urban subproletarian mass share this position.

The appearance of the phenomenon is desolating. "The marginal enclave, encysted in Latin American cities as the countryside's isolated vanguard, includes 30 million people—15 percent of total population, 25 percent of urban population, and a number expected to double in seven years."[28] Marginal sectors, because of their origins and society's inability to incorporate them, are huge groupings, "concentrated or diffuse, unsuccessfully attempting to infiltrate the secondary and tertiary sectors. A concept applies to them which reduces human life and social activity to a single meaning: 'populate,' in the Heideggerian existential sense 'desein,' 'without more.' "[29]

The marginal individual can only be comprehended as a person expelled from his place of origin and rejected by the modern urban world; he is a social "nobody" living in "no-man's land." Accelerated urbanization has become an adverse phenomenon in Latin America's stratified societies; it obstructs development rather than aiding it. Negative pressures distort housing, infra-structures, and services investments, which are out of proportion with those elsewhere in the country. And, despite these efforts, housing deficits, job shortages, insufficient educational and health services, undernourishment, and other manifestations of poverty continue to grow, widening the gap between city and countryside and making any definitive solution impossible.

Under present structural conditions, internal disintegration of Latin America's urban society is irreversible. Purely economic rationales have been used to counteract economic, political, and social deterioration, the best example being the integrationist line of ECLA and the IBD, which postulates continental integration as an antidote to the structural rigidities discussed above. While objective, these approaches have not considered the dispro-portionate weight of the marginal sectors vis-a-vis the human, technical, and financial resources needed to incorporate them into the process of development and structural change.

The marginal individual and group are so deeply immersed in their condition that, left to their own devices, they are incapable of self-realization.[30] Marginality is as pervasive as it is funda-mental. "It affects all aspects of human life, and all facets of the marginal person's social activity: political, economic, cultural, familial, and so on. Its effects reach beyond the marginal popula-tion to the whole society. This demands a perspective and a solu-tion as far-reaching as the marginality to be overcome."[31] By ignoring the integral nature of the process, by forgetting that the actors are marginal individuals on the one hand and to society as a whole on the other, Latin America's dominant groups have only aggravated the phenomenon and produced new disequilibria when the values and lifestyles they adopted have been inappro-priate for the real conditions and possibilities of developing countries.

As a general rule, dominant groups have selected policies unrelated to their country's circumstances. Examples abound: in education, highly theoretical and academic studies are juxta-posed with neglect of elementary and secondary instruction; capital intensive technology minimizes utilization of the human element; highly fashionable technical solutions to the housing problem cannot possibly work because they ignore economic and social limitations.[32]

Each time a step is taken accessible to the minority alone, the possibilities for social integration of the masses grow dimmer. A distorted society looms in the future, a society trapped in the cycle of underdevelopment, stagnation, and misery. Projecting current tendencies to 2000, Latin America will have disintegrated both internally and externally. Of its active population, 44 percent will be in the tertiary sector, but the region will still lack the technological and industrial impetus characteristic of developed nations. Manufacturing's employment capacity will be only 17 percent, foreshadowing disproportionate growth of services and unspecified activities (19 percent of the working population); petty, uncapitalized commerce would absorb many of the 15 percent in business and finances. Twenty to thirty percent of the population, mainly *campesinos*, will remain illiterate. Such figures suggest a marginal urban concentration of 80 to 120 million people, to which should be added almost 186 million in agriculture and related activities. This group's contribution to the national product is calculated at only 15 percent, inadequate for meeting even the most basic needs of the rural 30 percent of the total population. Specialists predict a massive increase in these imbalances: "There is no doubt that, within fifteen years, Latin American economies will be in a very precarious situation. Diverse bottlenecks will retard the development demanded by population growth and greater consumption desires, which are rapidly diffusing throughout the social structure."[33]

PROBLEMS AND PERSPECTIVES

It appears quite likely, then, that vital social sectors will remain or become marginal. According to Mayobre:

> In the twenty years since the war, Latin American development has been slow and unstable. In vast areas the process has deteriorated to the point where per capita income has grown by only 50 percent over the entire period, from a paltry $280 to about $430. If these tendencies are not modified, the 600 million inhabitants estimated for the end of the century will enjoy a per capita income of only

$650 . . . .This slow development, which implies such precarious material and cultural conditions for most Latin Americans, is all the more serious in that the figures just represent *average* incomes . . . .The amount is only a fifth of current per capita income in the United States, and slightly more than half that of western Europe and Russia; it is also below the figure for many other countries, capitalist and socialist alike. These differences will widen considerably. While Latin America has barely grown by one percent per year since 1960, other regions have grown two or three times as fast—without considering such extraordinary cases as Japan and some centrally planned economies. [34]

These structural deficiencies cause social marginality which, more than marginality vis-a-vis other social segments, represents a position peripheral to power and social benefits. Marginality refers to the participation of a group in society, both in the passive or receptive sense of access to goods and services, and in the active and contributive aspect of participation in decision-making.

Vekemans and Giusti note:

The Punta del Este Charter specifies that 'the process' must not only be measured by national per capita income, but also by other social yardsticks such as infant mortality, illiteracy, caloric intake per person, and so on. Goals for 1970 include at least six years of primary education for every child; a life expectancy five years longer; more equitable distribution of national income; land reform; reduced housing deficits; extension of secondary, vocational, and university education; and creation of more adequate health facilities. [35]

The 1970 goals are not being met, and will not be reached even by the end of the century without progress in cultural and material conditions. The deficiencies are reflected in the huge gulf between incomes here and in the hegemonic centers. "When income grows by 4 percent in the United States, its 192 million inhabitants can increase consumption by an average of $55; when Latin American incomes increase by 1.5 percent, its 230 million inhabitants can only increase spending by about $5 apiece." [36]

These contradictory forces and grave imbalances will foment an explosive "social tension between marginal sectors, whose expectations are growing, and the minorities, who retain power and receive almost all social benefits." In addition, there are the "adverse consequences of technical and scientific progress on developing economies, which cannot absorb modern technology fast enough."[37] The result will be atomization of Latin American society's human and material constituents; to overcome this, marginal groups must be immediately incorporated in effective programs to change economic and social structures. Real economic and political autonomy must be created to eliminate the internal factors which preclude organic or functional social integration.

CONCLUSIONS

Latin American underdevelopment reinforces economic and social stratification, internal colonialism, and external dependency. Herein lies the area's resistance to technological and political change, and thus the inability of our countries to organize and defend, before the developed nations, their right to participate in the benefits of the future. Under these circumstances, the only way to break the structure of domination is by going outside its traditional mechanisms.

This urgent situation demands a very specific type of action, geared to the following problems:

1. Given the failure of outer-directed development (based exclusively on traditional exports), and the discouraging results of attempts to establish inner-directed development (based on import substitution), Latin America must begin substitution for intermediate and durable capital and consumer goods, which are complicated to manufacture and require a much larger market than the nation.
2. A Latin American common market would allow rational division of labor in new substitution activities and would correct the causes of economic and social disequilibrium. But this idea clashes with economic stagnation and large scale internal disintegration in every Latin American country. Their structural differences and diverse levels of development hinder any unitary state economic action.

3. Marginality, by accentuating the disfunctionality of social relations within each country, also tends to reinforce regional isolation and to obstruct any organic national development policy. Drastic change in both values and culture is needed to overcome marginality. This implies a fundamental alteration of the traditional domination-subordination patterns which characterize the superimposed culture. Marginal sectors must both contribute and receive; the dominant elements must accept their participation.

4. Our fragmented and partial knowledge of Latin American reality allows neither formulation nor execution of a social policy that would systematically eradicate the causes of social marginality. Any action should begin by analyzing the inadequacies of the specific social system. Such diagnosis requires an empirical and theoretical base, as well as examination of historical causes. Only then can tendencies be recognized and projected in the context of a development model.

5. Such a major undertaking must incorporate all the social sciences in the tasks of diagnosis, policy formulation, and execution. It cannot be the work of one or a few isolated entities, but must rather result from the common effort of all.

NOTES

1. DESAL, *Marginalidad Social en América Latina: Un ensayo de diagnóstico* (preliminary version). Tomo I (Santiago, 1967), p. 3.
2. *Ibid.*, pp. 4–5.
3. *Ibid.*, pp. 9 *et seq.* The following synthesis primarily derives from this work. [Cholification is derived from the term *cholo* or half-breed. (Ed.)]
4. Pablo González Casanova, *La Democracia en México* (Mexico: Ediciones Era, 1965), p. 62; [published in English as *Democracy in Mexico* (New York: Oxford University Press, 1970)]. By the same author, "Sociedad Plural y Desarrollo: el Caso de Mexico," *América Latina,* No. 4 (1962). (Centro Latinoamericano de Pesquisas en Ciencias Sociales).
5. Carmen Miró, *La Población de América Latina en el Siglo XX* (Document presented at the First Panamerican Population Assembly, Cali, Colombia, in August, 1965). (Santiago: CELADE-Naciones Unidas, Serie A, No. 48) charts 1 and 12, pp. 2 and 36. To better understand

these projections, see also United Nations, *Provisional Report on World Population Prospects, as Assessed in 1963* (ST/SOA/SER.R/7).

6. Carmen Miró, *op. cit.*, p. 43.
7. Centro Latino Americano de Pesquisas de Ciencias Sociais, *Situacão Social da America Latina* (Rio de Janeiro, 1965).
8. Olga Mercado Villar and Patricio de la Puente Lafoy, *Característica del Proceso Migratorio en América Latina* (Estudio Preliminar). (Santiago: DESAL, 1968), p. 6.
9. *Ibid.*, pp. 8–10.
10. Jorge Graciarena, *Poder y Clases Sociales en el Desarrollo de América Latina* (Buenos Aires: Editorial Paidós, 1967), pp. 109–110.
11. Fernando Henrique Cardoso and José Luis Reina, "Industrialización, estructura ocupacional o estratificación social de América Latina," *Dados* (Instituto Universitario de Pesquisas de Rio de Janeiro), No. 3/2 (1967), pp. 4–5.
12. Ruben D. Utria, "Los Factores Estructurales del Desarrollo y el Problema de la Vivienda en América Latina," *Boletín Económico de América Latina* (United Nations), vol. 2, p. 267. For a more detailed treatment by the same author, *El Tugurio y el Hombre* (Consejo de Estudios Sociales), (Bogotá: Editorial Iqueima, 1965).
13. Jorge Graciarena, *op. cit.*, p. 110.
14. Celso Furtado, "Obstáculos políticos para el desarrollo económico del Brasil," *Desarrollo Económico,* Vol. 4, No. 16 (abril-junio, 1965).
15. Z. Slawinski, "Los cambios estructurales del empleo en el desarrollo de América Latina," *Boletín Económico de América Latina* (Naciones Unidas/CEPAL), Vol. X, No. 2 (oct., 1965), p. 164.
16. CEPAL, *Estudio Económico de América Latina, 1967: Rasgos Generales de la Evolución Reciente* (Naciones Unidas/CEPAL, mayor de 1968), vol. 1, pp. 90–91. Also see CEPAL, "Los cambios estructurales del empleo en el desarrollo económico de América Latina," *Boletín Económico de América Latina,* Vol. X, No. 2 (octubre, 1965), and *Estudios sobre la Distribución del Ingreso en América Latina* (E/Cn. 12/770/Add.1).
17. Herman Kahn and Anthony J. Wiener, *The Year 2000: A Framework for Speculation on the Next Thirty-Three Years* (New York: The Macmillan Co., 1967), charts III and XIV, pp. 139 and 161.
18. *Ibid.*
19. DESAL, *op. cit.*, Chap. 2, pp. 46–56.
20. Examples include ECLA's annual economic studies; the Panamerican Union's *El Estudio Social de América Latina,* published every two years; and DESAL, *América Latina y Desarrollo Social.*
21. In this sense see Centro Latinoamericano de Pesquisas en Ciencias Sociales, *op. cit.*
22. Pompeu Accioly Gorges, "Graos de desenvolvimento na America Latina," *Boletín CLAPCS;* Roger Vekemans and J.L. Segundo, "Tipología Socioeconómica de los Países Latinoamericanos,"

Revista Interamericana de Ciencias Sociales, Vol. 2, número especial (1963).

23. Works following this tendency include: Jorge Ahumada, "Hipótesis para el diagnóstico de una situación de cambio social"; and Frank Bonilla y J.A. Silva Michelena, "La investigación sociológica y la formulación de políticas," both in *América Latina;* Fernando Henrique Cardoso, *El Progreso del Desarrollo en América Latina* (Santiago: ILPES, 1965), "Proletariado e Mudança Social em São Paulo," *Sociología*, No. 1 (1960), and *Empresario Industrial e Desenvolvimento* (São Paulo: Difusão Europeia do Libro, 1964); E. Faletto, *Imágenes Sociales del Obrero* (Santiago: ILPES, 1966); and Gino Germani, *Estructura Social de la Argentina* (Buenos Aires: Raigal, 1965).

24. Illustrations of this approach include CEPAL, *El Desarrollo Social de América Latina en la Post-Guerra* (1963), introduction; and Jacques Lambert, *Latin America.*

25. Roger Vekemans, S.J. "La reforma social, o la reforma de las reformas," *Mensaje* (Santiago), No. 123 (octubre de 1963; edición especial); Roger Vekemans S.J. and Ismael Silva V., "Integración y reforma social," *Mensaje* (Santiago), No. 139 (junio de 1965; edición especial); Pablo González Casanova, *op. cit.;* Jorge Graciarena, *op. cit.*

26. Roger Vekemans, S.J., "Integración y marginalidad," *América Latina y Desarrollo Social* (DESAL).

27. Quoted in Jorge Graciarena, *op. cit.,* pp. 255–261.

28. Roger Vekemans, S.J. and Jorge Giusti, "Marginality and Ideology in Latin American Development," *Studies in Comparative International Development*, V, No. 11 (1969–70), p. 228.

29. DESAL, *op. cit.*

30. Roger Vekemans, S.J. and Ramon Venegas, *Seminario de Promoción Popular*, pp. 9 et seq.

31. Roger Vekemans, S.J. and Jorge Giusti, *op. cit.,* p. 229.

32. DESAL, *op. cit. (Marginalidad Social en América Latina)*, tomo II, p. 298.

33. Jorge Graciarena, *op. cit.,* pp. 213–214.

34. J.A. Mayobre, *op. cit.,* pp. 45–46.

35. Roger Vekemans, S.J. and Jorge Giusti, *op. cit.,* p. 227.

36. J.A. Mayobre, *op. cit.,* p. 46.

37. Raul Prebish, Communication to the Directing Junta of the United Nations Permanent Conference on Trade and Development, Geneva, August 16, 1967.

10. DEPENDENCY AND AUTONOMY IN LATIN AMERICA

HELIO JAGUARIBE
Instituto Universitario de Pesquisas, Rio de Janeiro

INTRODUCTION

This study is an introductory contribution to the interdisciplinary formulation of a Latin American development and integration model, undertaken as a joint effort by Latin American social scientists in the framework of CLACSO. In its initial and primarily economic aspect, this project relies on ECLA studies starting in the fifties and IDB investigations during this decade. There is a growing conviction that Latin America's problem of autonomous development and integration is not just economic; it encompasses, in equal or greater degree, political, cultural, and social variables, and requires interdisciplinary study. Preceding contributions, and those yet to come from diverse research centers, universities, and institutes (for example, ECLA and ILPES from the United Nations; the IDB and its specialized agency, INTAL, within the interAmerican system) are not to be minimized. But in the Latin American orbit and especially in CLACSO, the organization representing the region's social science, interest has centered on a more systematic, coordinated, ongoing, and cumulative effort. Students are working toward an autonomous development and integration model for the continent, at once practicable and theoretically valid.

It is clear that this type of model (hereafter referred to as MADIAL for Modelo Autónomo de Desarrollo e Integración de la América Latina) would emphasize autonomy, as well as national development and Latin American integration. Autonomous decisions would be formulated as much in the economic as the cultural and social realms, and only by Latin American actors and agencies. These independent decisions would be based strictly on Latin American interests as viewed from a Latin American perspective. Moreover, the model would itself be an autonomous symbolic system. It would not simply copy the "neoliberal" and Communist development models which now predominate, along with the concomitant ideological conflicts and academic rifts. The autonomous model would synthesize the elements of both "neoliberal" and Communist analyses appropriate to local conditions.

In its June meeting in Buenos Aires, CLACSO's Directing Committee asked me to prepare a document on Latin America's autonomous development and integration. The organizers of the Seventh InterAmerican Planning Congress requested a similar study for their October council meeting to be held in Lima, and for subsequent general discussion. This study is a partial response to these requests. It is just one introductory contribution to an imposing task, the interdisciplinary investigation and formulation of MADIAL. The choice to restrict myself to a preliminary analysis was imposed by obvious limitations: my lack of either personal competence or time for a fuller, more rounded study; and the problem's scope and complexity, which demand numerous successive contributions.

This study expands on my article, "Integración de la América Latina para el Desarrollo y para la Autonomía" ("Latin American Integration for Development and Autonomy"), of February of this year, which was distributed by IUPERJ to institutions affiliated with CLACSO. It also draws heavily on my earlier book dealing with economic and political development (in the revised and expanded English version recently published by the Harvard University Press), and on my current project, preparing a general theory of political development.

This study will attempt to analyze several fundamental considerations for MADIAL: 1. present Latin American structural tendencies; 2. The panorama of alternatives; 3. the alternative of dependency; and 4. the alternative of autonomy. Though the broad scope of this topic hardly encompasses all the problems to be examined, it has forced me to treat the material very schematically; simplifications are inevitable. There are almost no footnotes, other references to sources, or statistical illustrations.

The last preliminary note refers to my use of "Latin America." The term usually signifies the group of Iberian-origin countries lying south of the Rio Grande. I have explicitly and implicitly distinguished between 1. Latin America as a historical and cultural "horizon" conditioned by the past experiences of states in the area, and which—also for historical and cultural reasons—leads them to desire future integration (in this sense the term includes all the region's neo-Iberian countries); and 2. Latin America as an economic, political, and social reality capable of becoming an operative system either as a unit or within a regime of reasonably efficient international coordination. In this case, "Latin America" only includes the region's "viable" countries: Mexico and the South American nations. The three great powers, Argentina, Brazil, and Mexico, stand out because of their strategic importance and the decisive role—positive or negative—that they will play.

LATIN AMERICA'S BASIC ALTERNATIVES

The Three Alternatives

Modern Latin America suffers from stagnation, growing marginality, and denationalization. The area's historical process shows profound contradictions: between staggering population growth and economic, cultural, and social stagnation; between growing marginality among rural masses and the urban tertiary sector, and the possibility of a consensual government oriented toward social welfare; between denationalization, and maintenance of nation states and regional integration directed exclusively by Latin American countries.

These conflicts are more serious than the imbalances common to any other modern, complex society, and raise questions as to Latin America's viability. If we rule out advocates of the least codified forms of cosmopolitanism, in which all tensions are subsumed under an international Communist conspiracy oriented toward revolutionary war, students agree that the status quo is indefensible.

Current analyses suggest three basic alternatives—three idealized types—for Latin America's future. In no more than three decades, some form of these will materialize. The idealized types are dependency, revolution, and autonomy. We will examine each.

Two features stand out in contemporary Latin America. The first is common to all social macroprocesses: tendencies are defined in terms of past decisions and circumstances. Certain forces have prevailed over others, and their dominance has been cemented in new systems of power and development. As we will show, Latin America's main conflict will be resolved in a maximum of thirty years; the critical decisions that affirm one of the three alternatives will probably come within a decade.

Second, the sociohistorical process by which conflicts are resolved leads to situations of widely varying stability. Solutions can bring relatively stable ascendancy of one tendency, either because one force predominates, or because a higher level compromise reasonably integrates the conflicting poles. Future clashes will thus only arise from unforeseen situations. Alternatively, conflicts can result in the unstable predominance of some trend, where either the old conflict continues or a new one is generated on the basis of present antagonisms.

In Latin America, the poles of the dichotomy "relative stability" and "inherent instability" correspond respectively to the alternatives of autonomy, and of dependency or revolution. It is unlikely that Latin America can work out a stable dependency model. The intrinsically unstable alternative of revolution would plunge the region into a context of international conflict in which durable solutions are improbable. Unstable and reciprocally induced situations of dependency and revolution could alternate and clash far into the future if relative stability is not attained through autonomy.

Historical Time Periods

A final general point concerns historical time periods. Our comments are based on a triple hypothesis: 1. Sociohistorical processes show periods of acquisition and of prescription; though lacking the clarity of natural or juridical periods, their evolution and exhaustion eventually cement prevailing situations and tendencies; 2. the circumstances of a historical time period's formative moment benefit some forces and weaken their opponents; 3. contradictions in Latin America's status quo will be resolved in about three decades, the acquisition period for reaching a stable and autonomous solution. In an initial subterm of about a decade, as new situations take shape, minimum strategic decisions must be made to win autonomy in the following twenty years.

[Jaguaribe says that adducing a theoretical justification for historical periodization is beyond the limits of his study. He points out only that the divisions between historical periods are marked by "macrostructural" changes taking place in the world. The ability of an observer to understand the course of a particular period before it has ended is a function of 1. the level of sophistication of the social theory with which he is working; and 2. the degree to which the macrosocial changes in question are determined by observable processes. (Ed.)]

Proper use of the present critical moment for shaping the future demands systematic promotion of autonomous and integrated development in Latin America. Given present global tendencies, this objective will only remain viable for three decades; appropriate conditions must be generated, and decisions made, within about a decade. Efficient and goal oriented political, social, and economic regimes must be established in key nations. These must cause the GNP to triple within thirty years, achieve territorial and social integration, elevate educational levels, guarantee an efficient political process that represents popular aspirations, is consistent in executing policies, and so on.

The thirty-year deadline results from application of the first two hypotheses on historical time periods to current conditions. This term is only approximate, and many factors could alter it. The dominant tendency in a formative period can influence its duration—a trend toward autonomous development would increase prospects of continental change. Conversely, paralysis and dependency would impede future activity. Two factors are of decisive importance: 1. The realization, at least in key sectors, that time is running out for executing certain tasks; and 2. the lapse between such awareness and the initiation of serious efforts at implementation.

Latin America's Deadline

Latin America became aware of its underdevelopment, and of the causal link between underdevelopment and most of its problems, in the 1950s. While external limiting factors were poorly understood, there was acute awareness of the need for regional development before the gap between demographic and economic growth became insuperable. ECLA and progressive elements of the intelligentsia, partially supported by some political forces, helped diffuse this consciousness in the more important countries. There were, however, two serious problems. The new consciousness and its theoretical formulation had little effect beyond the intelligentsia. Parties and politicians adopted development slogans inconsistently, mechanically, and often just for their own ends. And the military intelligentsia, distracted into the deadend of anticommunism, failed to appreciate the problem of autonomous development. Both in theory and practice, development policies were initiated by populist politicians' superficial and self-serving support for change.

These delays in formulating Latin America's objectives have shortened the term for articulating an autonomous development and integration plan. The region's opportunity to direct its own destiny will probably end in another thirty years—one biological or two sociological generations. The period may not even be that long, given the external pressures opposing autonomous development and the passivity of important local groups. Without growing momentum for autonomous development, social forces will orient their interests to an alternative model, and ultimately strand those few groups advocating regional autonomy.

The next ten years, then, are crucial. In the key countries— Argentina, Mexico, Chile, and especially Brazil (because of its dimensions and influence)—the power structure must alter significantly in the next two decades; otherwise autonomous and integrated development may never reach fruition. Chances for autonomous integration will decline drastically; perhaps within just fifteen years, dependency and revolution will be the only remaining alternatives. Prolonged instability would follow, characterized by dependency, revolutionary outbreaks, and eventually by successful revolutions whose consolidation would be delayed by external circumstances. Stability could only be reestablished after a long and painful period, in which either this type of tumultuous revolutionary process were stabilized, or national identities were destroyed in a new "Roman Empire."

The Framework of Multipolarity

A new stratification of nations has paralleled the evolution from the Cold War's global bipolarity to a multipolarity with North American and Russian superpowers. Nations divide into those capable of full autonomy, those which may attain autonomous development, and those for which independent progress is unlikely.

[Jaguaribe then states that underdeveloped nations face seven alternatives: 1. peaceful autonomous development; 2. revolutionary autonomous development; 3. development by community incorporation within existing economic macrosystems; 4. balanced dependent development; 5. satellizing dependency or neocolonialism; 6. quisling dependency; and 7. coercive or provincial dependence. He concludes that satellizing dependency, or neocolonialism, describes contemporary Latin America most accurately. (Ed.)]

THE ALTERNATIVE OF DEPENDENCY

The Dependency Model

The United States is not purposefully preparing a model of satellizing dependency for Latin America. Only a small group of academics is examining the issue carefully or with any conceptual sophistication. Even Latin Americans who look favorably on this alternative lack analytical clarity. Objective historical tendencies, viewed in the current framework of interAmerican relations, form the background for satellizing dependency. Furthermore, although conceived in false terms which belie reality, and inconsistently pursued by its supporters in both Americas this alternative is at least in part a deliberate project.

The groups in the United States which stand to profit from satellizing dependency are the great multinational corporations, the business community in general, and the military establishment. Their Latin American counterparts are: 1. parts of middle sectors and the working class admitted into the dependent economy; 2. the sectors of the "national" bourgeoisie which, more or less deliberately, contributed to the conflict between national development and maintenance of a free capitalist order by choosing class interests over those of the nation; 3. elements of the consular bourgeoisie which have maintained links with the old semicolonial structure and, unconscious of the inherent contradictions, believe that satellizing dependency will prolong or restore semicolonial conditions; 4. alienated military groups, and/or those which have been converted by anticommunist ideology; and 5. the pretorianized military groups, converted into the foreign legion of a United States centered military system.

The scope of this study precludes analysis of each group; I will, however, sketch the two ideological justifications for satellizing dependency. Both feature a false consciousness, a self-protective adulteration to soften reality. The first has already been noted: anticommunism and its correlates of moralism, the supremacy of order, and authoritarianism. The second, in vogue among the bourgeoisie and the satellizing intelligentsia, is the theory of interdependent development, illustrated by the idealized case of Canada.

The Canadian model, which Roberto de Oliveira Campos has defended, stresses three concepts: 1. the theory that a) underdeveloped countries cannot produce needed investment resources without impractical sacrifice, so that the dynamic factor in national economic development is foreign capital; and that b) foreign capital will become available as long as receptor countries guarantee public order and regimes that permit and stimulate foreign investment; 2. the theory that economic development spills over into all other aspects of society, ultimately assuring balanced and generalized advance; 3. the theory asserting an interdependence and complementarity between countries producing raw material with investment opportunities, and nations that export capital and technology. Gradual development of the latter group constantly generates new forms of cooperation, which ultimately evolve into egalitarian associations among equally developed states. Canada is an illustration of this model.

Here I will note only the main fallacy of the "Canadian model," which might be labeled "economicist idealism." This concept, whose ideological counterpart is socialist Menshivism, could in some ways be considered a capitalist Menshivism. Menshivism postulated that capitalism, while producing economic development in bourgeois societies, would simultaneously engender the contradictions leading ultimately to socialism. The satellizing concept's economicist idealism presumes that a free economic process and its agents spontaneously generate economic development, in conditions of political, cultural, and social neutrality. Simultaneously, by a kind of inevitable harmony, they also bring political, cultural, and social development. The result is an automatic and mutually beneficial readjustment of relations between societies providing and those receiving capital and technology.

All the economic criticisms of the notion of spontaneous equilibrium are applicable to the Canadian model. In the larger realm of social theory it can be attacked as economicist, since the economic process is the independent variable assumed to determine all other social features.

The economic process does not spontaneously generate economic development. While this cause and effect sequence had some validity for Great Britian in the late eighteenth century, it has become less likely ever since. Industrial advance in the vanguard countries has obliged the more backward ones to work harder at deliberate and programmed development. Since their progress is increasingly dependent on state action, the autonomous decision-making capacity of national governments—the main strategic agents—has become more important. Simultaneously, the role of private investments in maximizing the profits of investment houses, with no concern for the receiving society, has diminished. Moreover, economic development does not guarantee political, cultural, and social development—autonomy in these areas is a requisite for economic progress. Neither does it guarantee equality or harmonious relations with the country supplying capital and technology.

The dependency model's predominance during the last decade has brought Latin America stagnation and marginalization as well as the model's inherent denationalization. Only an autonomous and nationalistic policy can allow the sacrifices necessary to educate and fully incorporate the marginal masses. Only such mass mobilization and incorporation can liberate sufficient production and consumption capacity for self-sustained and increasingly productive industrial development.

The dependency model both stems from and stimulates a circular causal relationship of alienation of the lite and marginalization of the masses. Latin American colonization established a cultural, political, economic, and social order in which the elites merely dominate, and are not functional leaders. Such systems, repressing mass aspirations to maintain equilibrium, tend to be static. The elite might consider popular demands if productivity increased, but stagnation precludes this possibilty.

Immobility, and the repression required to maintain it, produces increased dependency. Countries whose agricultural and mining exports are subject to deteriorating terms of trade, and which are unable to industrialize, tend toward balance of payments deficits. Correction requires external financing, which perpetuates both deficits and dependency. With low coefficients of education, technological innovation, and capital formation, and inability to mobilize local resources, the system also depends on imported capital and technology. Finally, external assistance must reinforce repressive capacity in proportion to growing mass demands.

Economic, scientific, technological, and military dependency, and internal repression generate a peculiar type of political fascism. Though it differs from the European pre–World War II variety in that the dynamic center is external rather than internal, both types follow a self-selected elite composed of middle class sectors associated with the bourgeoisie. This nontraditional leadership does not base its power on any existing popular delegation; it rather utilizes technical control to reconcile economic modernization with preservation of the political and social status quo. While one fascism is autonomous and endogenous, the other is dependent and exogenous. The latter could be labelled colonial fascism.

Latin America's dependent regimes are tending increasingly toward colonial fascism. The military establishments supporting present regimes in Argentina and Brazil, for example, refuse to recognize their real nature, and continue to be duped by anticommunist exhortations. The ruling order is accepted as legitimate, national security is equated with North America's, and dependency is identified with defense of Christian civilization. But the inability to leave the supposedly provisional phase of corrective repression and initiate self-sustained development is generating growing doubts within the military over the model's origins and their leaders' governing abilities.

In nonviable nations like Paraguay, military establishments confronted with the impossibility of national autonomy have grown cynical and corrupt. They have become pretorian forces in ossified regimes in which internal reform is almost impossible.

The Dialectic of Dependency

We will conclude our analysis of dependency by briefly characterizing its dialectic. We have already seen one of the main features: the circular causal relationship between stagnation and marginalization of the masses on one hand, and the system's compensation on the other—intensified repressive capacity and increased external dependence. But this deteriorating spiral cannot continue indefinitely, since denationalization and growing popular awareness are ultimately incompatible with national structures and existing mass–elite relations. From this decisive moment, the system faces two alternatives—revolution or stabilized dependency. These may long remain in latent or overt confrontation before one or the other prevails. Here we will concentrate on stabilized dependency.

Marx's theory of growing pauperization argues that the progressive marginalization of the masses (attributed by him to any form of capitalism) will necessarily lead to revolutionary explosion. If marginalization were carried to its ultimate conclusion, transformation could even be virtually nonviolent. However, stagnation and dependency can persist over extremely long periods. What produces revolutions, barring other circumstances, is not marginalization of the masses, but rather that of the subelite and elite sectors in a context of mass discontent. Totally marginalized masses lack the organization or technology for successful revolution. Spontaneous rebellions, however, can gain control of important parts of a country and thereby generate critical conditions for elite and subelite participation. But the masses are strategically and tactically incapable of overcoming the repressive machinery of a modern political system without the assistance of organizing cadres. This is particularly true if the system has not already become vulnerable by external or intrasectoral confrontations.

The serious flaw in the colonial-fascist model is that it tends to marginalize and disenchant even sectors of the middle class (the subelite) and the bourgeoisie. There are two reasons, the first economic. Inherent stagnation means no new jobs for the middle class; the colonial-fascist state must create parasitic public posts to compensate. This rapidly exhausts tax revenues, and the state must resort to inflationary measures which reduce real incomes and produce no economic growth. Since the model cannot correct this predicament, either the foreign hegemonic power must intervene or the system, unable to hold its subelite, becomes ripe for revolutionary mass mobilization.

The other reason for middle class marginalization is essentially cultural. Denationalization lessens capacity for self-determination or for creating symbols to evoke national solidarity and self-sacrifice. It becomes increasingly clear that the system is private, operates for the benefit of the dominant elite and the hegemonic power, and is only meaningful for those who profit from it. The more the system can reduce direct operating costs, by coercion and terrorism, the greater the passive resistance of nonparticipants. Efficiency will drop as indirect costs increase. Again, the system must be subsidized by the hegemonic power.

The dialectic of colonial-fascist regimes ultimately exhausts capacities for self-support, though large repressive capabilities may not be affected. In the last analysis, survival requires either the hegemonic power's resources and policies, or substitution of a simpler model. The second choice presupposes a small and very underdeveloped country.

Should the hegemonic power assume at least minimal financial responsibility for the system, primarily by funding jobs to prevent serious discontent in the subelite, the satellizing dependency model can persist indefinitely. With growing mass pressure, the system may have to both contain population growth and limit territorial mobility.

A few more years of the dependency model will require restrictions on rural-urban migration. This would entail an "apartheid" regime to confine the unemployed rural masses to a native superreservations in the hinterlands. Such policies would attempt to check the urban marginality which congests city life, sends the crime rate soaring, impedes public assistance services, and creates unbearable conditions for the middle class and gainfully employed sectors of the masses.

The hegemonic power's ability to aid dependent systems is, of course, limited. No matter how great its free resources, it cannot squander them or overspend. North America's available resources, those not essential for maintaining the country itself (including internal subsidies), could not possibly cover all the dependent systems; the funds are not even sufficient for Latin America. The great powers and superpowers can thus only selectively finance dependent systems. As the United States concentrates assistance on "quisling" systems, the Soviet Union is stressing the Cuban "showcase."

Options for the United States

The United States is involved in an imperialist process, though opinion polls and other surveys reveal that the many American people neither consider themselves, nor desire to be, imperialist. Even sectors with deliberate expansion projects, especially big business and the military, do not admit to imperialism. Economically, Latin American investment is considered the overseas extension of a business expansion process that is both ethical and beneficial, so long as certain rules of the game are respected. Politically and militarily, the spread of American power and influence is considered essential for national security, which is identified with the defense of democracy and the entire free world. Similarly, until the recent crisis of international communism, the Soviet Union equated defense of her own interests with that of socialism itself.

As in the communist bloc, the American people's ingenuousness—an implicit support for the status quo—cannot last indefinitely. Contradictions between national interests in the Communist bloc finally brought the general realization that socialism was not identical with the interests of the Soviet Union or of any other single country or group. The Soviet Union then had to choose between: 1. unilaterally sustaining its national interests and its ruling class oligopoly, a policy which would be imperialist and hegemonic and destroy the principle of socialist solidarity— as well as any illusions about the internal political oligarchy; or 2. adjusting to the new forces. The first alternative implies optimum use of reduced available resources, and growing external pressures. The second would permit maintenance of a greater resource base (including solidarity), while demanding a more equitable order of collective participation and increased internal political competition. The events attendant on the Soviet Union's decision on Czechoslovakia in August 1968 are significant. After agonizing doubts, and despite ratification of the Czech experiment in the Cierna and Bratislava accords, Russia could not tolerate the risks of a truly autonomous, democratic regime within the communist bloc; invasion was its response.

The United States will eventually face a similar decision vis-a-vis its area of hegemony. The alternatives will be to establish a new Roman Empire (as is actually happening now, despite the disclaimers of the American people); or to create an international community for development and defense, featuring more equitable modes of participation and corresponding readjustment of the internal order. It will become increasingly difficult to maintain the status quo as the contradictions of dependency and of North America's political system intensify. The need to choose between imperialism and community will become ever more urgent.

Whatever choice the United States makes will affect both the seven basic alternatives facing underdeveloped nations and the corresponding models. An American imperialist option would ultimately stabilize dependent systems. On the other hand, deciding for community would force these states to adopt either superior forms (autonomous models) or more rudimentary colonial-pretorian patterns in the few cases where this is feasible; they would otherwise be submerged in disruptive revolutions. I will outline each possibility.

The New Roman Empire.   With the imperial option (regardless of how it is chosen), the United States would face two basic problems with regard to the dependent systems: 1. the need to utilize their resources optimally; and 2. preventing the model's inherent deterioration from leading the dependent systems to revolution, which in turn requires ever growing subsidies. These problems can only be resolved by replacing spontaneous, private, and socially irrational modes of dependency with programmed and organized forms, following the example of the Roman Empire. This is the path from dependency to provincial dependency.

This course has two main consequences. Systematic imperial exploitation of provincial resources demands efficient administration. The system thus passes from a zero-sum or negative phase to one of provincial development, though for the benefit of an external center. Secondly, the old dominant elite, whose incompetence and vices allowed the empire to appropriate the system cheaply in the first place, is replaced by a functional leadership. This is partly formed by delegates of the empire, who advise the proconsul and local Herodian governors. The remaining delegates are selected by competitive recruitment among the local middle class, previously subjected to a "Romanization" process.

This last aspect of the transition from satellizing dependency to provincial dependency also has a Roman precedent. The Empire consolidated and institutionalized an "international" elite which, under the direction of the senatorial class and the high military command, formed the system's administrative subelite. It seems that an international "executive" class is now forming as "Romanized" contingents of the provincial middle classes are co-opted by the American middle class nucleus. Institutionalizing this tendency would offer the new Roman Empire a double advantage: the emerging class can perform necessary administrative services, both private and public; and the process will open new outlets for the dependent systems' middle sectors. These groups will replace the old elites as the systems' directors, assuring stability with progressively less coercion and greater incorporation of the peripheral masses.

The communitarian option. The United States has another option — community. In a new framework, under United States leadership but with more equitable participation, Latin America would develop autonomously, and with community mechanisms for cooperation and defense. As noted, this alternative is less likely because it would require major structural and attitudinal modifications in both the United States and the principal dependent systems. An alternative with many prerequisites has less chance of success than one which simply maintains the status quo.

Despite its lower probability, the communitarian option is neither impossible nor purely theoretical. It depends basically on two sets of conditions: 1. important changes in modes of participation and the decision-making process within the United States, which must result in new policies; and 2. adoption of the autonomous development model by some major countries within the North American sphere of influence, provided there is no strategic risk for United States national security. Likely Latin American candidates are Brazil or an Argentine-Chilean-Mexican coalition. This set of conditions will be examined briefly in the final part of the study. Here I will only mention a few main points.

For a communitarian option to work for the United States, its basic interests must be made compatible with free development in the rest of the world. Americans would balk at the notion; since they are unaware of their imperialist path, they judge that what is good for the United States is good for the free world. This attitude means that the uncontrolled growth of big corporations and increasing economic oligopolization will deprive the rest of the world of autonomous growth centers. This is as true within the United States as in other countries accepting this process (in practice, almost all those outside the communist bloc). Internally, all important decisions will be concentrated in an enlarged North American ruling elite.

The popular belief persists that tensions between Russia and the United States are due mainly to antagonistic ideologies and systems. The truth is precisely the opposite. Modern American capitalism cannot coexist with other autonomous capitalisms. But, excluding sociocultural and political military factors, there is no economic incompatibility between American capitalism and a socialist system—as long as they interrelate as autonomous and basically endogenous units, and carry on mutually beneficial trade in neonercantilist terms of comparative advantage.

Economic and political readjustment in the United States will face two obstacles: the extent to which viable alternative programs and structures are presented to the American people; and the strength of social forces which would support such changes. Recent investigations indicate that large scale redistribution of income and decision-making power would increase effective democracy and bring more balanced internal growth than that resulting from oligopolistic control of international markets. Growing numbers of highly educated Americans form the core of support for alternative policies; while they remain politically neutralized, though, the imperial option will become more firmly cemented.

We will close this discussion by outlining the implications of the communitarian alternative for dependent systems. The United States would refuse to subsidize the dependent systems; reorienting the North American economy to benefit its own people would also terminate expansionist pressures. New mechanisms would allow a more equitable community of autonomous nations.

The dependent systems would subsequently undergo decisive transformation, whether evolutionary, regressive, or disruptive. In some cases, and probably in most of Latin America's viable countries, the elites would initiate reforms ("We will make the revolution before the people do"), encouraging autonomous development and integration to protect their own position. With technological innovation and economic expansion, this policy would compensate for incorporating the masses and giving them, at last, their share in development benefits. In other cases oligarchic domination would follow the Paraguayan example and yield to colonial-pretorian models, even though new international conditions would preclude long term viability. Last, in countries like Colombia, with an important conservative sector, peaceful transition from dependency to an autonomous development model might be frustrated. Two conflicting, socially and geographically divided power centers could form, and civil war might result.

THE ALTERNATIVE OF AUTONOMY

The Revolutionary Model

Models divide between representational and operational types. The former are conceptual and/or mathematical symbolic systems which represent the most relevant variables of some reality. They are analogous to mechanical models which reproduce structures and processes on a small and simplified scale. Operational models are also conceptual and/or mathematical symbolic systems, but only start with representations of some empirical system. These models focus on the alterations necessary to bring specific results, which may include structural modification of the very system under consideration.

The most consistent representational and operational models for revolution, in political science terms, are those of Marxist derivation. Marx himself only outlined a representational model, synthesized in the Communist Manifesto. He was cautious and vague about any operational model; judging from the scanty written evidence, he seems to have envisioned something like the Paris Commune. It was Lenin, with Trotsky's strategic and tactical contribution, who formulated the first operational revolutionary model, theoretically consistent and confirmed by practice.

Other representational models of revolution include those of social science (for example, the works of Crane Brinton and conservative and reactionary positions which put forward the subversive concept of revolutions). This last interpretation has given rise to the operational antirevolutionary model of counter-insurgency.

Marxist-derived representational and operational models of revolution have significantly influenced events, completely conditioning both the representational model of subversion and the opposed, albeit mechanical and crude, operational model of counterinsurgency. Here I can only touch on these Marxist-based models, and what seem to be their weaknesses.

The theory of growing pauperization, corrected by the Lenin's analyses of imperialism, is the basis for the Marxist model of revolution. Its main fallacy lies in assuming that growing oppression inevitably generates a mass revolutionary explosion. Revolutions only occur when strategic sectors of the subelite are marginalized by the political system, and then find means to mobilize the masses. But the inherent weakness of satellizing or neocolonial dependency systems can be corrected when the hegemonic power becomes consistent in its imperial role, transforming satellizing dependency into provincial dependency and incorporating the provincial middle classes into the new international elite.

China and Cuba espouse the Marxist operational model of revolution, as amended by Lenin. Leninism's "Blanquist" aspect is even more pronounced in Latin America where, before Che Guevara's death, the objective conditions for revolution were presumed to exist. By this analysis, the only need was revolutionary mass mobilization through guerrilla warfare. While stressing Blanquism, the Chinese and Cuban model deemphasizes the urban proletariat and exalts the *campesinos*. Peasant masses form the true reserve army of underdeveloped capitalism; in semicolonial countries, they should perform the function which Marx and Lenin attributed to the proletariat in advanced countries.

The tragic deaths of Che in Bolivia and Camilo Torres in Colombia, and the containment of revolutionary guerrilla movements throughout the continent, attest to the flaws in this model. Here I will only summarize the problem.

Two main fallacies vitiate the revolutionary scheme. The first lies in the representational model on which it is based and the assumed correlation between pauperization, marginalization, and compression of the masses on one hand, and the ripening of objective conditions for revolution on the other. The second fallacy is the assumption that mobilized *campesinos*, aided from within by urban terrorists and guerrillas, would encircle and ultimately defeat the towns.

Not surprisingly, this strategic model has been heavily influenced by its historical precedents—China and Cuba. Both revolutions were unique: Cuba's could probably never recur, and China's only in two or three oriental countries and given several unlikely circumstances.

A basic condition of the Cuban model is that, in an area where it can apply virtually unlimited force, the hegemonic power does not intervene until the revolutionary war is won. Whatever Fidel's real intention, his revolution retained the image of a neo-Garibaldian democratic-liberal movement until after he gained power. This appearance prevented foreign intervention.

The North American security agencies have deficient analytical concepts and instruments, limited to the subversive theory of revolutions and the counterinsurgency model. But the United States must have learned from Cuba. Henceforth it can be expected to act pragmatically, as if all successful popular revolutionary movements in Latin America, regardless of aims and ideologies, will ultimately result in developmental socialist regimes.

This perspective prompts unilateral preventive interventions when, as in Santo Domingo, the hegemonic power deems them necessary. Limitations on this type of intervention are 1. the competence of the target country; 2. the extent of collaboration by Latin America's other dependent systems; and 3. the simultaneity and geographic range of interventions. Given present modes of collaboration by Latin America's satellite regimes, and the improbability of simultaneous rebellions in several countries, the only real check on American intervention is the strength and competence of the target country. Herein lies the main limitation of the Cuban model. It was and could continue to be effective in small countries where agrarian revolution has immediate repercussions in the cities, and where the regime's inability to quash rebellion can cause general demoralization. In Central America and the Caribbean, the developmental socialist model could swiftly solve internal problems. But, unfortunately, these are the countries in which preventive interventions are simplest, and where they can be effected with impunity.

In such large countries as Argentina, Brazil, and Mexico, one or a few peasant guerrilla focos have little or no effect on urban life or the modern sector. Preventive interventions in these countries would arouse vigorous opposition in important sectors of the middle class—including the military—which would consider foreign armed intervention a threat as grave as campesino insurrection. The armed forces of the large countries have the strength to repress peasant revolutions before guerrilla focos can muster revolutionary armies.

The Chinese model is applicable in only a few countries like India, Pakistan, and Indonesia. It presupposes an immense and relatively inaccessible peasant mass confronting an incompetent, inefficient, and alienated urban society. These conditions allow formation of an alternative, autonomous and endogenous system which can overthrow the official regime.

The United States was less advanced on the imperialist path at the time of the Chinese revolution. Today it would prefer the costs of preventive intervention, even in large countries, as long as 1. the revolutionary threat appeared within its hegemonic area; 2. logistics were relatively easy; and 3. there were little risk of counter-intervention or strong Soviet reaction. Thus, probably only the countries mentioned—India, Pakistan, and Indonesia— could replicate the Chinese revolution without triggering massive North American intervention. Clearly, no region would offer less resistance than Latin America.

The revolutionary model thus stands little chance of success, save in very special circumstances which do not now exist. Among the most important is that the outbreaks be simultaneous and widely-dispersed. The North American defense establishment, like any other, has limited capacities. Vietnam has demonstrated that finding manpower is the most critical problem. [1] As interventions cost more and more in terms of recruitment and combat losses, North America's anti-expansionist sectors are gaining support from a people who oppose personal sacrifice for an imperialism which does not benefit them.

Revolutionary warfare in Latin America, susceptible to intervention in small countries and internal containment in the large ones, would look quite different as a coordinated outbreak simultaneously affecting several countries. This would be particularly true if any of the most important countries were involved— Argentina, Brazil, or Mexico. Such large scale revolutionary mass mobilization would be an irresistible variant of the Chinese model.

Successful revolution depends on two main factors: the uprising must involve simultaneously several strategically located countries; and the masses must be thoroughly mobilized. A third condition, not essential but very advantageous, is that the revolutionaries quickly capture a major city. This would afford them belligerent status, the resources of a great urban center, and the chance to demonstrate the type of government they propose to install.

Though these conditions cannot now be met, continued deterioration may simplify their fulfillment. It is ultimately impossible, within traditional dependency, to create enough jobs for the middle class. Growing numbers are threatened with marginality, generating conditions in which revolutionary cadres can simultaneously form in some or all countries. Such circumstances make the revolutionary model increasingly viable.

Generalized decline is increasing the possibility of large scale revolutionary outbreaks. If the region's major countries do not soon opt for autonomous development, and if the United States does not anticipate spreading deterioration, the now unviable revolutionary model will inevitably be implemented within 10 to 30 years. The United States could effectively forestall revolution by opting for community, disadvantageous for dependency regimes and favorable for autonomy; or for imperialism, which ultimately converts satellizing dependency into provincial dependency.

The Autonomy Model

As a representational model, autonomy combines independent cultural, social, economic, and political development with a type of regional integration which does not endanger national identities or each country's maximum development. The framework is a coherent and harmonious system which multiplies members' resource and market bases and optimizes production and productivity in terms assuring endogenous regional development.

The model's main features include: 1. development of each member country as a national society; 2. maximization of national and regional decision-making autonomy; and 3. maximization of endogenous development and regional viability through a harmonious integration which multiplies national and regional resources, markets, and productivity.

The problem of interstate relations in a regional system is too complicated to treat here; I will mention only two aspects. One concerns the initial number of participants and their degree of involvement. (Operational aspects of this matter will be discussed later.) Integration which included all area countries at the outset would not necessarily succeed. Each member's sovereignty would have to be guaranteed in an association like the European Economic Community, with greater or lesser delegation of powers to the central organs.

The second aspect involves the subsequent phases of integration. Any Latin American association should set minimum goals of self-sustaining development and maintenance, without unrealistic anticipations of eventual supernationality or confederation; these will naturally result as the system evolves. IDB studies suggest that an association of this type must also include compensations for its smaller, relatively less developed members.

In the autonomy model, relations between member states and the regional system show three main characteristics. The first concerns the twin aspects of national development: members are embarked on a general process of cultural, social, economic, and political progess; and they are developing as *national* societies.

Overall development involves more than such economic considerations as the best use of productive factors and resources; it demands the optimized social rationality. This requires: (a) a rational scientific and technological culture, based on an ethic of liberty and social humanism; (b) equitable modes of participation for functional mass–elite relations which delegate authority according to merit and provide full and equal means of access to the ruling group; (c) the usual requirements of capital accumulation and optimal use of resources and production factors; and (d) an effectively repres. 'ational and generally efficient political order. National development will imply an association endowed with independent cultural values, based on self-determination, and oriented toward self-preservation and advancement.

The model's second characteristic is national and regional decision-making autonomy. Representative actors from within the system must be able to make decisions, requiring their prior agreement to establish necessary conditions.

Autonomy is the model's most essential feature. This involves in equal measure cultural possibilities of finalistic and operational rationality and its practical application, and a social order receptive to such self-determination. The system should also direct its own scientific, technological and economic progress.

National development requires profound alterations both in cultural values and styles and structures of participation, property, and power. Autonomy demands new relations between Latin American societies and the rest of the world—particularly the developed countries under North American hegemony, and above all, the United States itself. Institutional relations between nations must be altered, as well as those between local and external (especially United States) actors and agencies.

Latin American dependence on the United States, though often expressed in intergovernmental and interinstitutional forms—which include proconsular control in the smallest countries—is predominantly private. Ties include scientific, technological, economic, financial, and administrative dependency on the great North American multinational corporations. Overcoming this dependency will require a gigantic effort at scientific, technological, economic, and organizational modernization and innovation. New policies and norms must be ensured by state actions or sanctions. Inventions, patents, and foreign capital are among the most important areas susceptible to state control.

New standards must ultimately assure the absolute predominance of national and regional patents and capital; for now, they must gradually nationalize and regionalize already registered patents and current capital investments. Nationalization with conventional payments would exhaust the region's resources and abort its development. Expropriation, using taxes and related mechanisms, and automatic termination of privileged situations incompatible with Latin American development, would be necessary. In the former case, the very objects of expropriation would eventually produce the funds for indemnification.

The third aspect of the autonomy model includes endogenous growth and viability, and the multiple considerations for launching an integrated regional system. It contrasts with both preceding parochial stagnation and the present tendency toward satellized integration.

Latin America's old parochial stagnation needs no further comment. The Montevideo Treaty,[2] despite good intentions, is linked to this ethic. The Latin American Common Market was modeled on the least organic and most mercantile aspects of its European counterpart, which initially limited it to a relatively unimportant mechanism for facilitating regional trade, and did nothing to alter economic structures. The Association is now becoming the "clearing house" for multinational American corporations based in Latin America. This is the essence of satellizing integration, and contrasts sharply with the autonomy model. More from the momentum of events than by deliberate planning, LAFTA is rationalizing the system for distributing Latin America's markets and investment opportunities among North American multinational corporations. Such integration ultimately entails territorial organization of resources for a regionally based United States production and consumption system.

The essence of autonomy, in contrast, is to promote socioeconomic integration of the Latin American nations for their individual and collective benefit. The goal is to maximize each member's national capacity, along with that of the larger system. As a beginning, a large pool of human, technological, natural and financial resources could be formed to assure optimum endogenous regional development and viability. This would encourage maximum levels of large scale and highly productive industrialization, and corresponding trends in cultural, social, and political development. A large market for regional production should follow, allowing an ascending spiral of self-sustaining development in which growing demand stimulates higher production, and vice versa. Maximized endogenous development will ultimately ensure regional viability.

This viability is a function of both decision-making autonomy and the endogenous growth of scientific, technological, economic, and political potentials. These will give the continent a growing independent capacity for national and regional security.

A dependent Latin America lacks adequate security. The region is obviously incapable of nuclear confrontation. Internally, the existing order is neither national (its regimes are dependent) nor able to sustain itself. Continuing deterioration will lead the region either to revolution or to reduction to provincial status in the New Roman Empire. Opting for autonomy would create the conditions for endogenous growth and viability and an expanding independent security capacity.

Adequate security is critical for autonomous and endogenous development. The topic is large; here I shall only stress that a modern arms industry is an essential element. The military industry's technological and economic contributions would stimulate the growth of civil industry, as it did in the United States and Europe. Moreover, this military capacity would form a necessary bulwark for the regional autonomy.

Economic and military aspects correspond in both satellizing and autonomous regimes. Satellizing economic integration, in the current form of coordination of Latin American resources and markets by America's multinational corporations, corresponds militarily to the clandestine formation of an interAmerican defense force (FIP). Either way, Latin America supplies territory, resources, and manpower, while the United States retains equipment, control, and decision-making power. In the autonomy model, however, the relationship is reversed. Integration would bolster each nation's economic development, while combining arms manufacturing capacities and encouraging independent national and regional security systems directed by Latin Americans themselves.

Conditions for Establishing the Autonomy Model

We will now consider seven basic requirements for establishing the autonomy model:

1. Appropriate timing
2. National viability
3. Adaptation of the chosen political model to the target society's structural conditions
4. National and social adaptation to develop and maintain the process in countries where it begins
5. Mobilization of appropriate groups
6. Appearance of appropriate leadership
7. Absence of overwhelming foreign intervention

Appropriate timing. As we have seen, Latin American has a strict time limit for initiating autonomous and endogenous development. Though exact estimates are impossible, this goal will not be attainable after 2000.

National viability. In another study (*Economic and Political Development*, Cambridge: Harvard University Press, 1968), I analyzed this problem in greater detail. For obvious historical reasons, some Latin American countries are incapable of either individual or collective survival. Inadequate human and natural resources, the dependency of the elite on the United States, and precarious geopolitical situations, make the Central American and Caribbean countries unviable. An independent Latin American system, however, might eventually reabsorb these countries. States like Paraguay have seriously limited resources and are subject to colonial-pretorian regimes which appear immune to internal corrections. The destinies of such countries will probably remain uncertain, dependent on the region's success at autonomy. The viability of countries like Ecuador and Bolivia is also unsure. Though Uruguay's circumstances are different, her possibilities for national development are rapidly being exhausted; regional integration is urgently needed to open new horizons.

Adaptation of the chosen political model to the target society's structural conditions.   As I mentioned in the book cited above, political action is the only means to promote national development in countries that are underdeveloped but viable. It is important that the political model chosen be ﹐appropriate to the society in question. Three are possible in contemporary Latin America: national capitalism; state capitalism; and developmental socialism.

   Conditions deteriorated sharply after Latin America's first abortive attempt at deliberate development; thus pure national capitalism could not now be applied in any country. Mixed models, part national capitalist and part state capitalist, are called for in the more advanced nations, while forms varying between state capitalism and developmental socialism are indicated for the rest.

National and social adaptation to develop and maintain the process in countries where it begins.   The high demands of contemporary technology require concentrated resources. In Latin America, only Mexico, Argentina, and especially Brazil (because of its huge area) could hope for independent development. But any country would risk disastrous consequences by attempting development without North American approval. Should the United States choose the imperial option, as seems likely, it will have both the motivation and the means to use Latin America's dependent systems to quash any separatist take-off.

Thus we see the value of adopting a regional framework for Latin American development. This does not imply simultaneous mobilization of all countries; even excluding the unviable states, this would be impossible. It is also unnecessary in theory (though convenient in practice) that every Latin American country eventually participate. The process will inevitably begin on a limited scale; the example of Europe's "Outer Six" suggests that it could last indefinitely without incorporating all area states. It must, however, begin with the key countries, Mexico, Brazil and Argentina.

Mobilization of appropriate groups. Mobilizing competent groups is as important as choosing a suitable model. An adequate analysis would be too complex for this study, so I will make just two observations. Regardless of anyone's desires, the political developmental model appropriate for a country corresponds socially and politically to the cadres which can be mobilized. National capitalism stresses the empresarial bourgeoisie; state capitalism, the technical and administrative middle class; and developmental socialism, the revolutionary intelligentsia. Only separate analysis of each country can determine which factions and groups will be most easily mobilized within this general framework.

Second, there are very few groups which now support development. This is due to two related factors: 1. Latin American development has already experienced one serious setback; 2. the estimated 10-year limit for initiating the model means that strategic alternatives are rapidly running out. Existing factors must be used to best advantage to completely transform power, participation, value, and property structures in one or several strategic countries. Under these circumstances, the group that can be most instrumental in transforming the continent is that now holding power—the armed forces.

Mobilization should focus on progessive nationalist groups, untainted by officialdom, and dissatisfied with the satellizing dependency model. The Latin American military has been the object of extensive reactionary satellizing manipulation, and was used to destroy Argentine and Brazilian populism. The armed forces, ignoring the inherent limitations of these populist regimes, destroyed a nascent and autonomous regional development along with them. But this does not mean that the military, under new leadership, could not assume a different role.

The positions of privilege and control of both internal and external reactionary and satellizing forces have been under fire since the late fifties. Their only option appeared to lie in pitting the military against populist democracies. Though this effort was successful, the price may prove fatal. In the name of economic liberalism, the military concentrated enormous power in the state's executive branch; thus was created the structure for transforming Latin American societies. The only task now remaining is to imbue the structure with a new spirit, in a time period no longer than what these reactionary and satellizing forces have already enjoyed, and to substitute the ideology of developmental autonomy for that of satellizing dependency. The tanks must face in the opposite direction.

Students must be mobilized along with the military. Latin American youth is more dramatically aware of her problems than ever before, of the critical time period for resolving them, and of the catastrophic consequences if adequate solutions are not found. This contingent has never been so numerous, and its relative importance is unprecedented. New leaders must unite groups that are presently locked in a sterile and nationally suicidal confrontation. This leadership, together with the student and military vanguards, must initiate regional development.

Appearance of appropriate leadership. Social and political renovation obviously requires new leadership. Two factions (excepting students) are vying for this position. One represents the reactionary satellizing process established in the late fifties, which within a decade destroyed almost all existing populist

democracies. The leaders of this movement now hold power throughout Latin America, save for Chile, Venezuela in part, and—with qualifications—Mexico.[3]
Leaders overthrown in the onslaught of satellization constitute the other faction. Almost all were unable to comprehend, much less avoid, the weaknesses inherent in the populism of the fifties. They could not initiate irreversible, penetrating, and widely diffused development. Or, as with Carlos Lacerda, it was a matter of a *rescape* of reactionary-satellizing forces—by a unique combination of lucidity and unsatisfied ambitions, some politicians broke with satellitism. Lacerda, however, has failed to inspire confidence in the opposing camp.

There are no suitable political leaders outside the student ranks, and the students tend toward the revolutionary alternative. However, according to this analysis, revolution is impossible under the present circumstances. During the next decade, while autonomous development remains a possibility, existing forces will generate potential leaders for that process. The intelligentsia and nationalist military officers will be prime candidates.

This new leadership must determine the optimum deployment of existing forces and structures in a radical program of social, political, cultural, and economic renovation. The exigencies of the situation must be borne in mind; high costs or long time lags could make the reforms inoperative.

Absence of overwhelming foreign intervention. This is a final requisite for the autonomy model. I will conclude by correlating North American options and the prevailing tendencies in Latin America, and indicating likely consequences. Even if the United States chooses the communitarian option, which encourages autonomous development regimes, it will remain the hegemonic power. Renunciation of imperialism would be an enlightened choice in favor of its own social, cultural, economic, and political progress. And the United States would have the means, motivation, and justification for taking whatever preventive or corrective measures it deemed necessary to defend its option. Insofar as basic North American interests can be made compatible with those of the rest of the world, so can other countries, and Latin America in particular, initiate autonomous and endogenous development in harmony with the basic interests of the American people.

THE PROSPECTS

Covering our broad topic has demanded frequent schematization. I will conclude by outlining Latin America's prospects, which depend on tendencies in the United States and in Latin America. The hegemonic power has three options. The first is passive maintenance of the status quo, which we have seen cannot persist indefinitely. It could, however, last long enough for events to push the United States to one of the other alternatives. North America's expansionist forces — the large multinational corporations and the military—more or less consciously favor imperialism. The communitarian option resembles the official definition of North American foreign policy. This approach is disseminated in the American mass media, and many people assume their government is implementing it. Genuine supporters of this option among liberal and radical intellectuals, students, and social leaders, are critical of present policies; they assert that these contradict the communitarian ideal and will destroy its future prospects.

Latin America also has three possibilities. As in the United States, one is passive maintenance of the status quo. On our continent, however, this is tantamount to perpetuating satellizing dependency. This option is enforced by the region's armed forces, manipulated by anticommunist ideology or corrupted by colonial-pretorianism. It is supported by the consular bourgeoisie in particular, as well as by cartorial sectors of the middle class. Revolution, the second alternative, is supported by the radical intelligentsia, most committed university students, and the labor unions. Developmental autonomy, finally, is favored by progressive sectors of the middle class, the remainder of the national bourgeoisie, moderate elements of the intelligentsia, critics of revolutionary prospects, and some labor sectors.

There is every indication that a definitive decision will be made within a decade. If this does not happen, either north or south of the Rio Grande, present trends will produce irreversible consequences. There are three aspects of the process: 1.

confrontation of the three tendencies within the United States; 2. a parallel confrontation in Latin America; 3. the interaction between these confrontations, which will have a strong "feedback" effect on both and will ultimately determine the outcome. Neither the international situation nor events in Latin America are likely to prompt the United States to choose between imperialism and community; the present ambiguous status quo will probably continue for several years. Events surrounding the succession of President Johnson and through mid-1968 (when this study was completed), seem to confirm the deadlock of United States foreign policy. Clearly "communitarian" candidates, like Eugene McCarthy, could not dislodge the party bosses who controlled the Democratic Party machinery. Youth and radical pressure forced Johnson's reelection and immobilized imperialist forces. A clearcut decision has been postponed, and the outcome is yet to be seen.

In Latin America, however, alternatives are more urgent and thus will be debated more seriously. Passive maintenance of the status quo is coming to signify active support for satellizing dependency. Two sets of circumstances could prevent this option in the next few years: 1. Leaders able to initiate autonomous development may not appear, which would lead to confrontation between dependency and revolution; or 2. military leaders capable of producing a "Copernican revolution" in the armed forces may come to the fore. These groups could demonstrate that national security is no more than the military counterpart of autonomous development.

If, as was true in the first case, there is no mobilization for autonomous development, the imperial option will probably prevail in the near future. But if the United States continues to equivocate and fails to systematize its imperialism, Latin America's national and social structural decay will bring a generation of crisis in which revolution will become feasible.

North American indecision is in the interests of Latin American autonomy. A dangerous conflict would result if an American option for imperialism were coupled with a Latin American choice of autonomy. Depending on circumstances, the result might be imperial triumph, a communitarian compromise, or radicalized autonomy through a victorious revolution.

Chart I   Interaction of Tendencies in Latin America

Predominant Trends in the Next Ten Years

1. *In the United States*
1.1 Maintenance of the status quo
1.2 Imperial option
1.3 Communitarian option

2. *In Latin America*
2.1 Maintenance of the status quo (satellizing dependency)
2.2 Revolutionary option
2.3 Autonomy option

Probable Consequences in Latin America, and Long-Term Tendencies

1.1–2.1: Revolution—Establishment of an autonomous developmental socialist system

1.1–2.2: Repression—Provincial dependency in the New Roman Empire

1.1–2.3: Autonomy—International communitarian system, or:

Imperial reaction—Military intervention, premature quashing of emergent autonomy, and imposition of provincial dependency, or:

Conflict—with internal radicalization, conversion to socialism, and victorious resistance to the invader

1.2–2.1: Empire—Provincial dependency in the New Roman Empire

1.2–2.2: Imperial repression—Provincial dependency in the New Roman Empire

1.2–2.3: Imperial reaction—Provincial dependency, or:

Conflict—with internal radicalization, conversion to socialism, and victorious resistance to the invader, or:

Autonomous compromise—International communitarian system

1.3–2.1: Prolonged stagnation—Provincial dependency in the New Roman Empire, or:

Revolution and implantation of an autonomous developmental-socialist system

1.3–2.2: Reluctant imperial repression—Provincial dependency in the New Roman Empire, or:

Communitarian rebuilding

1.3–2.3: Autonomy—International communitarian system

NOTES

1. This problem will not exist in the New Roman Empire, in which a professional army will be formed from the "Romanized" provincial masses.
2. Treaty signed in 1960, setting up LAFTA. (Ed.)
3. Since September 11, 1973, when the military ousted President Salvador Allende, Chile ceased to be an exception. (Ed.)

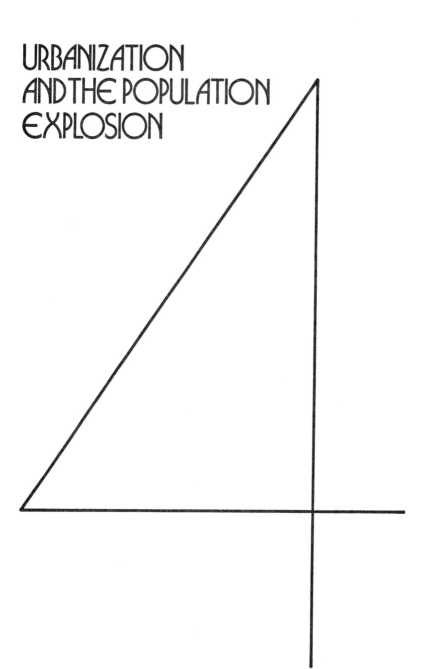

URBANIZATION
AND THE POPULATION
EXPLOSION

11. CITY AND COUNTRYSIDE IN LATIN AMERICA: AN ANALYSIS OF SOCIAL AND ECONOMIC RELATIONS[1]

JORGE E. HARDOY
Center for Urban and Regional Studies, Torcuato di Tella Institute, Buenos Aires

INTRODUCTION

Contemporary urbanization is accentuating the perennial distinction between densely and sparsely settled America. This urbanization is circumscribed within units of economically weak nation states which perpetuate the primary product export patterns initiated and consolidated during three centuries of colonial rule. Urbanization studies and projections, by choosing a national focus, disregard the continent's spatial context. If Latin America is correctly interpreted as a conglomerate—not even a simple sum—of differentiated units, it is entirely possible that the comparative advantages of localization will come to determine tendencies in urbanization and infrastructure development.

The future is hard to predict in this half-empty continent, where engrained patterns of territorial exploitation date from an epoch of political and economic dependence on external forces. Each country's urban system and hierarchy of population centers has reflected its economic orientation through successive historical phases; nations like Argentina, Chile, Peru, and Uruguay are typical of export oriented agrarian or mining societies, directed by urban minorities. They reflect state subordination to private interests and the absence of regional criteria for national development. Under these conditions, future urbanization patterns will depend on the region's future governments and their progress toward national and then continental integration, based on common interests and ideas.

Urban Latin America has increased in population and territorial scope for over 2000 years. Growth has intensified in the last fifty years, and the next half-century will continue the trend toward a larger urban population and a more extensive and effective hierarchy of centers. Latin America's urban societies have always derived sustenance and an economic base from the countryside; rural migrants are maintaining contemporary urbanization. Nonetheless, rural structural change and a new rural economic system have been delayed until recent decades. This reversal reflects the urban zone's expanding social, economic, and political influence, at least in the continent's most dynamic and industrializing areas. And so the moment is critical for both the zones themselves and for regional territorial integration. Consolidating a negative urban system of ambivalent and superimposed centers lacking clear roles would create a near-insuperable obstacle to national development.

A relationship as old as that between Latin America's cities and countryside can only be understood historically. The "New World" the Spaniards and Portuguese discovered was not new to 25 or 30 million Indians, many of whom lived in cities comparable to their European contemporaries. The nineteenth century republics were new politically, but both their economies and societies reflected the colonial heritage. Under present conditions, urbanization may be a means for reorienting development in individual countries and in the region as a whole, but only if it is sufficiently appreciated as a means to increase political participation, modify social structures, expand industrial production, and introduce — in both city and countryside — up-to-date technology and modern levels of education and participation. Last, urbanization demands redefinition of state functions with respect to both the individual and private enterprise.

THREE HISTORICAL PHASES [1]

Precolumbian urbanization, free from influences external to the continent, relied on indigenous populations and technology. It was based on the soil's productive capacity and subject to such primary localization factors as availability of water and land, distances to fields, and local topography. Defense was rarely a major consideration. The indigenous cultures built with local materials: stone in the highlands of Peru, Bolivia, Mexico, and Guatemala; adobe in coastal Peru; wood with straw roofs in Petén. Stone, often transported over considerable distances, was used in temples.

All Precolumbian cultures were based on agriculture. Most of the rural population clustered in largely self-sufficient villages whose size was primarily determined by the immediate area's productive capacity. Taxing the countryside helped maintain an urban society which probably included only 5 or 10 percent of total population. Urban ruling groups, bolstered by accentuated religious and military centralism, maintained political and administrative control over ever expanding territories. The Spanish conquest interrupted two great political experiments, the Aztec and the Inca, each of which centralized power in one person.

In ecologically favorable areas of Mexico and Guatemala, Latin American urbanization began at least 2000 years ago. Perhaps because of a more dispersed and smaller population, urbanization was delayed by several centuries in coastal and highland Peru and on the Bolivian altiplano. Precolumbian urbanization peaked in two epochs. The first coincided with the classic Mesoamerican cultures—Totonec, Zapotec, Teotihuacan, Mayan—in the middle of the first millenium A.D., and with Tihuanaco's expansion in highland and coastal Peru at the end of the first millenium. These were all interior cultures; Aztec and Inca expansions, after about 1430, were likewise directed from the interior with a regional perspective. Precolumbian cultures reaching the urban stage incorporated no more than 8 percent of Latin America's total area.

Two principal and independent urban regional systems, in the sense that there was a continuous flow of men and goods along well designed roads and between specialized urban centers of distinct hierarchy, existed around 1500—the Aztec and the Inca. Tenochtitlán, a city which may have numbered 150,000, was the capital of the Aztec confederation. Around it, joined by central Mexico's lacustrine system, arose a network of cities including Cuyuacán, Tácuba, Azcapotzalco, Texcoco, Ixtapalapa and others which, together, must have totalled about one million inhabitants.

From Cuzco, center of the Inca empire, the Incas determined the major aspects of a territorial policy oriented toward increasing regional production and satisfying the population's basic needs. Construction of roads, bridges, outposts, irrigation and drainage canals, terraces, warehouses, and so on, was ordered from .the capital, with execution and maintenance delegated to regional authorities. The Incas used the cities and towns of conquered cultures, and also built new cities in accord with specific objectives.

Elimination of indigenous governments, and the forced imposition of new values, precipitated the colonial disintegration. The Spaniards, to take advantage of established tribute systems, tried to maintain existing rural economic organizations during the first post-conquest decades. But new illnesses; the wars of conquest and resulting mobilization of, and hunger and death in, the indigenous population; new crops and grazing animals and their impact on land productivity; and large manpower levies for civic and religious construction—all produced a sharp drop in indigenous population. This has been estimated at 30 or 35 million around 1500; the causes cited brought rapid decline during the sixteenth century, and recovery began in the mid seventeenth century. Only in 1850 did population again reach the level estimated for 1500.

The distribution of Indian population influenced the location of the first Spanish cities. Some of these which still exist, like Mexico and Cuzco, Texcoco, Cholula, Mérida (Yucatán), Cuenca, and Cajamarca, were superimposed on Indian cities. Road alignment and plaza forms, and the location of churches and palaces, were affected by prior constructions of similar use. Most colonial Spanish cities like Guadalajara, Oaxaca, Guatemala, San Salvador, Bogotá, Tunja, Leiva, Caracas, Quito, Lima, Trujillo (Peru), Ayacucho, La Paz, Arequipa, Ica, and Huánuco, were founded in areas of dense Indian population—the Spaniards relied on the conquered peoples for subsistence and above all for developing the extractive and exporting economy which characterized the colonial period. These almost universally interior cities concentrated government and service functions hierarchically. A relatively small number were established in uninhabited or lightly populated areas. Some, like Cartagena, Havana, Portobelo, Veracruz, Panama, and Callao, were ports situated in terms of interests external to the continent, to ensure contact between the metropolis and its principal colonies. Others were mining centers, like Zacatecas, Guanajuato, Taxco, Potosí, and Huancavelica. There were also minor ports such as La Guayra, Campeche, Santa Marta, Guayaquil, Pisco, Buenos Aires, Montevideo, and Valparaiso, from which regional production was shipped to concentration points for the fleets and then to Spain. Finally, there were military posts and frontier stations like Monterrey, Horcasitas, Orán, and Arauco; settlements around religious missions; and other sorts of towns. The Spanish tended toward a city model characterized by the simplicity of its elements, the ease with which it could be laid out, and the relative balance it allowed in distributing urban lots.

Colonial cities were, in Richard M. Morse's words, "the centrifugal force for exploiting the environment." The criteria for this exploitation were set in the cities, residences for crown and church authorities, important merchants, mineowners, *encomenderos,* and *hacendados.* The country dweller was invariably Indian or mestizo, or a black slave imported when declining indigenous population disrupted regional economies. The rural Indian was usually obliged to work in the mines, to resettle in religious *reducciones,* or to fill *encomienda* labor exactions. Where this did not occur he attempted to maintain his life style, the values and practices inherited from ancient cultures. Spontaneous migration undoubtedly brought some to the colonial cities, though I believe that most of the urban Indian population originated in those accompanying the Spanish as members of auxiliary armies or as servants in the new settlements—individuals serving the colonial elite. The Spanish colonial city was primarily European and mestizo.

The total number of Spanish settlements has never been determined—there may have been thousands. Most numbered barely a few hundred inhabitants; around 1800, only Mexico and San Salvador had over 100,000 inhabitants. Havana approached this figure and Rio de Janeiro had a few thousand less; Lima counted less than 60,000; and Buenos Aires and Santiago had fewer than 50,000 each.

Brazilian colonization was different. The area was unique in lacking a docile and settled population, and mineral wealth was only discovered at the end of the seventeenth century. Portuguese colonization and the brief Dutch occupation of the Northeast in the mid-seventeenth century were essentially coastal. Both were based on sugar cane, whose cycle persisted until the end of the seventeenth century and generated a plantation society clustered around the export ports. Recife, Natal, Salvador, and other Northeastern cities were administrative and service centers for a lightly settled and little known interior, but primarily acted as points of exchange and contact with Portugal and Europe, where Brazilian sugar became a monopoly.

Mining in present day Minas Gerais developed during the eighteenth century. This cycle drew the economic center of gravity south, and accelerated urbanization around the port of Rio de Janeiro. Mining centers, including Ouro Preto, Diamantina, São Luis do Rey, Mariana, and Congonhas, were also founded. These were of an opulence then unknown in Brazil, and in them arose one of Latin America's most valuable sculptural and architectural movements. The French invasion of 1807 forced Portugal's royal family to flee to Brazil, and thus consolidated Rio de Janeiro's position as capital. A new economic cycle, based on coffee and centered on São Paulo, began shortly after independence was declared in 1821. Each cycle—sugar first, and then mining—left a declining region after losing its economic drive.

Throughout Latin America, long-lived urban systems persisted virtually unchanged until several decades after independence. Struggles for liberation and subsequent civil wars plunged the new governments into debt and disrupted regional economies, depopulating or immobilizing some old secondary centers. European powers including Britain and France, and the United States, replaced Spain as trading partners. European goods displaced the few regional products enjoying national markets, speeding the decline of interior cities. On the other hand, the concentration of new administrative, cultural, and commercial functions enhanced the primacy of national capitals, established in colonial administrative centers. Each country's interior remained a great void lacking adequate communications. Intensive cultivation and extensive livestock raising persisted where they had for centuries, while mining production declined. British, French, and German capital, and Italian, Spanish, and Portuguese immigrants (with lesser inputs of Jews, Syrians, Englishmen, Frenchmen, Germans, and Slavs) transformed the Atlantic countries after 1860. Within a few decades southern Brazil, Uruguay, and the Argentine coast were traversed by railroads, populated with new argicultural settlements, and dotted with hundreds of small towns responding to new crops—coffee in Brazil, wheat in Argentina and Uruguay—and to new forms of commercializing rural production.

The advantages of investing and living in Rio de Janeiro, São Paulo, Montevideo, Buenos Aires, and Rosario were clear by the end of the nineteenth century. Foreign immigration brought these centers accelerated growth, while their economies were diversified with foreign investments in railroads, transformation industries for agricultural production, banks, and urban services. Local capitalists seldom received the concessions granted foreigners. A few cities benefitted from public investments in ports and constructions financed with mortgage credits and with government debts guaranteed by foreign loans. Due to differences in natural and human resources and to greater distance from the European markets, similar changes were somewhat delayed in Chile, Peru, Mexico, Colombia, and Venezuela.

While important transformations occurred in some rural zones, *latifundia* and monocultural plantations restricted agricultural development throughout most of Latin America. Rent payment via personal labor; the rural worker's indebtedness to the patrón; cyclical and poorly paid employment in sugar, cotton, and banana plantations—all coexisted with *minifundism*. Miserable living conditions and lack of rural opportunities stimulated rural–urban migration, which reached significant volume during the 1930s. These movements are a basic factor in rapid urban growth, especially in industrial centers and the national capitals. Since about 1870, Latin America's spatial structure has developed in a manner characteristic of areas producing raw materials for an external market and consuming imported products and technology. Though each country has gradually gained geographic coherence, all reflect an external economic orientation and the lack of national objectives for regional integration.

THE CURRENT SITUATION

Latin American population densities are not excessive. Were territorial and other resources channeled toward development and improving socioeconomic conditions, area population could be several times larger. The historical trend is toward denser settlement of the continent's periphery with limited expansion toward the interior in Venezuelan Guayana, north-central Brazil, eastern Bolivia, central Paraguay, and southeastern Mexico. Current settlement patterns stressing Latin America's periphery and the Central Mexican and Central American highlands follow those initiated by the Iberian invaders and already well-defined by 1600. And these areas remain dependent, though in the nineteenth century the nature of this dependence shifted from politico-administrative, cultural, and economic to primarily economic, with strong political and cultural interference. Foreign oriented urbanization accompanied the change. This gradual and rather inefficient transformation of colonial urbanization "schemes" into national urban "systems" with regional interconnections did not substantially modify inherited patterns. As is apparent from their transportation systems, Argentina, Uruguay, Peru, Venezuela, Ecuador, and Chile figure among the "siphon" of "fan" countries; before the advent of modern communications, these nations' colonial "schemes" had not begun to cede to the now dominant urban "systems," which manifest no sense of nation.

Latin America's population density is very low. The figure was ten people per km^2 in 1960, when total population was 200 million; fifteen per km^2 are predicted for 1975, and thirty per km^2 for 2000, when total population will reach 600 million. But if 360 of the 600 million people of 2000 are urban, this group will be concentrated in less than one percent of total area (with, of course, different densities and concentrations in each country); population density in the rest of the continent will average twelve people per km2.

Large areas of Latin America are unsuited for permanent settlement because of aridity, excessive altitude, unfavorable climatic conditions or other reasons, and have only been settled to exploit natural resources. Two-thirds of Argentina receives less than 500 mm. of rainfall and lacks water; expansion of arable land on the Peruvian coast requires expensive irrigation works; northern Mexico and northern Chile, coastal Peru, and southern Argentina, contain some of the world's most important deserts. Erosion has destroyed large areas of traditional monoculture in regions like northeast Brazil and northwest Argentina. And general ignorance as to the location and real potential of mineral deposits, soils, and water resources (especially subterranean), makes prediction even more difficult. Less than 5 percent of the continent is geologically mapped. One specialist asserts that we know almost nothing about "over 70 percent of the minerals considered important for modern industry," and that "only 8 to 10 percent of the region's soils have been reconnaissance mapped." Assessing alternatives for territorial occupation in 2000 is thus almost impossible, as is predicting how new integration systems might affect population distribution.

Historical tendencies and existing projections suggest: 1. denser settlement of already occupied and developed areas around the continent's principal industrial connurbations with limited territorial expansion; 2. persistence of extremely low population densities in the region's vast uninhabited or sparsely populated areas (less than 1 person per km2), despite plans, studies, and various expensive and not always high priority projects of national or continental infrastructure; and 3. somewhat higher densities in such areas of intensive cultivation and relatively low industrialization as Argentina's Cuyo region, Cochabamba in Bolivia, Peru's coastal valleys, and parts of Mexico favored with investments, preferential attention, and so on.

Accelerated urbanization is the continent's most striking demographic and ecological feature. None of the world's main regions is growing or urbanizing as rapidly as is Latin America. South America's overall growth rate is slightly less than Mexico's and Central America's.

National differences are critical, insofar as policies and programs must relate to each country's urbanization potential. An urbanization classification into categories of stable, moderately stable, unstable, and very unstable in terms of three indicators— percentage of rural population, growth rate of rural population, and growth rate of urban population—reveals a varied and intensely interesting picture. Uruguay is the only stable country (18.5 percent rural population, 0.00 percent rural growth, 2.10 percent urban growth). Argentina (32.4 percent, 1.05 percent, and 2.53 percent), Chile (36.3 percent, 1.05 percent, and 3.18 percent), and Cuba are moderately stable. Venezuela figures among the "unstables" (37.1 percent, 1.00 percent, 6.40 percent). And very unstable countries include Ecuador (67.0 percent, 1.85 percent, and 5.41 percent) and Brazil (59.7 percent, 1.76 percent, 5.67 percent).

Even Uruguay will have to absorb 423,000 new city dwellers between 1968 and 1980, but Brazil will have to contend with 27, 655,000.

These relative orders of magnitude reveal wide variations between current urbanization levels, urbanization rates, and urban potentials. Until recently, most metropolitan growth focused on industrial centers of regional, national, or global importance. But industrialization is not accompanying rapid urbanization in developing economies. Urbanization, per capita income, energy consumption per capita, and percent of GNP produced by the industrial sector are correlated, but the figures for Latin America's most industrialized, urbanized, and developed countries are far below those for developed countries. Urban growth may slow without further industrialization, since neither commerce nor finances nor public administration can provide enough jobs to maintain high urban population.

Through urbanization, governments can redistribute population according to regional or national development plans. By coordinating investments to exploit new regional resources, countries could select levels of centralization or decentralization in accord with their possibilities, requirements, and development goals. Continuing the historic pattern means accepting dependence. Slowing urbanization means cutting off the most dynamic economic sectors. But gradually redirecting urbanization toward a few national and, perhaps in the near future, continental foci of regional development, is an alternative within each country's investment capabilities.

Rural population continues to grow in every country except Uruguay, even though less rapidly than the urban population. Paraguay, which lacks both a basic transportation network and an adequate urban system, has a population 60 percent rural and disproportionately concentrated in primary activities (relative to the primary sector's share of GNP). But its rural service centers of 2000 to 5000 people are developing as well as the capital, the only city numbering over 100,000. In Brazil, the intermediate centers in closest contact with the countryside are growing faster than the great state capitals; they are also favored by a tradition of spontaneous regionalism rooted in geographical and historical factors. On the other hand, the primacy of cities like Buenos Aires, Lima, and Montevideo is intensifying. Despite the long and relatively homogeneous colonial heritage, not only cultural roots but also development patterns and phases vary widely between countries. In 2000, the inhabitants of Latin America's cities will number more than current total population, while rural population will not have declined in absolute terms. This is what makes it so important to direct future population distribution, particularly in the urban zones.

URBANIZATION WITHOUT INVESTMENT RESOURCES

Latin American cities annually receive billions of dollars of hidden and direct investments, both public and private. These involve numerous activities including industry, commerce, defense, public works, housing, sanitation, and education. Short range programs promote jobs, services, housing, transportation, communications, education, health, recreation, and so on; they cover the full range from public to private development, financing, and execution. No one really knows how much is invested, and the uncertainty heightens in considering the variable but significant expenditures in spontaneous home construction, communal projects, and community services. These investments share a relatively short time range and limited territorial scope. (Urban area in the region's largest countries, Brazil, Argentina, and Peru, is less than 1 percent of the total, while it varies between 3 and 4 percent in smaller ones like El Salvador and Uruguay, depending on definitions of urban, suburban, and rural.)

Coordination and control of all private and public investments is essential for greater efficiency and, more importantly, to achieve nationally articulated economic systems. But without a clear idea of amounts and destinations of urban investments, and with no more than general notions of the state of goods and services, the job market, and urban operating costs, it is almost impossible to project the necessities which must form the basis for an ordered and coordinated investment plan. Latin American center-cities are not old, but they have decayed prematurely due to lack of conservation or renovation. And all the errors of unguided and uncontrolled urban growth are mixed in the peripheral districts, which reflect the injustices of divided and highly stratified societies in which the masses have almost no voice in the decisions affecting their lives. These areas also reveal the State's failure to prepare the people for the problems of urbanization, and its inability to direct private investment.

Even if such education and regulation were quickly established, with state backing and a more favorable public opinion, our cities would face a graver problem. Urban Latin America has been developing and expanding for 2000 years, and there are neither economic, social, nor political reasons to suggest that the process will stop in any country before reaching a level compatible with economic structure and functions. Urbanization is passing through a different phase in each Latin American state; the smoothness of the process depends on urban potentials and responds to factors of urban attraction, interurban mobility, and abandonment of the countryside. The quantitative implications have been signaled repeatedly. But do area countries control investment resources sufficient to face urban growth of 270 million in 40 years; to provide jobs, housing, and indispensable services for new city dwellers? Can future investments be directed to high priority sectors, and linked to national development strategies? I am pessimistic, since rational action is impossible in the political administrative systems of many countries and, in others, any action is blocked by outdated power structures. Without development and an equitable income distribution, national savings are impossible; without increased savings, investment capacity must stagnate. And the amounts needed simply to provide for projected urban population and to begin urban renewal are far beyond the means of any Latin American country.

Buenos Aires is a case in point to which we can limit ourselves for our purposes here. The metropolitan area includes seven million people and is growing at 2.7 percent per year; this is the continent's most extensive and heavily populated urban conglomerate, though its growth is much slower than some other major centers. Next year (1969), Buenos Aires will have to assimilate 189,000 people—people needing housing and water, sewers, electricity, transportation, education, and basic health services. According to housing specifications used by internationally financed Argentine institutions, these facilities cost about $2000 per person.

Buenos Aires also has a housing deficit for 700,000 people— 10 percent of the total—now living in provisional structures, shanty towns or *villas de emergencia*. Another 700,000 share rooms in *conventillos* slums or live in houses decayed beyond repair. These percentages are not the worst among Latin American cities. A conservative program might annually relocate 4 percent of these 1,400,000 people, or 56,000. Finally, about 2 percent of housing becomes unusable each year, so the 140,000 people forced to abandon their dwellings must also be resettled.

To sum up, in 1969 Buenos Aires will have to contend with: 189,000 new inhabitants; 56,000 people resettled as part of a program to eradicate the present housing deficit in 25 years; and 140,000 people who must abandon their present dwellings—a total of 385,000. At $2000 apiece, $770,000,000 is needed just to provide housing and the basic services mentioned above. And this ignores more pressing investments in new jobs, regional infrastructure, university education and scientific investigation, urban supply services, and metropolitan government. Such a large outlay to create economic housing which, in accordance with Latin American construction techniques, will barely last the fifty years I have assumed, is totally out of the question. Argentina's overall urban needs in 1969 will include: 350,000 new inhabitants; 4 percent of the 20 percent now living in provisional dwellings and *conventillos* (16,371,000 total, or 130,968); and the 2 percent forced to abandon decaying housing each year, or 327,420. So that the country would have to resettle 808,388 people, signifying an outlay of $1,616,776,000—a sum not including investments to really advance the nation. These estimates also disregard rural needs, which would involve about a third of total population. And, to repeat, these figures are based on approximate real costs of housing and services installed with international financing in accordance with the standards set by international organizations.

With this outlook for Argentina, a "moderately stable" country in urbanistic terms (32.4 percent rural, 1.05 percent rural population growth rate, 2.53 percent urban growth rate), and with one of the region's highest and best distributed per capita incomes, prospects are bleak indeed for a country like Brazil (59.7 percent, 1.76 percent, 5.67 percent), which must construct a city of 1,846,000 in 1968 just to fix the new urban population, and another, slightly larger in 1969, and so on until 1980 when it will have to settle 2,611,000 people just to stay even with urban growth.

My thesis is that any urbanization policy must consider several facts:

1. Under present political and economic conditions, urbanization will continue to lack necessary investments.

2. The situation will tend to deteriorate further, making long-range solutions even less likely, unless immediate steps are taken to maximize investment returns and to create conditions minimizing the frictions of urbanization without investment.

3. The urban-rural gap in opportunities and living conditions makes the cities—especially the national capital and regional centers—the goal of country dwellers and inhabitants of small towns.

4. Urbanization involves positive and negative aspects, both of which require further analysis. It has incorporated vast sectors into national life, even though its failure to advance national integration has exacerbated uneven regional development.

5. The countryside is becoming increasingly isolated from nascent urban-regional systems.

6. Urbanization carries basic political implications which will affect the future power structure.

A second main point concerns urban investments, the priorities of which should be set by a national socioeconomic plan developed in accordance with a long range strategy. Very few Latin American countries have planned their development; most have four, five, or six year plans which lack legislative sanction, remain unpublished, or are being written toward an uncertain future. Last year, in examining various national plans from South America, I was struck by the near universal unconcern for urban investment programs, even under traditional sectorial designations. Only Brazil is attempting local planning integrated with socioeconomic plans elaborated at other levels of government. Venezuela's Direction of Public Works is battling to pass an urbanism law. The International Committee of Economic Development (CIDE) plan for Uruguay includes useful thoughts on territorial structure, but lacks legislative approval. Chile has been developing a regionalization policy of national scope for two or three years. The General Direction of the Ministry of Housing and Urbanism, functioning since December, 1965, has concerned itself with plans for rural and urban housing and with supervising, coordinating, and regulating all aspects of urban planning. Argentina has seen only isolated and local urban planning initiatives, completely removed from the decision-making powers.

THE NEED FOR A GENERAL THEORY OF RURAL AND URBAN DEVELOPMENT

A general theory of rural and urban development is urgently required. The task is complex, but essential for any urbanization policy that is not to lose contact with the problem's complexity, dynamism, and newness on the present scale.

1. Most Latin American urbanization studies interrelate cities by contrasting them with rural areas. In a grave interpretive error, the countryside is analyzed as a dependent area in territorial isolation from urban and regional systems. Urbanization is exclusive to individual countries to the extent that massive international migrations are unauthorized and unimportant in Latin America. Urbanization, then, must affect each nation's countryside. Its impact is seen in the new relationships between what is urban and what is rural. The process also penetrates rural areas with more advanced technology, better and more varied services, improved administration of productive activities, and rapidly expanding consumption patterns. As agriculture's importance in GNP decreases, services, institutions, means of communication, and structures until recently unique to the big cities are appearing in rural centers. Though limited in area, the urbanization of nation, society, and economy is nonetheless growing in scope. The Argentine, Uruguayan, Venezuelan, and Chilean countrysides—save for isolated and underpopulated pockets—already function as centers for communications, services, transport, and rural socioeconomic change.

2. National economies have turned on external demand for agricultural and mining production for nearly four hundred years. Each country's urban network and systems of roads, railroads, telephones, ports, and basic industries, have reflected primary production's responsiveness to external demand. Oil and gas pipelines and high-tension power lines perpetuate such tendencies. Excepting a few areas of touristic interest, overland communications within the continent have been and remain precarious. Historically, each country developed an internal system converging on one or two centers, usually coastal, and responding to external investment and demand. At the turn of the century, when some began import substitution for consumer goods, the new industries were established close to these potentially large markets. As shown in the historical sketch, interior regional centers did not then develop. And timid recent attempts at promoting

alternatives to the one or two main cities have failed to generate more balanced regional development. Sharp regional discontinuities are revealed and explained in any study of national development—Furtado's on Brazil, Ferrer's on Argentina, Pinto's on Chile, or Brito Figueroa's on Venezuela, to cite some examples.[2] Almost every country includes a developed area with high incomes like Argentina's industrialized coast, southern Brazil, central Chile and central Mexico, and Venezuela's Caracas-Valencia-Maracay connurbation; and an underdeveloped and poorly articulated interior. Some regions have clearly advanced at the expense of others, without any full explanation of how these imbalances have affected overall national development.

3. The primary sector's stagnation and vulnerability become apparent as traditional agrarian economies urbanize and industrialize. The lack or poor location of certain basic natural resources, such as fuels in Brazil and Chile and iron and coal in Argentina, is another grave problem. Since resources can only be evaluated for 2 percent of the continent, possibilities remain uncertain. Erosion due to bad agricultural technique annually destroys, even in the best endowed countries, areas comparable to those brought under cultivation. Development of the continent's interior and preliminary "horizontal development" of each country requires more than foundations and costly symbolic public works, and demands incorporating and utilizing new land and resources. Such colonization and urbanization is doubtless more costly than intensifying exploitation of already settled zones. Nonetheless, though concentrating on the interior may decrease short range economic returns, it seems the best route to long term national economic diversification and integration, without which there is no hope for international integration.

4. Low agricultural productivity combined with isolation, traditional patterns of organization, and low living standards, all push people from the countryside toward the cities. Modern technology and marketing facilities in rural areas are handicapped by the lack of roads, communications, and dispersion centers, and by tiny plot size per family. These three factors weigh enormously in low argicultural productivity. Low incomes force rural

families to invest almost exclusively in basic necessities, and they remain outside traditional rural credit lines. Various studies have concluded that the quest for jobs and for generally better opportunities is the main motive for migrating. These studies also show that single men and women, relatively highly educated for the area they leave, preponderate among migrants.

Opportunities remain scarce in rural settlements, with their generally stagnant artisanry, and small industry and commerce. New road construction and the expanding effective radius of banks, insurance companies, and agricultural machinery and basic consumer goods industries, are spontaneously reordering these small towns. While some decline, a few regional centers will grow in accord with comparative advantages of location. Given the importance agriculture will continue to have in regional GNP's, and the complementarity between rural change and urbanization on a national level, rural restructuring is essential for regional development.

5. Primary and secondary education are underdeveloped. Universities continue to stress law and the humanities over engineering and the sciences. Technical training and the preparation of middle level professionals are substandard and unattractive to youth. Education can motivate entire communities to increase production, but only when oriented to national development needs. Human resources must be mobilized and trained according to national education and investigation policies which consider the phase of development and future professional and technical needs. The bottlenecks of secondary and technical education, and adult training, must also be eliminated. And area countries must encourage engineering, agriculture, and the sciences, and prepare bureaucrats and administrators to boost returns in both public and private enterprise. Achieving these objectives will constitute a revolution against traditional prestige patterns, and be a decisive step in overcoming low human productivity. Industrialization requires substantial reordering of traditional priorities in investigation, university instruction, and technical and secondary education. Each country must develop its own strategy in accord with its resources and level of development. Moreover, mobilizing professionals, researchers, and

technicians is a solid base for regional cooperation and advance. Even within nations, professional mobility and mobilization are needed to overcome delays and the technical limitations of regional efforts due to scarce human resources in strategic fields. Urbanization like that described in the preceding section cannot import all of its technology. The housing standards of international financing bodies have proved unadaptable, as has insisting on ineffective regulative plans to control urban development, or constructing costly hospitals which are useless in areas lacking even rudimentary preventive facilities.

6. Certain political practices continue to impede development. Idealistic national constitutions have suffered from discontinuities of personnel and policies in the highest executive, legislative, and judicial spheres, and cooperation is rare between political parties. Many countries have even faced systematic attempts to subvert public functions to facilitate the private sector's selling out to foreign interests, and reflecting its lack of vision, patriotism, and executive capacity. In recent decades, power groups based on agriculture and mining have been displaced by others based on banking, industry, and foreign trade and with strong international associations. These new groups control politics, directly or more commonly through military puppets. Political apathy is marked in the most advanced countries, while widespread political marginalization persists in the least developed ones. Such circumstances breed skepticism vis-a-vis development plans and reform. The power holders simply have no interest in sacrificing immediate profits and privileges in a search for a more representative system. Terms like "agrarian reform" are accepted, but the effects are limited. In cases like the even more essential urban reform, the words still lack force.

7. Various political administrative systems are inappropriate for current development needs. But decentralizing decision making may limit future alternatives, and may not be advisable as either a system of regional representation or a check on often-feared centralism. One possibility is new forms of representation and participation stressing the now nonexistent "regional governments" and the expansion of autonomous or semiautonomous

entities to evaluate problems more accurately and execute programs more efficiently.

These seven points affect both rural and urban development; their interdependence reflects the need to analyze urbanization within a broader theoretical framework.

CONCLUSIONS

The city is a form of life accepted by contemporary societies independently of industrialization. Most of each country's investments, governing institutions, educational facilities, and technical and scientific establishments are concentrated in cities; cities also afford the quickest channels of social mobility.

Each city is a system of spatial interrelations. Functional regions require urban centers. Such urbanization of society affects national deveopment, and it reflects and helps determine regional development. But orderly guidance of urban development on a microregional or urban-regional level is impossible without first establishing criteria for maximizing investments, especially in human and natural resources, new industries and services, and regional infrastructure. An urban policy, treating one aspect of territorial organization, is thus a basic element in national socioeconomic plans. Regional disaggregation of national plans is a fundamental problem from both political and technical viewpoints; it concerns the distinct roles which, in a federal state, pertain to nation, region, province, and municipality. Solutions to this problem remain distant. Difficulties begin with inadequate regional statistics, are aggravated by the lack of technicians in needed specialities and of criteria concerning responsibilities of different levels of government, and culminate with the unclear notions of national planning bodies on regional and sectoral priorities.

National development should be buttressed with an urbanization policy incorporating criteria for economic localization in terms of regional economic activities, at least for the main cities. This policy should also include social and demographic criteria for the economic distribution and characteristics of urban and rural populations; economic and social criteria for delineating ur-ban-regional systems and their physical interaction; and an insti-tutional structure to sustain the three previous aspects.

Since accelerated growth in Latin America's larger centers (over 100,000 inhabitants) has occurred at the expense of inter-mediate centers and the countryside, an urbanization policy should respond to regions as well as to the entire nation. An urbanization policy should integrate future urban-regional sys-tems based on more efficient regional and national hierarchies, as well as developing new centers and subcenters of rural advance-ment.

The state's role, decisive in elaborating and executing this policy, begins when a government decides to plan its develop-ment and to incorporate urbanization as a spatial and socio-economic variable in projections and investment programs. It continues when, to better comprehend national problems, mobilize support, improve efficiency in development programs, and compensate for seasonal productivity variables, the nation is divided into regions. Finally, sectoral growth goals must be estab-lished for each one, and financial and institutional support pro-vided to achieve them. The region's role in modern and planned states, if not fundamental in decision making, is nonetheless essential in analyzing and evaluating decentralized national development.

Such a national urbanization policy, with its regional consid-erations, forms the basis for an urban development policy. The latter's effectiveness depends on the extent of the former and the precision with which it is implemented. Economically, an urban development policy should set the terms for enterprise locating in a city and assure adequate site selection. Socially, it should create, locate, and maintain essential services, including housing, in accord with economic exigencies. Physically, with infrastruc-ture and soil uses determined by functions, densities, and rela-tionships of open and builtup spaces, it will determine the city's internal structure and thus assure the fulfillment of economic and social ends. And institutionally, it must bolster low level planning units within the national planning system. Municipalities, alone or in association (where their regional importance is slight), and metropolitan governments or prefectures, where such is the appropriate scale, must orient themselves more technically to attain planning goals. The relationship between regional and urban development plans should parallel that suggested for disaggregating national plans.

Urban development plans must allow for problems more constant and more dynamic than those anticipated in an urbanization policy. They must create participatory organs to integrate urban society. Decision-making organs must anticipate the incorporation of urban development plans within the urbanization policy—the municipality cannot obstruct the more ample criteria of regional development, but rather must adjust its plans to these.

Urbanization and urban development policies do not assure an improved urban situation, but they do indicate an attitude favoring more rational use of financial and technical resources by means of better coordinated investments and decisions. They also provide a flexible means for detecting problems, evaluating regional plans, and developing more effective programs.

The model of Latin America's future city, built with inadequate financing, is hard to predict. The multiple factors affecting urban form, and the possibility of new technology, new social concepts of property rights, and the breakdown of traditional power factors, make any prediction liable to grave error. Furthermore, it is unclear whether urbanization can be financed without investment resources, when city building is generally disdained in favor of supposedly more dynamic investments.

One possibility is cost reduction, combined with continuing to demand at least fifty years of life from a building. Massive and massively financed projects, using technology appropriate to each country's level of development, may facilitate this goal. But credit can no longer be scattered on an isolated basis. Improved construction, transportation, and communications technology is required, as well as possession of appropriate sites. Costs can also be cut by diverting urbanization's profits from speculators and lucky landowners to society in general. Yet another means is to perfect construction techniques for the inevitable provisional housing, increase its livability, and encourage voluntary construction on sites previously supplied with basic services. The consideration underlying these three suggestions, all feasible for the short term, is that urban development demands an energetic, continuous, and visionary land acquisition policy to impose order and discourage speculation.

State control of land for urban expansion guarantees that cities can be reconditioned to meet needs still difficult to foresee, and that technology now too expensive for developing countries can be incorporated. Although my concept of a city built without adequate investment resources is minimally architectonic, it is attuned to social and economic realities. I do not mean that aesthetics should be forgotten. But a less individualistic and less monumental aesthetics must be found, an aesthetics based on strong, concentrated, and very "urban" elements, combined with use of the natural countryside in areas where precarious construction techniques constitute a challenge or limitation so far unrecognized by urban designers.

Anticipating future expansion of Latin America's urban peripheries offers numerous advantages if the land market is adequately regulated and if *barriada* formation can be controlled, with essential services provided beforehand. Under these conditions, the physical and to an extent the social environment can be improved. More difficult, though not impossible, is using modern technology to create jobs in the new *barrios*, in activities integrated with housing and reflecting appropriate phases in the individual's country–to–city transformation.

Urbanization of the countryside and ruralization of the city now seem simultaneous and complementary. Proposed agrarian reforms are directed at increasing production, creating stability and improved living conditions for rural workers, and actively incorporating country folk into national political and institutional life; urban reforms, not now under consideration but equally urgent, have complementary goals. These are: to make the city a site of progress and social change, a stimulus to national development with better integrated and more complementary urban and rural societies and economies, and a model for massive qualitative changes; and to promote radical reform of power structures without which any attempt at real development will be severely limited and distorted.

NOTES

1. Author's condensation of the original version.
2. Celso Furtado, *The Economic Growth of Brazil: A Survey from Colonial to Modern Times* (Berkeley: University of California Press, 1965); Aldo Ferrer, *The Argentine Economy: An Economic History of Argentina* (*Berkeley: University of California Press, 1967*) Anibal Pinto Santa Cruz, *Chile, Un Caso de Desarrollo Frustrado* (Santiago: Editorial Universitaria, 1962); Federico Brito Figueroa, *La Estructura Económica de Venezuela Colonial* (Caracas: Instituto de Investigaciones, Facultad de Economía, Universidad Central de Venezuela, 1963). (Ed.)

12. THE FUTURE OF URBANIZATION IN LATIN AMERICA*

JOHN FRIEDMANN
University of California—Los Angeles

THE URBAN PROSPECT: CORE AND PERIPHERY

Urbanization in Latin America is an irreversible process. Previously dispersed population is being reassembled in a limited number of urban centers, leading to fundamental changes in the ecological structure of the continent. Some countries, such as Chile, Argentina, Uruguay, Cuba and, more recently, Venezuela, have already passed through their urban revolutions and are now working out the multiple consequences of this historical process. Other countries, among them El Salvador and Bolivia, have not yet experienced the full violence implicit in the uprooting of rural populations and their resettlement in cities. Still other countries — Brazil, Mexico, Peru — are even now undergoing the trauma of accelerated urbanization (Wingo, Jr., 1967).

The statistics are dry, but they reveal the stark dimensions of the process. In 1950 urban population in centers with 2,000 or more inhabitants represented 39 percent of the region's total; by 1960 it had risen to 46 percent; and the current figure is perhaps close to one-half. But the limit that is gradually being approached hovers somewhere around 80 percent, or roughly the percentage

---

*Published by permission of Transaction, Inc. from *Studies in Comparative International Development,* Volume 5, Number 9, copyright © 1969-1970, by Transaction, Inc.

corresponding to Uruguay in 1960 (Wingo, Jr., 1967: Table 1). [1] If current growth rates continue, this limit may be reached within another generation. [2]

We cannot with any precision know the future of city growth in Latin America. [3] In the process of continued urban expansion, and under the impact of the rising use of the automobile for private transportation, it may be that the inherited image of the city will be fundamentally altered. [4] In the metropolitan countries, this process is already far advanced. The basic phenomenon is the appearance of large deconcentrated urban regions, each of which may contain more than one and often several tightly interconnected cities. A variety of terms have been used to describe this new phenomenon: Jean Gottman refers to a specific set of urban regions as *megalopolis*; John Friedmann and S. M. Miller call a single unit within this set the *urban field*; Brian Berry, referring principally to the labor market aspects of the urban field, speaks of the *functional economic area*. I see no reason why much the same forces operating in Latin America should produce significantly different results for ecological structure. [5] In saying this, I am aware of the inverted ecological pattern in Latin American cities where, contrary to the experience in the United States, the poor occupy not only the center but extend in massive *poblaciones* around the outward edges of the urban core (Schnore, 1965).

It is also quite likely that the urbanization of the countryside will continue at an accelerated pace. [6] The term refers to the increasing capitalization and commercialization of agriculture in the region, the organization of peasants into syndicate and cooperative forms of organization, the extension of urban communication media (newspapers, radio, television) into rural districts, higher educational levels for rural populations and their more active political participation in national affairs, transport improvements from rural areas to urban markets, gradual adoption of selected items of urban consumption and, more generally, the acceptance by the rural farm population of selected urban values, attitudes and ways of living. These changes will occur at vastly different rates in different countries, being positively related to both levels of demographic urbanization and rates of city growth. The overall effect, however, will be to blur traditional distinctions between rural and urban and, consequently, to create a totally new configuration of economic, social and political life in the region (Quijano, 1967).

As William Nicholls (1967) has pointed out, we can expect to see many of these changes mediated by distance to large urban concentrations, so that the process of urbanization of the countryside is likely to be accelerated near metropolitan centers and especially within the "urban field" itself.

The future geographic distribution of urban populations in Latin America cannot be accurately predicted. Nevertheless, there is good reason to suppose that by far the greater part of urban growth will occur at the points of greatest potential for information exchange or interaction. (Friedmann, 1968a and 1968b). What is important to recognize, however, is that the basic regional structure of potential interaction values is already laid down. This is so, regardless of whether we take countries individually or Latin America as a whole under an assumption that national boundaries will progressively decline in importance as barriers to trade and other forms of interchange. Future urbanization will tend primarily to reinforce this basic structure.

The points of greatest potential interaction will tend to coincide with the principal core regions of the area. Core regions may be defined as territorially organized subsystems of society which have a high capacity for steady economic expansion. They are also areas whose institutions are capable of exerting a farreaching influence on the economic growth of their dependent peripheries. [7]

Core regions are not necessarily single cities or metropolitan areas. They are ecological subsystems that may include a set of several cities with a high degree of interdependency among them, together with the intervening nonurban spaces and the immediate hinterland (or urban field) of every city in the set.

Peripheral regions are similarly conceived as territorially ordered subsystems of society, but their path of economic growth is in large measure determined by the decision of core region institutions. With respect to their peripheries, core regions may therefore be called autonomous; with respect to core regions, peripheral areas will be dependent.

Both autonomy and dependency, however, are relative values. Since core regions can be shown to be organized in the form of a nested hierarchy, so that superior cores control certain of the developments in lower level core regions, most core areas are situated in the periphery of other, more controlling ones. In this way, the condition of a given periphery may appear to be doubly dependent—directly upon its immediate core region and indirectly upon a core region situated at a higher level. An example of a doubly dependent periphery is given by the copper-mining areas in the north of Chile. The key industries there are managed by North American concerns some of whose influence is exerted through related Chilean Santiago. In addition, Santiago exerts a controlling influence in national affairs over this same periphery (for example, through Corporación de Fomento de la Producción-Norte). The people living in the northern parts of Chile, however, have practically no guiding influence at all over their own future.

Autonomy and dependency appear as reciprocal but asymmetrical relations. Autonomy is nearly always modified by the ability of dependent areas to bring pressure to bear on core regions. The relation is an asymmetrical one, however, insofar as autonomy implies an ability on the part of core regions to influence events in the periphery that is greater than the latter's capacity to determine its own future. Symmetry in autonomy and dependency relations would be achieved only between low areas of approximately equal power. In this case, we may speak of *interdependency* in their relations.

The decisive criterion for distinguishing between cores and peripheries is, therefore, the focus of effective decision making power. In the case of dependent subsystems of society, this power is primarily external, and their development is consequently induced exogenously. More autonomous subsystems of society, by contrast, are more able to steer their own development. And this ability increases as one rises through the hierarchy of core regions.

Both autonomy and dependency relations may be limited to only a few areas of activity, or the influence may be pervasive, covering a large portion of the possible spectrum of economic, political, cultural and social activities. But where a measure of dependency is present, the relation is nearly always a "colonial" one of exploitation. For all practical purposes, altruistic dependency may be ruled out in interregional relations. Concretely this means that certain economic resources will be transferred from dependent areas to the relevant cores in order to strengthen the economies and political power of the latter. Income may be transferred through consistently unfavorable terms of trade between core and periphery; capital may be transferred to the core in the absence of opportunities of a propitious climate for investments in the periphery; and labor may be transferred out of the periphery because of the greater economic, social and cultural attractions of core regions. These resource transfers, however, are impeded, on the one hand, by international boundaries and, on the other hand, by a certain rootedness, especially of labor resources. It is only in the frictionless world of classical economics that an initial symmetry is maintained through the unhampered operation of the relevant markets for capital and labor.

In contrast to a condition of dependency, autonomy means essentially a capacity for self-direction, that is, a capacity for mobilizing and using resources in the service of self-defined objectives. Resources may be mobilized either through certain instruments of control directly from dependent peripheries or, alternatively, through a procedure of bargaining involving other core regions or relatively strong peripheral areas, usually secondary cores. It is important to note that the objectives into whose service these resources are pressed may be either those of individual core region institutions or of the core population as a whole (as in the case of public objectives). What permits us to extend the concept of autonomy to a region as distinct from particular institutions is that each region constitutes a subsystem of society showing high connectivity, so that a major institution *in* this system is also integrally a *part* of it and thus capable of influencing the nature and direction of the changes to which it is subject.

One of the principal features of core region growth is its self-reinforcing character. This is especially pronounced above a certain threshold size which, for the United States, appears to lie around 250,000 inhabitants (Berry and Schwind, 1967: 25-55). I shall not enter here into a detailed analysis of the possible reasons for this. It is generally believed, however, that increasing external economies, internal market development and the appearance of certain specialized services and facilities above the threshold size (culture, government) play a decisive role.

A recent study by Pedersen and Stöhr (1969) demonstrates the overall stability of core region structure under various assumptions for emerging common market arrangements in Latin America. [8] Regardless of the assumptions used, major urban concentrations clustered around the Rio de Janeiro–Belo Horizonte–São Paulo triangle and the axis connecting Buenos Aires with Montevideo continue to be the major poles of continental attraction, especially if integration should occur chiefly through maritime transport. Pedersen and Stöhr write: .

Emphasis on maritime transportation will . . .give the existing urban agglomerations locational advantages both over the interior of the continent and less developed coastal regions. Planned development on the maritime transportation network being attempted by the LAFTA and the Andean Group might eventually result in an improved locational situation for the less developed coastal regions, but current shipping policies seem mainly geared towards improvement for the biggest harbours.

Removal of custom barriers will be of greater importance where transportation costs are smallest. When reliance is placed on maritime transport, it will therefore strengthen the tendency towards geographic concentration. Development of Latin America based only on maritime transport will thus lead to a concentration of economic opportunities; and an integration of Latin America relying only on maritime transportation will mean little to those 75 percent of the population who live away from the principal harbours. [9]

Similar results are obtained if it is assumed that sea transportation will be complemented by a system of efficient air cargo service. It is around the large air terminals—the new communication nodes—that major increments in urban growth tend to occur. They are preferred as a location by those activities—the leading ones in any modern economic system—that depend on rapid and efficient contact with multiple centers throughout the world. There is no reason to suppose that the results for Latin America will be radically different from this established world-wide pattern.

The picture of Latin American urbanization that emerges from these projections is one in which a relatively small number of important core regions will experience self-sustaining growth and, through their economic and political institutions, exert an increasing dominance over dependent peripheral areas. Within an economically integrated Latin America, these tendencies would be accentuated, with a set of hierarchically ordered and powerful core regions holding sway over a continental periphery (and subperipheries) whose economic and political existence would be largely derivative of core region growth, and whose principal function would be to contribute to the wealth and power of the central areas with their own resources.

THE FUTURE OF THE PERIPHERY IN LATIN AMERICA

The remainder of this monograph is devoted to the question of whether the projected pattern of growing core region dominance is also the only desirable and possible "scenario." To jump ahead of the argument, the answer will be that it is neither. A strategy model will then be presented as a basis for countervailing public policies and programs capable of strengthening the internal capacities of selected peripheral areas to accelerate their economic growth and reduce their dependency on core regions.

Those of us who live in core regions tend to view the world through very special glasses. Our perceptions tend to ratify, and our evaluations to justify, the status quo. The poor are poor because they deserve it; the rich are the elect. If peripheries are dependent and show a low potential for economic expansion, it is because they are morally weak and incapable of organizing themselves for development. If some resources are nevertheless transferred from the center to the periphery, this will often be regarded as the price of political support and national unity but not as "rational" policy on grounds of economic advantage. This view-point, however, may well be the result of a fundamental distortion of perceptions and valuations according to which a given relation of power is regarded as "in the nature of things" and therefore inescapable. Are there perhaps countervailing forces that might encourage the evolution of a spatial pattern of urbanization in Latin America that would significantly depart from the one that has been sketched?

Four broad trends may be projected that would tend to oppose the further concentration of people, wealth and power in the principal core regions of the continent. The first of these concerns the basic infrastructure for economic growth. [10] As Pedersen and Stöhr (1969) have shown in their study of the possible effects of the common market on regional structure, improvements in the internal road network of Latin America will tend to increase the attractiveness of peripheral over core areas. [11] This transport effect would be reinforced by prospective changes in the management of communications and electric power services. Both are likely to be extended gradually in the form of regional, national and even international networks, with the result that existing differences in locational advantage between cores and their peripheries will gradually diminish. The tendency will be for power and communications to become more nearly ubiquitous services, available in most places at roughly similar levels of efficiency and cost.

The second set of opposing trends concerns the urbanization of the countryside to which allusion has already been made. Again, the projected changes would progressively diminish differences in locational attractiveness between core regions and their peripheries.

The third trend concerns the diseconomies of urban growth which tend to appear beyond a certain city size. There is some evidence for the rising capital costs of municipal services required for absorbing increments of population with increasing city size (Busca and Cafiero, 1966). Although we are not yet able to relate these curves on the costs of urbanization to others that measure its economic benefits, it seems likely that net advantages will disappear beyond a size which has been estimated to lie between 500,000 and one million inhabitants. [12] Benefits may continue to accrue to individuals and firms beyond this threshold size. Nevertheless, a point may be reached where some activities will prefer locations *away from* existing large metropolitan centers. These activities would become potentially available for settlement in the periphery.

The fourth set of factors favoring the periphery over the core has to do with the former's increasing consciousness of discriminatory growth—a consciousness that may lead to divisive political tensions with existing cores. In the context of Latin American integration, these tensions would become evident in the resistance of certain countries—peripheral to the main continental cores—to further economic integration. Their resistance might be attenuated, however, by extending to them, in the form of compensatory payments, some of the benefits of core region development.

These considerations lead up to the question of whether unrestrained core region growth is, from the standpoint of public policy, to be preferred as the single long run strategy for national and international development (Matus, Vuskovic *et.al.*, 1967). A number of countervailing trends have been identified which, in principle at least, would tend to increase the relative attractiveness of peripheral areas for productive investment. But greater accessibility and higher mobilization rates in the periphery may also have precisely the opposite effect of accelerating core region growth, since they will tend to increase the peripheral population's propensity to migrate to the core. The trends discussed, therefore, will not by themselves produce an outcome different from the projected pattern of growing core region dominance. It remains to be seen whether a model for the growth of peripheral economies can be presented which does not depend exclusively on comparative locational advantage. This is the task for the next section.

A MODEL FOR SOCIAL DEVELOPMENT

According to a widely accepted theory, economic growth of a depressed or newly settled region is initially brought about by expanding its production for export to other regions (North, 1964:chap. 12). The income generated by this activity within the region, as well as the stimulus given to local enterprise by supplying the endogenous export sector with certain commodities and services or by enabling it to purchase the output of the export sector at a lower cost, will tend to increase the rate of regional production. As a result, production for intraregional demand will gain relative to production for export so that the economy becomes increasingly self-sustaining and less dependent on extraregional markets.

This theory may be challenged on two grounds. First, the regional multiplier effects of the initial export activities may be very low. This typically happens when the export sector employs a small amount of highly skilled labor, as in modern mining operation, or where it uses larger amounts of relatively unskilled labor at low wage rates, as in plantation economies (Baldwin, 1964: chap. 14). The regional multiplier effect will be further reduced where the export investment is in the hands of extraregional interests that will channel most of the profits earned to places outside the region. Finally, "backward" and "forward" linkages of the initial export activities may be established with industries that are located, not within the region itself, but in one or more of the existing cores (for example, processing facilities for raw material from the periphery).

The second challenge skirts these particular difficulties but argues that the regional multiplier depends chiefly on the capacity of a region to organize itself for economic growth.

The ways leading to the economic growth of a region are limited. They include: [13]

1. the discovery and capture of new markets for old products;
2. the introduction of new ways to produce old products (that is, changes in the production function giving more output per unit of labor and capital input);
3. the production of new or improved products and services;
4. the establishment of new types of organizations for production (for example, cooperatives, corporations, associations or firms);
5. the buildup of local physical infrastructure directly relevant for production activities (for example, roads, supply of electric energy, port facilities);

6. the creation of local savings and investment institutions;
7. the development of human resources: labor supply and its skills;
8. the development of local natural resources and improvement of locational advantage; and
9. the development of institutions and services to provide more or better information and knowledge useful in planning and production (for example, universities, research stations, telex, market research services, planning offices, mass media).

Some of these ways require nothing more than the existence and ingenious use of individual entrepreneurial capacity in the sense of Joseph Schumpeter's classical model of risk-taking entrepreneurship. But the majority call for cooperative, organized activity that involves more than one segment of the regional population. Cooperation is needed, for example, to pull outside capital into the region for investments that will strategically advance the long term interest in economic growth (for example, a new university, a tourist hotel, a shipyard, a research center). Organized action is also needed to mobilize local resources for special purposes or put existing capital to more efficient use (for example, a regional planning office, development-conscious regional and local authorities, improved management of natural resources, local institutions for investment credits to small and medium sized industries). Where concerted action fails to appear in sufficient volume, where it is misdirected or where participation is restricted to only a small and self-serving elite of families, selfgenerated, sustained regional economic growth will fail to occur.

On the basis of these amendments to regional growth theory, it becomes possible to distinguish between "active" and "passive" peripheries (core regions are by definition active). To facilitate the analysis, passive peripheries will be treated as residual areas after the active and potentially dynamic regions have been identified.

I shall refer to active peripheries as *social development poles* or areas of concentrated settlement (usually cities of some minimum size) which have a high potential capacity for organizing themselves to achieve sustained economic growth. I propose that we call this their capacity for social development. This concept of social development is meant to include all processes endogenous to a region that contribute and lead up to increases in production and productivity in the use of regional resources. Within a given area, this may include a growing ability to perceive and seize economic opportunities given in the environment, to mobilize resources for production, to diagnose common problems accurately, or organize successfully and carry through programs looking towards an "improvement" of the physical environment and, more generally, to experiment with new ideas, new approaches and new forms of organization in dealing with the tasks at hand. Among sociologists today, the capacity of an area to generate and absorb continuous change is accepted as a distinctive sign of successful modernization. Social development, then, refers most generally to continuing increases in the capacity of a territorially based subsystem of society to deal with problems of innovative change. In most cases, this will involve responses on the part of broad segments of the population.[14]

This view of social development is distinct from one which classifies investments in housing, health and education as "social" or which regards improvements in consumption patterns, social participation, conditions of work, infant mortality and similar measures as relevant indicators.[15] It may be useful for certain purposes to single out these aspects of development as "social," but this would imply a substantially different concept from the one I am proposing here. The present concept refers to a process that is distinct and analytically separable from but, at the same time, also functional for the economic growth of an area.[16]

If we accept this point of view, it is clear that economic growth may be achieved indirectly by promoting and strengthening certain facilitating social processes internal to a community. The alternative to this would be to implant artificially into an area productive facilities which can be sustained with only minimal involvement of the local community. This might occur, for instance, with the erection in some remote region—say in the Chilean province of Magallanes—of an oil refinery whose capital is entirely in the hands of external interests and which can be operated with only minimal local adjustments as a "foreign" enclave in the region. More generally, it is the case of all "neopatrimonial" cities whose growth is the result of initiatives originating in the capital city with little, if any, meaningful participation of local populations.

Social development is conceived here as occurring primarily in cities of microregions. To the extent that active peripheral areas become linked to each other as well as to core regions, the economic growth of an entire system of cities and regions would tend to occur.

THE PATTERN VARIABLES: PSYCHOSOCIAL INFRASTRUCTURE OF A REGION

We know very little as yet concerning the configuration of conditions that makes some regional "communities" more capable of organizing for economic growth than others. The following complex variables, each composed of subvariables forming a pattern, are suggested as a basis for working hypotheses in the empirical study of social development:

1. *Regional consciousness*, or the desire and will of populations to promote the economic growth of their area; a group-focused image of economic growth.
2. *Information transfer*, or the "openness" of leading sectors of the population to information external to the region and their capacity to reinterpret and use this information in ways that will make it relevant to local economic growth.
3. *Autonomy*, or the ability of local populations to make effective decisions relating significantly to the economic growth of the area.
4. *Innovative propensity of the social system*, or the affinity of local leadership for patterns of social organization conducive to sustained innovative activity.
5. *Organizational capacity*, or the ability of local populations to organize themselves effectively for the solution of common tasks related to economic growth.

Following Janusz Ziolkowski (1967: 19–32), we may call these pattern variables of social development the "psychosocial infrastructure" of a city. [17] To clarify the relations among them, the following two-by-two matrix may be set up.

Pattern Variables	Individual	Collective
Motivational	• regional consciousness • innovative propensity (leadership)	• regional consciousness
Facilitating	• information transfer • organizational capacity (enterprise)	• information transfer • organizational capacity (community) • autonomy • innovative propensity (social org.)

These pattern variables refer exclusively to ecological subsystems of society or regions (microregions, cities). They are therefore relative measures of internal capacity for social development. The matrix of the larger societal system (nation) in which they are embedded establishes the basic norms from which regional subsystems will deviate. To the extent that regions are closely tied into the national system, they can be expected to partake of many of its norms. If the political organization of the system is highly centralized, for instance, nearly all regions will, to a large degree, be externally dependent and capable of organizing primarily to petition the central authorities for assistance in local projects. The number of significant deviant cases, as well as the degree of deviation, will be relatively small. More open and decentralized systems, however, will give the regions greater initiative and power to act on their own behalf. System parameters, therefore, must be viewed as establishing the limits to social development at subsystem levels. If these limits are both rigid and narrow, structural change in the parameters is the only path that is likely to permit more rapid economic growth in the periphery. But if they are relatively wide and flexible, the number of deviant cases—and the degree of deviance from system norms—will increase, and social development in the active periphery will be more likely to lead to the results desired.

Each pattern variable at the regional level is, in turn, composed of a constellation of subvariables or major components that are identified and discussed below.

Motivational Variables

Individual

Regional consciousness

1. Political participation: in democratic politics, local interests find expression through the political process and specifically through the election of politicians to office. Active participation in local politics, as measured for instance by voting behavior, may be taken as a rough indicator of concern with public affairs; a nonparticipant population will tend to be alienated from the larger community and difficult to enlist for social development.

2. Regional commitment (a group-focused image of change): some pride in and identification with a local area would seem to be prerequisite for most kinds of socially oriented action. Regional commitment, particularly on the part of local leadership groups, has its national counterpart in the ideology of nationalism. A dependent internal proletariat, as well as noncommitted residents whose principal orientation is towards centers and groups outside the area, will not be likely to devote much energy to promoting local economic growth.

Innovative propensity (leadership)

1. Leadership attitudes (dominant): every social system may be divided into a dominant and nondominant (dependent) sector. Attitudes of the dominant groups towards change, the proper role of system elites and "modernization" will be important for economic change. Also relevant are elite attitudes towards the dependent sectors of population, the legitimate aspirations of these groups and expectations regarding their proper relationship to the dominant sectors. Elite understanding of society as a fluid, open, participant, horizontal system, characterized by free collaboration rather than by authority and compliance will have positive meaning for the social development of an area.

2. Leadership attitudes (nondominant): attitudes similar to those for the dominant leadership are important here. Of special relevance will be the perceived—as well as desired—degree of autonomy of nondominant groups, their sense of social power and their desire to collaborate freely in the process of regional economic growth.

Collective

Regional consciousness

1. Institutional orientations: institutions such as local centers of higher education, local political party organizations and business and manufacturing concerns may be oriented predominantly towards advancing their own interests, the interests of the region or extraregional interests; they may also be more or less inclined to accept changes in the traditional social order. Both are important motivational variables in the process of social development.

2. Mass media orientations: questions similar to those immediately above may be raised also with respect to the performance of the principal mass media (newspapers, radio, television) which serve the local population.

Facilitating Variables

Individual

Information transfer

1. Educational level: the educational level of local populations will be one of the determining factors in the process of innovation, facilitating or hindering the transfer of information from sources outside the immediate area. In general, an educated population will tend to be better prepared for generating and absorbing innovations than one that is less educated. Its perceptions of problems and opportunities for action will also tend to be more realistic.

2. Number of professionals in the population: professional people and technicians nearly always have a university education. As such, they play a special role in the transfer of information, being in more direct contact with the outside world and generally better equipped than others to lead the process of community change. Their specialized skills are also needed for many types of social development.

Organizational capacity (enterprise)

1. Available "managerial" skills: the distribution of management abilities in the population—whether in private enterprise, the cooperative movement, civic organizations, labor unions, housing projects and the like—serves as a significant index of the "ability to organize" for economic growth. Communities deprived of significant organizing skills will tend to have a low potential for dealing effectively with forces of external change.

Collective

Information transfer

1. Centers of higher education: universities, technical schools and similar institutions will generally function as "transmission belts" for scientific, technical and cultural information from out-

side the local area. They will also be capable of rendering specialized services to the community. Their presence, size, vocation
and efficiency in carrying out their local mediating role constitute
significant measures of the social development potential of a
region.

2. Mass media: the number and types of mass media available to
a community and the size of their audience are all relevant indicators of social development potential.

Organizational capacity (community)

1. Community organizations: the number of self-generated
organizations in an area—neighborhood unit councils, clubs,
civic associations, labor unions, housing cooperatives and so
forth—constitutes, together with their membership, a direct
measure of local organizing ability and of experience with collab-
orative action. Important additional information should be
obtained concerning their programs, stability, intensity of activity
and ability to satisfy the specific needs of their members.

Autonomy

1. Extent of autonomous decision-making powers: if social
development is conceived as a process occurring in distinct
localities, it may be reasonable to insist that a significant proportion of the vital decisions which affect economic growth must be
made by local authorities and other organized groups in the region. This ability is partly a function of the institutional framework for decision making and the financial resources and skills
available to the region for specific undertakings.

Innovative propensity (social organization)

1. The structure of social organization of a city will be a major
factor in its development. Two basic models of organization may
be distinguished: one emphasizes hierarchy, authority, permanence and limited access to information (the elitist, bureaucratic model); the other stresses horizontal relations, shifting pat-

terns of collaboration, free association, and radical openness to information (the democratic, nonbureaucratic model) (Friedmann, 1968c). The second of these models tends to reveal a higher propensity for innovative change than the first. To the extent that its social organization conforms to the second model, a city will tend to have a high degree of social development potential.

The foregoing account of pattern variables may be summarized by saying that subsystems of society in which some or all of these structural conditions are present. will be expected to demonstrate a significantly higher capacity for social development than subsystems where only a few or none of them exist, or where their intensity is weak.

As a corollary, the presence of the structural components identified would be reflected, first, in the character of local economic development (auto-directed, responsive to local needs and aspirations) and, second, in the rate of local economic development (a function partly of the ability to mobilize resources). These two sets of consequences, however, need not coincide. It is entirely conceivable that local economic development is intense without being responsive to local interests (where investments, though locally promoted, are exogenous and controlled by core regions); it is also possible to imagine a situation where local development, though responsive to local needs, will be relatively low in intensity.

The economic growth of an ecological subsystem of the society may therefore be either *exogenous* (imported and outer-directed) or *endogenous* (locally generated and self-directed). In both cases it may appear as a result of social development, but only in the second instance would always be true. The study of the conditions for social development and the processes by which social development occurs is thus of fundamental importance for industrializing societies that, in their entirety, may lie within the peripheries of international core regions. It is of special importance for the formulation of appropriate policies directed at coping with underdevelopment in national peripheries. For if a peripheral region is to break out of its condition of colonial dependency, it will have to choose the path of social development to economic growth. The nature of the data required is such that they do not readily lend themselves to factor analysis. What is needed, therefore, is the construction of community "profiles" composed of the fourteen variables listed and an interpretive judgment on the meaning of each city profile for social development. Cumulative evidence should make it possible to assign proper weights to each component and reduce the number of relevant indices of an area's "psychosocial infrastructure" to those that are truly critical for its ability to organize itself for sustained economic growth.

SOME CONCLUSIONS FROM EMPIRICAL RESEARCH

Exploratory studies on the conditions affecting the capacity for social development of two cities in southern Chile have recently been carried out under the guidance of the author and Ernesto Cohen.[18] Valdivia and Puerto Montt were selected on the basis of several considerations. Both were settled initially by German populations; their sizes—73,000 and 66,000, respectively, in 1960—were roughly comparable; they are located within three hours' driving distance from each other; both are coastal cities serving a larger region; and both are distant from Santiago (855 and 1090 kilometers, respectively). Despite these external similarities, however, the two cities showed marked internal differences in their score on a number of components of the pattern variables described. Of 28 cities examined, Valdivia ranked eighth and Puerto Montt 27th with respect to the sum of 11 surrogate measures used.[19] There was thus a presumption that Valdivia would exhibit a relatively greater capacity to organize for economic growth than Puerto Montt. The overall quantitative index of social development was not taken too seriously, however. The research itself attempted to shed light on the validity and meaning of the pattern variables for social development.

Four individual studies were carried out in the two cities. Clinton Bourdon's interest was in the performance of the local economic elite groups; Diva Dinovitzer studied organizations of the so-called *sector popular*, that is, the dependent, low income population; Margarita Diggs did a study of the reactions to a devastating earthquake which struck the southern part of Chile in 1960, in the hope of discovering significant differences in the responses of Valdivia and Puerto Montt to a disaster that left no sector of the population unaffected; and Nancy Zimmerman concentrated on the region serving role of the Universidad Austral, a medium sized private university located in Valdivia.

Before proceeding, it is necessary to describe briefly some salient features of the national system which, it was subsequently discovered, exerted a decisive influence on certain aspects of social development in the two regions. Economically, Chile occupies a middle range between the already industrialized and newly industrializing nations. Its *per capita* income is variously given as somewhere between $450 and $550, placing the country near the top of a list of Latin American nations, immediately following Argentina, Venezuela and Uruguay. Politically, Chile is considered a unitary state. The only government mediating between the citizen and the national government is the municipality, which has an elected city council; provinces and regions are simply units serving administrative convenience. Municipalities, however, are exceedingly weak and are able to spend an average of only $10 *per capita* per year, most of which goes for the salary payments of local officials. Nearly all effective power is therefore wielded from locations in Santiago, where it is divided among the Chief Executive, the National Congress, national political parties, the national administration and a number of nationally organized pressure groups. Local interests are not clearly represented in the Congress, whose legislative acts are steered principally by partisan and ideological considerations that have no clear relationship to local interests and needs. A good deal of the time, however, the system operates on the basis of reciprocal favors through extremely complex chains of personal contacts which help to meliorate what otherwise would be a rather inflexible pattern of administrative behavior.

The structure of Chilean society has traditionally been held together by the so-called principle of authority, according to which it is the right of the few to govern and the duty of the many to obey. It is a system of ascriptive status, cast in the mold of a bureaucratic (hierarchical) model of organization. Although the system is now being challenged from many sides, it still retains considerable strength and vitality.

Our studies in Valdivia and Puerto Montt revealed the immense weight and influence of this national system on local social organization. The principal conclusions with respect to the social development model presented earlier are best summarized by looking separately at the responses of the dependent and dominant sectors of the population.

The *dependent sector* accounts for between 65 and 95 percent of the population in both cities; a more precise estimate is not possible because an unambiguous criterion of "dependency" is lacking. The dependent sector might also be called the passive or excluded population. In Chile it is common to refer to it indiscriminately as *población marginal* or *sector popular*. Armand Mattelart (Mattelart and Garretón, 1965: tables 17 and 18), a Belgian demographer, uses employment characteristics of the active male population as part of a broader definition (table 1).

Table 1 Occupational Stratification of Active Male Urban Population, 1960

(Percentages)

	Valdivia	Puerto Montt
Urban Managerial Groups, Medium-Sized and Large Enterprises	0.8	1.3
Upper Administrative Class	4.5	3.9
Independent Professionals	0.5	0.5
Self-Employed Managers (*Empresarios*)	1.2	1.6
Lower-Middle Administrative Class	8.2	8.2
Autonomous Lower-Middle Class	8.4	9.5
Subtotal, Urban Middle Class	23.6	25.0
Dependent Working Class	67.9	62.8
Autonomous Working Class	8.5	12.2
Subtotal, Urban Working Class	76.4	75.0

SOURCE: Armand Mattelart and Manuel A. Garretón, *Integración Nacional y Marginalidad* (Santiago: Pacífico, 1965), table 18.

According to Mattelart, approximately 75 percent of the male labor force in both cities can be classified as blue collar. Family income statistics, unfortunately, are not available. If they were, a possibly smaller percentage than Mattelart's might reasonably be called "dependent." In any event, the phenomenon of dependency is a matter of degree rather than of absolute judgment. What can be asserted with confidence is that it refers predominantly to low income groups whose social participation is limited to membership in such organizations as soccer clubs, mothers' centers, syndicates, neighborhood *juntas*, cooperatives and mutual aid associations. These organizations are typically small, local and often unaffiliated. In 1966 about one-half of the *sector popular* in the two cities studied were not members of *any* organization and consequently were excluded altogether from any meaningful participation in the affairs of their community. Between them and the all-powerful central government, there were no mediating institutions of any sort. But the participation of the remaining 50 percent was also exceedingly restricted. For certain types of organization, only small numbers of the population from which recruits might potentially be drawn in fact held formal membership in them (Table 2). Less than 15 percent of the adult women belonged to mothers' clubs; between 40 and 60 percent of the men did not participate in athletic organizations; less than one-fifth of the workers were organized into unions; less than 40 percent of the families in the dependent population were represented in neighborhood councils; less than 10 percent belonged to mutual aid associations. The resultant defenselessness, if not anomie, of the vast majority of the low income population can be readily imagined.

The data in Table 2 also show that the "dependent" populations in the two cities showed no significant differences in the overall pattern of their organization. Furthermore, and important from the standpoint of our concept of social development, popular organizations of the type found in Valdivia and Puerto Montt had very little to do with economic growth as such or, for that matter, with any of the truly vital concerns of the dependent population. Sport clubs organize to play soccer; mothers' centers receive cooking and sewing classes; neighborhood organizations form to present their needs—the paving of a street, the construc-

Table 2   Data on Community Organizations for the Dependent Sector, 1966

	No. of Organizations		Av. No. of Members		% of Org. Affiliated		Total Membership		% Members of Rel. Pop. Base	
	V	PM	V	PM	V	PM	V	PM	V	PM
Mothers' Centers	82	68	35	28	76	66	2,902	1,958	15	11
Soccer Clubs	82	72	129	104	63	49	11,432	7,551	58	41
Syndicates	55	23	69	99	46	39	3,803	2,286	19	12
Neighborhood Juntas	38	41	112	102	50	44	4,287	4,190	35	39
Mutual Aid Associats.	16	20	88	100	50	75	1,411	2,008	4	6
Others[a]	26	27	73	106	58	56	1,910	2,886	5	8

a. Include cooperatives and cultural, youth and welfare organizations.
SOURCE: Census of *Organizaciones de Base,* Consejería Nacional de Promoción Popular, 1966.
Percentages in the final column were estimated on the basis of the relevant population group from which membership might conceivably be drawn and represent rough orders of magnitude rather than precise measurements.

tion of a playground, the provision of emergency housing—to the authorities; labor unions organize according to craft on a shop basis to press limited demands against employers or to plead their case directly with the authorities. There is no conceivable way by which these modest collective activities can be joined to matters that relate to life in the larger "community"—the city as a whole. The street, the neighborhood, perhaps the *barrio* command some loyalty and are capable of being conceptualized, but not the city and its future. Only one case was discovered where syndicates and neighborhood *juntas* collaborated in any sense with the dominant elites on a matter pertaining to the economic growth of the area. This was a special committee set up in Valdivia to pressure the government into locating a shipyard in the area. This collaboration was clearly an instance of complementary interests. A shipyard would create jobs and income for workers who therefore acquired a stake in the project.

More notable differences in the capacity to organize for economic growth were found between the dominant elite groups of the two cities. In neither city did the elites exploit the possibilities for concerted action to the maximum feasible extent, but Valdivia clearly showed more ability in this regard than Puerto Montt. Valdivia's superior showing could be ascribed, in part, to a greater identification of the local elites with the region, a more accurate perception of problems and a more adequate understanding of what would constitute effectively instrumental action, a greater capacity for concerting interests, a large managerial tradition and the presence in Valdivia of education and research institutions that could be relied upon to give technical advice when needed.

Even so, the difference is only one of degree. The elite groups of both cities tend to organize, if at all, primarily to achieve specific economic ends through petition and pressure on the central authorities. In spite of their greater organizational skill, for instance, the elites of Valdivia have so far failed to assure themselves of a long term supply of high quality forests for their wood product industries, nor have they taken any steps that would mobilize local capital resources for industrial expansion in the region. And although Austral University came into being as the result of local initiative by a few wealthy Valdivian families, this center of higher education has traditionally served only individual clients by making its specialized expertise in agriculture and forestry available to those able and willing to purchase it; only recently has it begun to play a more active leadership role in the region.

In both cities the dominant elite groups appear to find the conceptualization of city- or region-wide interests exceedingly difficult. Under the pressure of disaster, as immediately following the devastating earthquake in 1960, the atomistic character of the local social system becomes strikingly clear. Individual families and groups of related families suddenly revealed themselves as the basic and, indeed, the only active agents in the locality. Oblivious to wider concerns, they advanced their own self-interest quite without shame by exploiting as best they could the network of reciprocal favors that operates outside, but parallel with, the formal system of the State bureaucracy. The rhetoric they used was communitarian, but the benefits they sought would accrue to themselves exclusively.

Thus, although Valdivia appears to have the edge on Puerto Montt in the city's potential for social development (in the highly specific meaning of the term used in the monograph), the difference is nowhere near as pronounced as we were led to believe on the basis of purely formal criteria. We had initially given insufficient weight to the influence of the national system as setting up

the limits for effective local organization. In Chile these are un-
usually narrow and inflexible. We had also overlooked the importance for social development of the internal social and political
structure of the areas we studied. This structure was evidently not
neutral with respect to the ability to organize effective actions for
economic growth. The mass-elite structure, common to both
Valdivia and Puerto Montt, effectively excluded the great
majority of the population from any meaningful participation in
the larger affairs of their communities and left them with a small
number of highly personal concerns of relatively marginal significance to their own sense of well-being. More pluralistic or
communitarian structures of local society—American and
Yugoslav models come to mind as prototypes—might lead to a
more active involvement and to reorientation of basic societal
values. In Chile, where economic power is to a large extent in the
hands of the State, effective action is restricted to a small group
of elite families that has direct access to the nerve centers of the
State management apparatus. The internally dependent masses
do not have significant economic power, are consequently at the
mercy of the State and of the elites linked into its machinery for
compliance and are limited to sporadic interventions through
direct action, such as strikes and demonstrations. In a recent inci-
dent, nine *pobladores* were shot down by the police during an
attempted land invasion in Puerto Montt.

Where economic power is concentrated in the hands of the
State, therefore, self-generated local development will be limited
essentially to an ability for organizing petitions to channel public
investments to the region. To the extent that economic power is
concentrated in the hands of a small group of elite families, self-
generated local development will depend on certain characteristics of the local elite groups, namely, their education level, their
cosmopolitan outlook, their connections with national elite
groups, the extent to which their behavior is self- or group-
oriented, the degree of their class or community consciousness,
the extent of their identification with the future of the local area
and their capability for rational appraisal of local opportunities
and limiting conditions. Where elite groups define their interests
narrowly, do not identify with the local area and are more class-

than community-conscious, the local economy is likely to stagnate. Where elite groups are poorly connected with national elite groups, little social development can be expected. Where elite groups are unrealistic about what can be achieved, their efforts are likely to be misdirected, with equally negative results for local economic growth.

TOWARDS A STRATEGY FOR SOCIAL DEVELOPMENT

The future of Latin America is, we assume, partly open to deliberate choice. What I am therefore proposing is a strategy that would accelerate the economic development of the continent's present peripheries by a directed effort to realize the potential for social development of especially promising areas. This would be complementary to efforts to reinforce normal core region growth—a strategy which, at least for the more important areas, will in any event be followed.

To begin to order thinking on the development of Latin America's peripheries, it will be helpful to distinguish between already existing and new social development poles and to subdivide the latter into spontaneous and planned. This classification may be crude, but it is useful; separate public policies must be formulated for each set.

I shall have little to say about new social development poles. Many of them appear in areas of ongoing colonization along the settlement frontier, especially along the emerging internal highway systems of Latin America (carretera marginal de la selva, carretera Belém-Brasília). These roads and their adjacent areas are now attracting large numbers of settlers and are stimulating the founding of new cities. It may be possible to direct this vast city-forming process and to encourage the formation of social development poles that can be pushed over the minimum threshold size of population necessary for sustained growth. A combination of planned and spontaneous settlements in new colonization areas may offer the best solution.

Rather than deal with the problem of the settlement frontier, I shall pass in brief review some of the measures that may be applied to already existing social development poles. [20]

Since "active" centers are encapsulated within larger "passive" peripheries, the basic strategy should center on efforts to accelerate migration from the latter areas to the development enclaves. In this way, ever-increasing numbers of the population could be incorporated into dynamic subsystems of society. [21] Deliberate urbanization in this sense can be achieved by concentrating investments in basic services capable of absorbing the new population (housing, schools, water and sewerage systems, hospitals, clinics, transport services and the like) in areas which have a demonstrated high capacity for social development.

Returning now to the variables that together compose the psychosocial infrastructure of an area, the major thrust should be towards improving the performance of what I have called the facilitating variables; not much can be done—at least within a democratic framework—by way of direct influence to improve the structure of motivations if these should be unfavorable to economic growth. Indirectly, however, deliberate development efforts can positively reinforce attitudes that are receptive to modernization. To obtain such results, external assistance should avail itself of local capabilities for development; induced development should be viewed as an effort to strengthen local leadership and enlist the active collaboration of local groups and organizations from all social strata. The identification of problems and the ordering of priorities should, when possible, be locally determined.

Going beyond this general approach in extending development assistance, the strategy should focus on the improvement of the facilitating variables. Education opportunities (secondary and technical) should be expanded and the curriculum made more immediately relevant to local needs. The emigration of professionals to the principal core regions of the country should be reduced by creating within the local community conditions attractive to professional persons. This would involve action to provide adequate housing, expansion and upgrading of provincial university centers, expansion and improvements in the use of communication media (the communication needs of professionals tend to be much greater than for the population at large) and the promotion of cultural activites, such as concerts, lecture series, theater, libraries and museums, that would break down the sense of isolation and cultural improverishment typical of the elites in the provincial urban centers.

Of particular interest would be the improvement of management skills already present in the community. This can be accomplished partly through the organization of intensive training courses for different leadership and managerial groups such as labor union leaders, political cadres, leaders of housing cooperatives, selected neighborhood council members and small businessmen and industrialists. These courses are likely to produce a lasting impact if, at the same time, opportunities are created for exercising the newly acquired skills. Wherever possible, courses should be related to specific development objectives.

Another line of action would involve the expansion of existing university centers (or the establishment of new ones where they do not already exist). Equally important, however, would be attempts to relate the activities of the university more specifically to regional needs. This refers not only to the types of professional (or subprofessional) courses of study offered but also to the role of the university as a center of cultural and scientific activity.[22] A somewhat similar approach may be adopted with regard to the mass media and their function in the community as mediators of external information and as modernizing agents. Special training may be given to radio, newspaper and television staffs and assistance offered in devising programs related to the interests of local groups taking part in the development program.

One of the most significant aspects of the strategy proposed here concerns the enlargement of local autonomy in the social development poles selected. This may involve legal action (for example, the setting up of special development districts related to an increase in local decision-making powers), the channeling of development funds to local authorities and/or organized groups with specific development objectives and training programs to improve the technical and administrative ability of local officials.

The concept of social development which has been used in

this monograph presupposes the existence of objective opportunities for increasing production. If they do not exist, no amount of induced social development will yield appreciable economic results. For this reason, the strategy of social development must also be concerned with the objective conditions for economic growth, even though this would appear as a secondary goal relative to the preoccupation with strengthening the social conditions for development.

Two approaches seem paramount in this connection. First, access to core region markets as well as to local influence areas should be improved, including in this the major modes of communication (transport, telephone, telex, radio, television). As a subsidiary strategy—and for a later stage of implementation— linkages among existing and new social development poles should be strengthened in a similar fashion. Second, special measures should be adopted to encourage the formation and inflow of enterprise capital. Extending special lines of credit, granting exemptions and temporary subsidies (direct or indirect) to local enterprise and the establishment of local development organizations—all deserve careful study.

The proposed measures would, of course, have to be adjusted to local as well as national conditions. But their consistent application over long periods of time should lead to the more complete realization of social development potentials of peripheral areas and eventually to the transformation of these potentials into increased production.

To carry out such policies, new institutional and legal arrangements may be required. This may not be an impossible hope should Latin American countries decide to make the conquest and vitalization of the periphery the major "social project" of the next generation. Pioneer settlement, city founding and city building are all within the great tradition of Latin American culture (Morse, 1962). It does not seem unreasonable to think that the next 30 years will enter history as a great new age of city building in which the public effort was primarily directed towards the internal ordering of core regions and the creation and expansion of social development poles in the periphery within the context of national and multinational policies of development.

APPENDIX: SOME ASSUMPTIONS REGARDING TRENDS IN THE DEVELOPMENT OF LATIN AMERICAN NATIONS TO THE YEAR 2000

A General Cautionary Note

There are very few generalizations that can be made about Latin America as a whole that still retain sufficient information to be meaningful and useful. More appropriate would be to approach the subject through a study of regional groupings of countries, but this would require an effort far beyond what is possible here.

Another problem is that we have as yet no means to make long term projections for historical systems as a whole. I say "as yet," but in fact I believe we shall never have this capacity. Science enables us to make predictions for single variables or small clusters of variables under controlled conditions; but when the conditions themselves become variables, our ability to make predictions is rapidly reduced to zero, and we substitute philosophy, hope and belief for knowledge.

In the Latin American setting, these considerations are especially valid, since the countries of the continent are still in formation and the parameters are not yet fixed, as they are, for example, in Europe and to some extent also in the United States. Furthermore, in contrast to the metropolitan world regions, Latin America's future is very much more dependent on external events—events whose nature and timing are also obscure. To know what will happen in Latin America is to know first what will happen in the world. And here again we are reduced to philosophy, hope and belief.

Our actions, however, are influenced by what we expect to happen. The expectation may turn out to be wrong, but this we shall know only later. Meanwhile, we can try to make some guesses about the future conditions in Latin America that will constitute the framework for our actions now and in the near future. The consequences of those actions will themselves be incorporated into the future and therefore will change it in ways that differ from our original expectation, changing the balance of forces that will determine the outcome at a certain time. Following, then, are some abbreviated comments on what I believe or expect to happen in Latin American countries over the next generation. My certainty in these beliefs is rather weak, though the actual strength of belief varies a good deal from issue to issue: I have not set out to trace a range of possible outcomes in the form of either alternative "scenarios" or of "surprise-free" projections. I think that the future will be full of surprises, and this "knowledge" will itself condition our actions.

The Assumptions

1. *Greater political autonomy.* The United States, though it will continue for some time as the world's most powerful nation, will be less able and less inclined to impose its own political solutions on the countries in Latin America. The "cultural revolution" now occurring in the United States means that for a considerable period to come United States policy will be more concerned with internal than external matters; a new isolationism appears to be in the offing. Moreover, there will be a series of new powers, in addition to the United States and the USSR, which will be able to exert, if not world influence, at least influence at the regional level. Japan and Germany are obvious candidates; Mexico and Brazil will play increasingly important roles in the Latin American concert of nations; the world role of China is still uncertain though one is inclined to believe that this gigantic nation will be too much concerned with its own internal problems over the next 30 years to pay a great deal of attention to the outside world.

The vacuum of power created by a withdrawal of the United States from active interference in the politics of the developing nations means that they will gain new options. National forces will be strengthened. There will be less reluctance to experiment with national forms of socialism which depart from the inherited liberal-democratic political framework.

2. *Social mobilization.* The continuing, rapid urbanization in Latin American countries is likely to lead to an even more rapid social mobilization of populations, both urban and rural. By

social mobilization is meant a set of phenomena which leads to increasing participation of previously excluded populations in the development process. Reference is to rising literacy rates, higher levels of education, participation through the increasing use of mass media of communications, membership in different types of functional organizations and increased political participation (voting, strikes, demonstrations). One immediate result of social mobilization is a level of consumer wants rising more rapidly than the ability of national economies to satisfy. The other, intimately related, is the emergence of political parties whose strength derives from their ability to give effective expression to these wants at the level of national policy.

3. *Decline of liberal democratic institutions.* The pressures generated by social mobilization in a situation of growing political autonomy will bring liberal-democratic institutions under severe stress. These institutions which until now have defended the rights of the individual vis-à-vis the community are managed, largely for their own benefit, by organized interest groups representing the rural oligarchies, and the urban middle sectors will become increasingly incapacitated to deal with many-sided conflicts generated by accelerated urbanization. The popular, broadly based political movements which will challenge the dominance of traditional interests will do so in the name of the nation and of an ethos that will stress inclusive egalitarian and distributive values in place of production, achievement motivation and competition. The free enterprise system, so closely associated with the philosophy of liberalism, will give way to some form of communitarian management. This shift in ideology will tend to reinforce social mobilization, particularly insofar as local participation in decision making is concerned. Strong regional and local (municipal) organizations for development will be commonplace throughout most Latin American countries by the year 2000.

4. *Economic growth.* Given a political system organized more around the value of social justice than of production suggests that gross national product annual growth rates in Latin America will most likely fall within the range of 1 to 3 percent on a per capita

basis. Most countries will be able to achieve growth rates that do not exceed 2 percent a year. This means that over the next generation per capita incomes will increase only by 50 to 150 percent, resulting in income levels that will range from a low of perhaps $150 (for Haiti) to $2,500 (for Venezuela). (By comparison, United States per capita income will be more than $4,500.) Since the number of countries with sustained 3 percent growth rates will be relatively small in Latin America, one can reasonably conclude that existing income inequalities among the American states will be exacerbated. The countries most likely to register high growth rates include Mexico, Venezuela, Brazil and Argentina. This differential growth will bring the Inter-American system under severe strain and will inhibit efforts to create a Latin American common market.

5. *Industrialization*. Relatively modest economic growth rates are compatible with fairly high rates of increase in industrial production (6 to 12 percent per annum). The new industrial technology, however, is typically capital-intensive, with the result that industrial employment will maintain a relative strength of between 15 and 20 percent in relation to total employment. The social impact of industrialization will thus be severely circumscribed. Social development, one may conclude, will occur largely independent of industrialization. This would reinforce the political trend toward communitarianism (or national socialism).

6. *Hyperurbanization*. In most countries urbanization will continue at a super-rapid pace from 4 to 7 percent a year. The more probable exceptions to this are Chile, Argentina, Uruguay and Venezuela—where existing urbanization already includes two-thirds or more of the population. Economic growth (including industrialization) will lag significantly behind, with the result that the accumulating urban proletariat will make its demands felt with increasing vehemence. The resulting "crisis of inclusion" will reinforce the trend leading to a decline of liberal democratic institutions. Last-ditch efforts may be made by the traditional Establishment to counteract the swing to popularly based political movements, but these are not likely to provide stability in the absence of strong support by the United States (see hypothesis 1).

7. *Center-periphery structure.* Economic development and urban growth will continue to favor the existing major Latin American core regions centered on Buenos Aires–Montevideo–Pôrto Alegre and São Paulo-Rio de Janeiro. But increased accessibility to these centers (through gradual lowering of tariff barriers and internal road improvement) will lead to a significant expansion of core areas, with portions of the present periphery brought into the radius of core region influence (Santiago-Concepción, Asunción, Belo Horizonte–Brasilia and Salvador [Bahia]). This will mean some opening up of Latin American continental interior (which has considerable economic development potential) in those areas which have greatest access to core region markets and encourage more economic interchange among the countries concerned (Brazil, Uruguay, Argentina, Chile). At the same time, it will put the remaining Latin American countries at a disadvantage. Central America and countries such as Mexico, Venezuela, Colombia and perhaps Peru will seek closer commercial and diplomatic ties with the United States, in part to counteract the spreading influence of a consolidated Latin American core region. This will contribute further to the breaking up of the Latin American system as one with a unified and effective political voice.

8. *Rise of cosmopolitan culture.* Economically and politically, Latin American integration on a continental scale is unlikely to make much progress over the period under consideration. But considerable unity may be achieved at the intellectual and professional levels. The main forces facilitating this development are metropolitan growth (by 2000, Latin America may have 20 and perhaps more metropolitan regions with over one million inhabitants), supersonic continental jet service, satellite communications systems, continental modern telephone-telex system and the continuing trend towards the establishment of Latin American professional reviews as well as other large-scale publishing ventures. By 2000 a highly developed continental intellectual system may have become established. Through this system Latin America will be linked with the rest of the world, particularly with the emergent metropolitan powers. In the physical sciences Latin America will probably continue to plow in the backwaters of scientific advance, but it is quite possible that major world contri-

butions will come from the social sciences, not only because of proven competence in this area but also because Latin American social scientists will be more "in tune" with the problems besetting other developing countries than those of the older regions.

NOTES

1. The corresponding figures are substantially reduced if a cutoff point of 20,000 is taken as the definition of urban. Thus, the average for Latin American countries having 1950 and 1960 data would decline to 28 percent (1950) and 36 percent (1960). See Durand and Peláez (1965: 167, table 1).

2. A current estimate projects Latin America's urban population to 73 percent by the year 2000 (Olivos, 1969). Country projections of urban population to 1985 appear in CELADE (1969: table 2). For a general discussion of urbanization trends see Browning (1967: 71-116).

3. A framework for the long-term projection of major variables in Latin American development is set forth in the Appendix. See also *Economic Bulletin for Latin America* 6 (1961).

4. The future rate of increase in the use of automotive transport in Latin America may be estimated at two to three times the rate of increase in population, that is, at between 5 and 9 percent a year. This implies doubling rates of between eight and 14 years.

5. In recent years, the first steps towards the large-scale planning for urban regions have been taken in a number of Latin American countries. In Chile, for instance, a region centered on Santiago but comprising an area roughly 160 kilometers in diameter is currently under study by the National Planning Office. See also Oficina Nacional de Planeamiento Urbano (1967).

6. Involved in this is a process of spatial diffusion for urban innovations. The basic literature is discussed in Rogers (1962). A fundamental geographic contribution to the subject is the recently translated work by Hägerstrand (1968).

7. See Friedmann (1967) for an elaboration of the core-periphery concept.

8. This finding is consistent with results from many other studies which emphasize the structural stability of spatial frameworks.

9. The Pedersen-Stöhr analysis refers only to South America. The citation is taken from a preliminary version of the paper and may be slightly altered in the final publication.

10. For the concept of "infrastructure" or "overhead capital" see Youngson (1967).

11. This gain in relative advantage, however, may not be sufficient to transform the basic pattern of core region dominance.

12. This size range is suggested on the basis of Australian studies by Neutze (1965). A very complete study of urbanization in relation to value added and employment has recently been carried out in India (Stanford Research Institute et al., 1968). Although the results of this study cannot be generalized to other countries, it provides evidence, at least for India, that the urbanization costs of economic expansion in metropolitan centers are not appreciably lower than for smaller cities. Thus, an economically powerful argument exists for a policy of decentralizing growth to provincial cities on the basis of primarily social considerations.

13. This list was suggested to me by Mr. Clinton Bourdon to whom I am also indebted for his many critical insights into the process of regional economic growth.

14. For a full statement of the implications of this model see Eisenstadt (1967: passim). Eisenstadt's model, however, suffers from being excessively elitist in its orientation and from not giving sufficient emphasis to the creative role of social conflict.

15. This appears to be the prevalent view supported in official publications of the United Nations, such as its periodic Reports on the World Social Situation. The present definition is also distinct from one that would stress the increased "participation" of different groups in societal processes and their increased access to decision-making power as characteristic elements of social development.

16. The concept of social development in the sense of the internal capacity of a region to organize for economic growth was first suggested to me by the experience of Hong Kong, a region almost completely deprived of natural resources and distant from major export markets, which nevertheless has been able to sustain an astoundingly high rate of economic growth for two decades. This result, it seemed to me, could be ascribed only to the organizational ability of the Chinese and British communities of the colony. Also noteworthy is the existence of regions in the northeastern United States which, flourishing in the bygone era of coal and iron, were subsequently unable to make a successful transition to a postindustrial economy. For their failure to respond adequately to modern challenges, they have become distressed enclave economies (for example, Buffalo, New York).

17. In his illuminating paper, Ziolkowski describes contrasting forms of recent industrialization efforts and related urbanization in Poland—one which was imposed on a town by the center in neopatrimonial fashion and another (similar to our social development poles) which grew "organically." The paper is especially worth reading not only for the support it lends to the model presented in these pages but also for the salient points of difference. The general issue is posed in the following extract: By having set in motion the mechanism of spatial and social mobility and by moving large masses of rural population to the towns, where they were introduced to the system of industrial work, it has reached—often in a dramatic manner—the deep differences existing between individual regions in relation not only to the material and technical but also to the psycho-social infrastructure. Among the distinguishing features of this psycho-social infrastructure are the ability of organized cooperation, tradition, culture and discipline of work, sense of responsibility and general standards. It is precisely this infrastructure, so frequently lightly dismissed and neglected in investment policy, that largely determines the effects of this policy; in this light it is easier to understand . . . the ostensibly strange phenomenon that the commissioning of a new industrial enterprise in one region takes such a short time in comparison with a similar project elsewhere or that in factories in one part of the country the shift to a new technology or a new line of production requires so little time while in another it causes so much difficulty, or that productivity and quality of production is higher in one case and lower in another [Ziolkowski, 1967: 22–23].

18. These studies were done with the support of the Centro Interdisciplinario de Desarrollo Urbano y Regional (CIDU) of the Catholic University of Chile. It is expected that they will be published by the Center in the near future.

19. The measures included road distance from Santiago; population increase between 1940 and 1960; percent of labor force in 1960; average annual municipal income per capita, 1960 to 1965; number of students registered at local universities, 1967; percent of population with secondary school, technical and university education in 1960; percent of eligible population voting in the congressional elections of 1965; and percent of the labor force in mining and manufacturing industries, 1960.

20. I shall exclude from consideration here any changes in the structural characteristics of the national system of which the subsystem is a part. This is done, not because it is thought to be a matter of

secondary importance, but because space prevents me from dealing adequately with this subject.

21. See Friedmann (1968b) for an analysis of the broader consequences of this policy.

22. For an excellent appraisal of the role of a regional university see Hamilton (1968).

REFERENCES

Baldwin, R.E. (1964) "Patterns of Development in Newly Settled Regions." In J. Friedmann and W. Alonso (eds.) Regional Development and Planning. Cambridge, Mass.: The Massachusetts Institute of Technology Press.

Berry, B. J. L. and P. J. Schwind (1967) "The National Space-Economy and Urban Fields in Iowa's Urban Future." Cities of the Future. Proceedings of the Fourth Annual Urban Policy Conference, 26–28 October. The University of Iowa, Institute of Public Affairs.

Browning, H. L. (1967) "Urbanization and Modernization in Latin America: the Demographic Perspective." in G. H. Beyer (ed.) The Urban Explosion in Latin America. Ithaca, N.Y.: Cornell University Press.

Busca, A. and S. Cafiero (1966) "Costo Social del Asentameinto." Cuadernos de la Sociedad Venezolana de Planificación 4, no. 8 (August): 35–45.

Celade (1969) Boletín Demográfico, Año 2, vol. 3 (January).

Durand, J. D. and C. Peláez (1965) "Patterns of Urbanization." The Milbank Memorial Fund Quarterly 63, no. 4, part 2 (October).

Economic Bulletin for Latin America 6 (1961) "The Demographic Situation in Latin America," no. 2 (October): 13–52.

Eisenstadt, N. S. (1967) "El Estudio del 'Fenómeno de Urbanización en Venezuela' y los Problemas de Desarrollo de una Sociedad Moderna." Ensayos y Exposiciones 3d ser., no. 4. Caracas: CENDES.

Friedmann, J. (1968a) "An Information Model of Urbanization." Urban Affairs Quarterly 4, no. 2 (December): 235–244.

Friedmann, J. (1968b) "The Strategy of Deliberate Urbanization." Journal of the American Institute of Planners 34, no. 6 (November): 364–373.

Friedmann, J. (1968c) "Bureaucratic and Innovative Models of Urban Life." New York: Paper presented at the Annual Meeting of the Latin American Studies Association, 8 November. Mimeo.

Friedmann, J. (1967) "A General Theory of Polarized Development." Mimeo.

Hagerstrand, T. (1968) Innovation Diffusion as a Spatial Process. Chicago: The University of Chicago Press.

Hamilton, N. L. (1968) "A Preliminary Analysis of the Role of the Regional University Centers of the University of Chile in Regional Development." Santiago: Centro Interdisciplinario de Desarrollo Urbano y Regional, Catholic University of Chile (May). Typescript.

Mattelart, A. and M. A. Garretón (1965) Integración Nacional y Marginalidad. Santiago: Pacífico.

Matus, C., P. Vuskovic et al. (1967) "Polémica sobre el desarrollo del interior de América Latina." Santiago: ILPES (September). Mimeo.

Morse, R. M. (1962) "Some Characteristics of Latin American Urban History." The American Historical Review 67, no. 2 (January): 317–338.

Neutze, G. M. (1965) Economic Policy and the Size of Cities. Canberra: The Australian National University.

Nicholls, W. (1967) "The Transformation of Agriculture in a Semi-Industrialized Country: The Case of Brazil." New York: National Bureau of Economic Research (December). Preliminary.

North, D. C. (1964) "Location Theory and Regional Economic Growth." In J. Friedmann and W. Alonso (eds.) Regional Development and Planning. Cambridge, Mass.: The Massachusetts Institute of Technology Press.

Oficina Nacional de Planeamiento Urbano (1967) Plan de Lima.

Olivos, L. (1969) Políticas de Población y Desarrollo para el Año 2.000. Washington, D.C.: Departamento de Asuntos Sociales, Unión Panamericana (January 13). Mimeo.

Pedersen, P. and W. Stöhr (1969) "Urbanization, Regional Development, and South American Integration." American Behavioral Scientist (May).

Quijano, A. (1967) "Urbanización y Tendencias de Cambio en la Sociedad Rural." Santiago: División de Asuntos Sociales, CEPAL (April).

Rogers, E. M. (1962) Diffusion of Innovations. New York: The Free Press.

Schnore, L. (1965) "On the Spatial Structure of Cities in the Two Americas." In P. M. Hauser and L. F. Schnore (eds.) The Study of Urbanization. New York: John Wiley and Sons, Inc.

Stanford Research Institute et al. (1968) Costs of Urban Infrastructure for Industry as related to City Size in Developing Countries. India Case Study (October).

Wingo, Jr., L. (1967) "Recent Patterns of Urbanization Among Latin American Countries." Urban Affairs Quarterly 2, no. 3 (March): 81–110.

Youngson, A. J. (1967) Overhead Capital. A Study in Developmental Economics. Edinburgh: University Press.

Ziolkowski, J. (1967) "Sociological Problems of Regional Development." Proceedings of the First Scandinavian-Polish Regional Science Seminar. Warsaw: PWN—Polish Scientific Publisher.

13. DEMOGRAPHIC PROJECTIONS AND THEIR IMPORTANCE IN PLANNING

ANA MARÍA ROTHMAN
Centro de Investigaciones Sociales, Instituto Torcuato di Tella, Buenos Aires

Introduction

All projections are, to a certain extent, only approximations—they indicate a tendency, a range within which actual values fluctuate, rather than precise predictions for specific years. And thus one may question the extent to which development planning should take population projections into account. But while increasing time spans expose absolute magnitudes to a growing probability of error, demographic projections are indispensable for planning in that they can anticipate structural changes.

Projected population growth is certainly relevant for estimating future demand volume and the structure of the labor force and student population, as well as all manner of needs like housing and foodstuffs. However, overall demographic projections are not adequate by themselves—other variables must be considered besides age and sex structure, such as the population's changing urban–rural composition and development related changes in behavior patterns.

Demographic analysis, therefore, though it has limitations, is nonetheless important in formulating development programs. Latin America's basic demographic data, especially those derived from censuses, have improved significantly in the past twenty years. But the information remains inadequate for such ends as projecting trends for specific subgroups or for certain characteristics of the population such as the urban–rural dichotomy. The first part of this study summarizes the demographic situation expected in Latin America and its diverse regions around 2000, as well as placing the continent in a world perspective. Given the great discrepancies between Latin America's population structures, aggregate figures have only relative value. Notable variations exist even within the region's subzones, linked to different socioeconomic situations; any planning study analyzing demographic factors in relation to socioeconomic variables should consider each country individually.

With this in mind, our analyses of possible demographic repercussions on such variables as education or economic participation are limited to Argentina, for which there are population projections by sex and five-year age groups from 1960 to 2000, and which with Uruguay represents a unique situation in Latin America in terms of the current demographic transition.

LATIN AMERICA IN 2000

In 1963–64, the United Nations Secretariat used recent information, including census results from around 1960, to estimate world population by regions for the period 1960–2000. (This study, entitled: United Nations: *Les Perspectives d'Avenir de la Population Mondiale evaluées en 1963. Etudes Demographiques* ST/SOA/Series A/41, was published in 1966.)

The UN study includes "weak," "median," and "strong" estimates; we will consider only the "median" series, the most plausible considering each region's past and present characteristics.

Chart 1 gives population data for the world's seven main regions for 1960, 1980, and 2000; it also includes information for Latin America's four subzones. As these estimates show, Latin America's 212.4 million inhabitants of 1960, corresponding to 7.1 percent of the world population, held fifth place among the regions (Chart 2). The continent's population is expected to increase most up to the year 2000, tripling, and advancing to third place among the seven regions. The total will be 638.1 million, or 10.4 percent of world population (Chart 2).

Chart 1 Estimated Population For World Regions (1960-1980-2000)
(In Thousands)

Regions	Years		
	1960	1980	2000
World Total	2,988,180	4,330,037	6,129,734
Asia	1,659,391	2,461,355	3,457,918
Europe	424,657	479,391	526,968
USSR	214,400	277,800	353,085
Africa	272,924	448,869	767,779
North America	198,664	261,629	354,007
Latin America	212,431	378,437	638,111
Tropical South America	112,479	209,506	361,985
Central America	46,811	90,433	165,901
Temperate South America	32,796	46,221	60,514
Antilles	20,345	32,277	49,711
Oceania	15,713	22,556	31,866

SOURCE: United Nations, "Les Perspectives d'Avenir de la Population Mondiale," ST/SOA/SERIES A/41. Appendix 3, Table A3.2, p. 152.

Average annual growth for all of Latin America, 2.84 percent in the period 1960-65, the world's highest, is expected to decline to 2.41 percent by the end of the century, when it will rank second to Africa's (Chart 3).

Growth rates in Latin America's four subzones will vary widely. The fastest increase will occur in Central America, with rates of 3.2 percent per year between 1960 and 1965, and 2.8 percent in 1995-2000. At the other extreme, South America's temperate zone shows 1.8 percent growth in the first period, and 1.3 percent at the end of the century.

Changes in fertility and mortality explain growth trends and levels; migrations may also have an effect, though their expected actual importance will range between slight and negligible.

Chart 2 Regional Proportions of World Population and Subregional Proportions of Latin American Population (1960–1980–2000)

	Years		
Regions	1960	1980	2000
World Total	100.0	100.0	100.0
Asia	55.3	56.9	56.4
Europe	14.2	11.1	8.6
USSR	7.2	6.4	5.8
Africa	9.1	10.4	12.5
North America	6.6	6.0	5.8
Latin America	7.1	8.7	10.4
Oceania	0.5	0.5	0.5
Latin America	100.0	100.0	100.0
Tropical South America	53.0	55.4	56.7
Central America	22.0	23.9	26.0
Temperate South America	15.4	12.2	9.5
Antilles	9.6	8.5	7.8

SOURCE: Chart 1

The projections all assume declining mortality, in regions where rates are already low (Europe, the USSR, North America) as well as in those with high mortality in 1960 (Africa, Asia, and Latin America)—the sharpest drop is expected in Latin America. This decline is not apparent in crude mortality rates derived from projections for regions like Europe and the Soviet Union, due to their "older" age structures.

Fertility levels generally lower than 1960's are expected at the end of the century, though crude birth rates will remain high in regions like Africa (40 per thousand in 1995–2000), South Asia (27 per thousand), and Latin America (30 per thousand).

Within Latin America, birth rates likely in 2000 range widely from Central America's 32.6 per thousand to temperate South America, whose 21.0 per thousand will approximate North America's 22.2 per thousand.

Chart 3 Average Annual Regional Growth Rates, According to Estimated Populations

(Percent)*

	Periods		
Regions	1960-65	1980-85	1995-2000
World Average	1.80	1.84	1.64
Asia	1.93	1.86	1.54
Europe	0.72	0.51	0.43
USSR	1.49	1.32	1.06
Africa	2.30	2.67	2.68
North America	1.41	1.58	1.45
Latin America	2.84	2.81	2.41
Tropical South America	3.09	2.95	2.50
Central America	3.16	3.30	2.76
Temperate South America	1.84	1.48	1.28
Antilles	2.22	2.30	2.00
Oceania	1.76	1.90	1.59

*Calculated with the formula: $r = \dfrac{P_t - P_o}{P_t + P_o} \cdot \dfrac{2}{t}$

SOURCE: United Nations, "Les Perspectives d'Avenir de la Population Mondiale", ST/SOA/SERIES A/41.

The previously cited levels of and variations in demographic rates in large degree determine each country's age structure, and are in turn influenced by this. Chart 4 details population distribution by major age groups for 1960, 1980, and 2000.

Population under 15 varied between 26 percent and 46 percent of the total in 1960, with the high value corresponding to Central America; those 65 and over ranged between 3 percent and

Chart 4 Population Structure by Major Age Groups for World Regions (1960–1980–2000)
(% of Total Population in Each Age Group)

Regions	0–14 years			15–64 years			65 years and over		
	1960	1980	2000	1960	1980	2000	1960	1980	2000
World Average	36.4	35.8	32.4	58.7	58.4	61.2	4.9	5.8	6.4
East Asia	36.6	32.2	26.5	59.7	62.4	66.1	4.2	5.4	7.4
South Asia	41.0	41.7	34.6	55.9	54.7	60.9	3.1	3.6	4.6
Europe	25.7	23.0	22.9	64.5	63.9	64.0	9.8	13.1	13.1
USSR	30.8	26.1	27.1	63.0	64.4	61.7	6.2	9.5	11.2
Africa	43.1	43.6	42.3	54.2	53.6	54.5	2.7	2.8	3.2
North America	31.3	29.9	29.8	59.7	60.7	61.3	9.0	9.4	8.9
Latin America	41.7	42.1	38.0	55.0	53.9	57.7	3.3	3.9	4.3
Tropical South America	43.1	43.6	38.8	54.2	52.9	57.3	2.7	3.5	3.9
Central America	45.5	45.3	40.5	51.1	51.5	56.0	3.4	3.2	3.5
Temperate South America	32.5	30.7	27.9	62.6	61.9	63.2	4.9	7.4	8.9
Antilles	39.9	40.0	35.5	56.2	55.9	59.8	3.9	4.1	4.7
Oceania	31.7	30.8	31.6	60.5	60.9	59.9	7.8	8.3	8.5

SOURCE: United Nations, "Les Perspectives d'Avenir de la Population Mondiale" ST/-
SOA/SERIES 4/41. Chap. 7, Table 7.4, p. 40.

10 percent; and the "active" age group (15–64) accounted for between 51 percent and 65 percent, the low value corresponding to Central America.

In 2000, the under-15 age group will vary between 23 percent and 42 percent of the population; the 65 and over age group between 3 percent and 13 percent; and the 15–64 age group between 55 percent and 66 percent. Latin America will thus participate in the general trend toward relatively fewer minors and greater weight in the active group, although the wide variations just cited indicate considerable intraregional differences.

In 1960, the highest value for the relation between potentially active population and economically dependent population (persons under 15 or 65 and over) was Central America's 953 dependents per thousand actives between the ages of 15 and 64. Temperate South America reached only 599 per thousand, not far from levels in Europe, the Soviet Union, and North America.

This high dependency quotient is expected to decline sharply by 2000, reaching 784 per thousand in Central America and 734 per thousand in Latin America as a whole. Discrepancies within the region will decrease, since zones with low levels in 1960 will show little further decline due to their "aging" populations.

The great differences between Latin America's subzones merit special note with regard to the demographic situation in 2000. According to the "median" projection, which assumes continued mortality decline and a moderate drop in fecundity, two sharply contrasting zones will persist in 2000.

Crude birth rates in tropical South America and Central America will average around 32 per thousand, with crude death rates about 6 per thousand, and growth of 2.5 per thousand. In contrast, temperate South America's birth rate will average 21 per thousand; her crude death rate, 8.5 per thousand; and overall growth, 1.25 per thousand.

These differences will generate contrasting age structures; in 2000, those between 0 and 14 will range between 41 percent of the total population in Central America and 30 percent in temperate South America; and those 65 and over between 3.5 percent and 9 percent for the respective zones.

Notable national variations in association with varying socioeconomic conditions are to be expected even within these contrasting demographic zones. As we have noted, any attempt to correlate demographic variables with socioeconomic factors for planning purposes should treat each country separately. Projections by age and sex for individual countries are presently available only up to 1980, though the Latin American Demographic Center is working to extend them to 2000. The following section, as an example, uses projections for Argentina to analyze population growth and its repercussions on two important planning variables: labor force and education.

ARGENTINA'S PROJECTED POPULATION

This study is based on projected population by sex and age groups from 1960 to 2000, elaborated in the light of past trends of mortality, fecundity, and migrations, and on the base of the 1960 census as differentially corrected for omissions according to sex, age, and origin. [1]

Historical trends reveal more or less pronounced declines in fertility and mortality, both of which reached relatively low levels in the period 1960–65 (crude birth rate 23 per thousand, crude death rate 9 per thousand). Nonetheless, recent tendencies and socioeconomic conditions suggest that the decrease will continue.

The projection thus assumes: a) declining mortality, with life expectancy at birth (e) of 66.5 years for both sexes between 1960 and 1965, reaching 70.3 years by the period 1995–2000; b) a constant crude reproduction rate of 1.53 up to 1975–80, followed by a decline to 1.15 in 2000; c) net annual immigration of 25,000 persons from 1965 on.

Chart 5 gives the projection's results by sex and five-year age groups for 1960, 1980, and 2000.

Chart 6 shows gross birth and death, migration, and overall growth rates for the initial period, 1960–65; the middle period, 1980–85; and the end period, 1995–2000.

Chart 5 Argentina: Projected Population by Sex and Age Groups (1960–1980-2000)

(In Thousands, on June 30)

Age Groups	Both Sexes			Males			Females		
	1960	1980	2000	1960	1980	2000	1960	1980	2000
0 — 4	2,254	2,925	3,054	1,159	1,488	1,559	1,095	1,437	1,495
5 — 9	2,166	2,764	3,027	1,103	1,405	1,545	1,063	1,359	1,482
10 — 14	1,980	2,549	2,996	1,006	1,295	1,529	974	1,254	1,467
15 — 19	1,761	2,346	2,970	890	1,191	1,515	871	1,155	1,455
20 — 24	1,635	2,248	2,927	831	1,155	1,488	804	1,093	1,439
25 — 29	1,612	2,175	2,768	818	1,108	1,405	794	1,067	1,363
30 — 34	1,617	1,988	2,545	815	1,011	1,293	802	977	1,252
35 — 39	1,504	1,767	2,336	759	894	1,185	745	873	1,151
40 — 44	1,273	1,620	2,213	638	823	1,133	635	797	1,080
45 — 49	1,195	1,561	2,100	601	786	1,060	594	775	1,040
50 — 54	1,075	1,509	1,865	551	744	931	524	765	934
55 — 59	901	1,331	1,584	470	644	772	431	687	812
60 — 64	691	1,046	1,353	354	488	644	337	558	709
65 — 69	501	885	1,178	258	401	537	243	484	641
70 — 74	352	681	988	175	302	423	177	379	565
75 — 79	196	453	703	92	198	282	104	255	421
80 — 84	91	238	391	39	97	144	52	141	247
85 and over	46	132	276	18	48	89	28	84	187
TOTAL	20,850	28,218	35,274	10,577	14,078	17,534	10,273	14,140	17,740

SOURCE: CONADE, Instituto Nacional de Estadística y Censos.*Proyección quinquenal de la población 1965-2000.* Buenos Aires.

Declining average annual growth, from 15.7 per thousand in 1960–65 to 9.5 per thousand toward the end of the century, results from the combination of decreasing natality (from 23.4 to 18 per thousand in the forty years) and the expected trend of mortality.

Because of Argentina's elderly age structure, the real decline in mortality indicated by the already cited figures for life expectancy at birth is not apparent in crude mortality rates, which will have climbed from 1960–65's 8.8 per thousand to 9.4 per thousand by the end of the century.

Age structure by major groups reveals how lower natality will "age" the population—between 1980 and 2000, importance of the

Chart 6 Argentina: Crude Natality, Mortality, Migratory Growth, and Overall Growth Rates, Derived from the Population Projection (1960-1965/1980-85/1995-2000)

(Per Thousand)

Both Sexes	1960-1965	1980-1985	1995-2000
Natality	23.36	21.02	18.11
Mortality	8.84	8.92	9.35
Migration	1.15	0.86	0.73
Growth	15.67	12.96	9.49
Life Expectancy at birth (years)	66.5	69.6	70.3

SOURCE: CONADE, Instituto Nacional de Estadística y Censos. *Proyección quinquenal de la población 1965-2000. Buenos Aires.*

0-14 and 15-64 age groups will decrease relative to that of the 65 and over age group.

SOME IMPLICATIONS OF ARGENTINE POPULATION GROWTH FOR ITS ECONOMICALLY ACTIVE AND STUDENT POPULATIONS.

The demographic variables we have considered have varying impact on sex and age structure; we must focus our attention on the latter to study the demographic aspects of, for example, economically active and student populations.

The Economically Active Population

The potential economically active population can be considered that between ages 15 and 64. Argentina's projected population to 2000 affords the following observations about this group:

1. Its proportion with respect to total population will climb slightly, from 63.6 percent in 1960 to 64.3 percent in 2000 (both sexes.) (See Chart 7.)

Chart 7 Argentina: Population Structure by Sex and Major Age Groups and Dependency Quotient (1960–1980–2000)

	Age Groups											
	0 — 14			15 — 64			65 and over			Dependency Quotient		
Years	1960	1980	2000	1960	1980	2000	1960	1980	2000	1960	1980	2000
Sex	(Proportion in each age group)									(Percent)		
Both Sexes	30.7	29.2	25.7	63.6	62.3	64.3	5.7	8.5	10.0	57.2	60.4	55.7
Males	30.9	29.7	26.4	63.6	62.9	65.2	5.5	7.4	8.4	57.2	59.2	53.5
Females	30.5	28.6	25.1	63.6	61.9	63.3	5.9	9.5	11.6	57.2	61.7	57.9

SOURCE: Chart 5

2. Although the general trend is toward slower increase in both total population and that of the active age group, the 15 to 64 group will grow faster than total population in the periods 1980–85 and 1995–2000. (See Chart 8.)

3. The relationship between those of active ages and those outside this group is the "dependency quotient." In Argentina, this figure was 57.2 percent in 1960; it will decline slowly toward 2000, since lower natality and fewer minors will compensate for the large relative increase among those over 65. (See Chart 7.)

   This dependency quotient is quite low with respect to Latin America's overall level of 80 percent in 1960. However, the calculation underestimates the true "dependency level," the full weight of inactive persons on the working population, since within the productive age group there is considerable unemployment and underemployment among males, and only a small percentage of working women.

4. This last point shows that the analysis must be extended by projecting the economically active population by sex and ages to measure more accurately the structural variations within the active group.

Chart 8 Growth of Total Population and of Population in Active and Student Age Groups (1960–1965/1980–1985/1955–2000)

Population by Age and Sex	GROWTH RATES* (PER THOUSAND)		
	1960–1965	1980–1985	1995–2000
TOTAL POPULATION			
Both Sexes	15.62	12.95	9.50
Male	14.51	12.59	9.47
Female	16.77	13.32	9.53
POPULATION 15–64			
Both Sexes	15.49	13.42	11.96
Male	14.42	13.50	12.08
Female	16.60	13.33	11.84
POPULATION 6-12	10.80	13.40	1.95
POPULATION 13–18	23.09	17.47	2.20
POPULATION 6–18	16.14	15.18	2.06

*Calculated with the formula: $r = \dfrac{P_t - P_o}{P_t + P_o} \cdot \dfrac{2}{t}$

For methodological purposes, two projections were made for the economically active population. The first assumes constant activity rates, so that variations in the economically active population reflect only changes in population structure; the second assumes variable activity rates, to analyze the combined effect of demographic variables and of changing activity patterns.

Two hypotheses were made with respect to activity rates: hypothesis A, with constant rates equal to those calculated from 1960 census data; and hypothesis B, with variable rates. Variable activity rates were projected considering activity patterns by age and sex in 1947 and 1960, and the changes during the intercensal period. The evolution of these rates in more highly developed countries is also pertinent. Reduced male activity rates among those under 20 and higher levels among those over 54 are expected by the end of the century. Female activity is harder to predict, since social mores as well as industrialization levels and forms of the productive structure are involved. Nonetheless, a growing activity rate is anticipated during the rest of the century; relatively large changes are likely in female rates and patterns. (See Chart 9.)

Chart 9 Argentina: Activity Rates by Sex and Age, Calculated for 1947 and 1960 and Projected for 1980 and 2000

Age	Sex and Year	Males				Females			
		1947	1960	1980	2000	1947	1960	1980	2000
10-14		5.9	5.19*	4.10	0.80	3.5	2.84*	1.80	0.80
15-19		76.8	75.57	72.40	59.40	36.7	34.78	32.10	26.70
20-24		91.0	93.61	91.50	90.40	31.3	40.06	41.82	43.60
25-34		96.3	97.95	96.70	96.70	22.3	26.99	28.00	32.00
35-44		97.8	97.74	97.74	97.74	21.6	22.15	28.40	35.20
45-54		96.4	91.59	95.90	95.90	19.5	17.64	26.60	33.10
55-64		87.9	65.67	72.20	78.70	14.2	10.75	19.00	23.60
65 and over		57.7	38.61	37.70	36.10	7.3	5.20	6.40	7.90
Gross Activity Rate	Constant Hypothesis			59.31	61.87			16.08	16.59
	Variable Hypothesis	59.46	59.50	60.95			16.56	18.60	21.56

SOURCE: 1947: United Nations, Aspectos demográficos de la mano de obra, ST/SOA/SERIES A/33, pp. 61, 64.
1960: Calculated from 1960 census data.
1980: Males—Average activity patterns for industrialized countries in 1950 were used as a model.
Females—the 1950 average for the U.S. and Canada was used as a model.
2000: Males—French model, 1954.
Females—U.S. model, 1950.
*Estimated value, since the census only registered actives of 14 and over.

Chart 10 offers projections for the economically active population with constant rates (hypothesis A) and variable rates (hypothesis B), by age groups and sex, as well as proportional distributions for 1960, 1980, and 2000.

Changes in the first projection are due exclusively to variations in age structure. These are minor, with a relative increase in the number of those over 55, due to the population's aging, and near-constant levels for men and women. And thus the growth rate of the economically active population projected with constant rates for the three periods considered—1960–65, 1980–85, and 1995–2000—closely parallels that of population in active ages (15–64) for the same periods. (See Charts 8 and 11.)

However, the projection assuming variable rates—hypothesis B—reflects changes in both age structure and patterns and levels of participation. Not only do proportions of the active population in certain age groups vary (less in that under 20, more in that over 55), but there is also a sex differential.

Significantly faster growth of the economically active female population is anticipated using variable rates. (See Chart 11.) By 2000, the economically active female population will have grown by 126 percent over 1960 levels, as compared with only 71 percent for males.

To conclude, major changes in Argentina's economically active population produced by structural changes in the population's sex and age are not likely before the end of the century, according to expected trends in basic demographic components like mortality and fecundity, though these may have greater impact over a longer period. Changes which may occur will result from new patterns of participation in economic activity, directly related to industrialization and urbanization, as well as to new work laws and legislation on such matters as the length of obligatory education.

Student Population

School-aged population will be considered in two groups. The first includes ages 6 to 12, or elementary school age; the second includes ages 13 to 18 and is more closely linked to secondary

Chart 10 Argentina: Projection of Economically Active Population, by Sex and Age (1960–1980–2000) (Hypothesis A: Constant Rates; Hypothesis B: Variable Rates)

Sex and Age Groups	Hypothesis A						Hypothesis B			
	1960		1980		2000		1980		2000	
	Abs.	%	Abs.	%	Abs.	%	Abs.	%	Abs.	%
Both Sexes										
10–14	80	1.0	103	1.0	121	1.0	76	0.7	24	0.2
15–19	976	12.2	1,302	12.3	1,651	12.0	1,233	11.2	1,288	8.9
20–24	1,100	13.8	1,519	14.3	1,969	14.3	1,514	13.8	1,972	13.6
25–34	2,031	25.4	2,628	24.6	3,349	24.3	2,621	23.7	3,446	23.6
35–44	1,671	20.9	2,048	19.3	2,760	20.0	2,152	19.5	3,051	21.0
45–54	1,252	15.7	1,673	15.7	2,172	15.7	1,877	17.1	2,562	17.7
55–64	624	7.8	877	8.3	1,094	7.9	1,054	9.6	1,473	10.2
65 and over	256	3.2	474	4.5	676	4.9	480	4.4	695	4.8
TOTAL	7,990	100.0	10,624	100.0	13,792	100.0	11,007	100.0	14,511	100.0
Males										
10–14	52	0.8	67	0.8	79	0.7	53	0.6	12	0.1
15–19	673	10.7	900	10.8	1,145	10.6	862	10.3	900	8.4

20-24	778	12.4	1,081	12.9	1,393	12.8	1,057	12.6	1,345	12.6
25-34	1,600	25.4	2,076	24.9	2,643	24.4	2,049	24.5	2,609	24.4
35-44	1,365	21.7	1,678	20.1	2,266	20.9	1,678	20.0	2,266	21.2
45-54	1,055	16.8	1,401	16.8	1,824	16.8	1,467	17.5	1,909	17.9
55-64	541	8.6	743	8.9	930	8.6	817	9.8	1,114	10.4
65 and over	225	3.6	404	4.8	569	5.2	394	4.7	532	5.0
TOTAL	6,289	100.0	8,350	100.0	10,849	100.0	8,377	100.0	10,687	100.0
Females										
10-14	28	1.6	36	1.6	42	1.4	23	0.9	12	0.3
15-19	303	17.8	402	17.7	506	17.2	371	14.1	388	10.1
20-24	322	18.9	438	19.2	576	19.6	457	17.4	627	16.4
25-34	431	25.4	552	24.2	706	24.0	572	21.7	837	21.9
35-44	306	18.0	370	16.3	494	16.8	474	18.0	785	20.5
45-54	197	11.6	272	12.0	348	11.8	410	15.6	653	17.1
55-64	83	4.9	134	5.9	164	5.6	237	9.0	359	9.4
65 and over	31	1.8	70	3.1	107	3.6	86	3.3	163	4.3
TOTAL	1,701	100.0	2,274	100.0	2,943	100.0	2,630	100.0	3,824	100.0

SOURCE: Charts 5 and 9.

Chart 11 Projected Growth of Economically Active Population: 1) With Constant Rates, Hypothesis A; 2) With Variable Rates, Hypothesis B (1960-1965; 1980-1985; 1995-2000)

Active Population	Growth Rates [a] (Per Thousand)		
	1960-1965	1980-1985	1995-2000
HYPOTHESIS A			
Both Sexes	14.92	13.25	12.10
Males	14.62	13.20	12.35
Females	16.03	13.43	11.18
HYPOTHESIS B			
Both Sexes	16.67	13.99	13.17
Males	14.76	12.29	11.67
Females	23.56	19.19	17.41

a) Calculated from the formula $r = \dfrac{P_t - P_o}{P_t + P_o} \cdot \dfrac{2}{t}$

school attendance, future university demand, and the future labor pool.

The growth of the age 6-12 population resembles that of the population as a whole in 1960-65 and 1980-85, while the age 13-18 group grows more quickly, reaching its highest level—23.1 per thousand—in the first period. (See Chart 8.) This results from the transitory natality increase between 1945 and 1950, survivors of which formed part of the age 13-18 group in 1960-65. This generation will weigh heavily on the educational system and contribute to an elevated labor pool.

But in the long run, the assumptions of declining natality after 1975 will be reflected in the school-aged population in both subgroups. The growth of the age 6-12 population between 1995 and 2000, 1.95 per thousand, is markedly below that registered in the middle and initial periods, as well as beneath the overall growth rate toward the end of the century (9.5 per thousand). (See Chart 8.)

Chart 12   Argentina: School-aged Population of Both Sexes[a]
(In Thousands)

Age	1960	1980	2000
6	440	561	607
7	434	553	605
8	428	545	604
9	421	536	603
10	413	527	602
11	405	519	600
12	397	510	599
6 to 12	2,938	3,751	4,220
13	387	501	598
14	378	492	597
15	368	484	596
16	359	474	595
17	351	467	594
18	344	462	593
13 to 18	2,187	2,880	3,573
6 to 18	5,125	6,631	7,793

a) Population by five-year age groups was opened to intermediate ages using Sprague's multipliers.
SOURCE: Conade, Instituto Nacional de Estadística y Censos, op. cit.

In addition to trends in demographic components and the resulting age structure, changes in student population depend on patterns of school attendance. Argentina's 1960 enrollment rates (the proportion of persons of a given age attending elementary or secondary school) for specific ages from 6 to 19 were used to project student population; rates of an economically developed country like France in 1954 were accepted as theoretically attainable for 2000, and linear progress was assumed between the two levels. Chart 13 gives estimated enrollment levels for 1960, 1980, and 2000. Chart 14 contrasts constant enrollment rates, hypothesis A, and variable rates, hypothesis B. The first series signals the increase in students expected from demographic growth alone—44 percent between 1960 and 2000. The second estimate measures the increase which will occur if educational authorities undertake a thirty-year program to match attendance levels of economically developed countries, and if school-aged population grows as anticipated.

Chart 13 Argentina: Estimated Rates of Primary and Secondary Enrollment (1960–1980–2000)

Age	1960	1980	2000
6	89.2	94.2	99.3
7	90.0	94.7	99.4
8	94.1	96.6	99.2
9	92.8	95.9	99.2
10	92.9	95.9	99.1
11	86.9	92.8	98.7
12	87.0	92.7	98.4
13	70.6	84.4	98.1
14	60.1	63.1	66.0
15	41.6	45.6	49.6
16	31.4	36.4	41.4
17	22.2	23.5	24.7
18	12.8	12.8	12.8

SOURCE: 1960: Conade Sector Educación, 1980–2000: Tasas Proyectadas en Función de las Tasas en 1960 y las Tasas "Teóricas" Adoptadas para el Año 2000 a saber: Tasas de Escolaridad por Edad, Totales de Enseñanza Primaria y Media Registrados en Francia 1954.

Chart 14 Argentina: Projected Primary and Secondary Student Population (Hypothesis A: Constant Rates; Hypothesis B: Variable Rates)
(In Thousands)

Age	1960	Hypothesis A		Hypothesis B	
		1980	2000	1980	2000
6	392	500	541	528	603
7	391	498	545	524	602
8	403	513	568	526	599
9	391	497	560	514	598
10	384	490	559	505	597
11	352	451	521	482	592
12	345	444	521	473	589
6 to 12	2,658	3,393	3,815	3,552	4,180
13	273	354	422	423	587
14	227	296	359	310	394
15	153	201	248	221	296
16	113	149	187	173	246
17	78	104	132	110	147
18	44	59	76	59	76
13 to 18	888	1,163	1,424	1,296	1,746
6 to 18	3,546	4,556	5,239	4,848	5,926

SOURCE: Charts 12 and 13.

The effect of increased enrollment rates in the period 1995–2000 is clear in a comparison of results for the two hypotheses. (See Chart 15.) Argentina's primary school enrollment, already around 90 percent in 1960, will change relatively little. Larger increases are to be expected in secondary enrollment rates, corresponding to the age 13–18 group. Overall, projected student population for 2000 will have increased by 67 percent over 1960 levels.

Chart 15   Argentina: Growth of Primary and Secondary Student Population According to Hypotheses A and B.

(Rates Per Thousand)
1960 -1965/1980-1985/1995-2000

		Hypothesis A		Hypothesis B	
Age	1960-1965	1980-1985	1995-2000	1980-1985	1995-2000
6 to 12	10.62	13.44	1.90	15.64	4.11
13 to 18	22.53	17.28	1.98	22.43	6.52
6 to 18	13.67	14.43	1.92	17.48	4.82

SOURCE: Chart 14.

But neither these projected increases, nor larger ones, can negate the absolute limit on school-aged population set by the anticipated drop in natality.

SOME FINAL CONSIDERATIONS

All Latin American development efforts must be undertaken with full awareness of the impact of changing fertility and mortality on population composition by age, sex, activity, and so on.

The continent's varying population structures mean that aggregate figures have only relative value. The probable evolution of Argentina's population and its consequences for the economically active and student populations analyzed in this work may well apply for Uruguay, another country with low birth, death, and growth rates. The Argentine case may also prove illustrative for countries with moderate growth like Chile and Cuba. But the other Latin American countries, representing 80 percent of the region's population, are characterized by totally contrasting demographic conditions. Rapid growth in these nations results from swiftly declining mortality and high and constant fecundity, which generates a population constantly rejuvenating itself.

Such significant demographic variations within Latin America reflect different levels of development; projections must consider the interrelations between demographic factors and socioeconomic variables. These include both demographic consequences of economic development and the possible impact of changing demographic components on economic variables. Those who project the effects of industrialization on fecundity and mortality have generally assumed a process similar to that in Europe or the United States. But probably more pertinent now is independent study of Latin America's experience. Rather than limiting itself to the region's most developed countries, such analysis should focus on each country individually, for example, by contrasting urban and rural zones.

But this requires trustworthy and complete basic information, for units as well as aggregates. The task now before us is to collect and analyze this information.

NOTES

1. CONADE, Instituto Nacional de Estadística. *Proyección quinquenal de la población 1965-2000.* Buenos Aires.

14. POPULATION AND DEVELOPMENT

BENJAMÍN SAMAMÉ P.

Ministerio de Trabajo, Lima

INTRODUCTION

Predicting the future is risky, especially in this age of intense social change and of man's growing dominion over nature and attempts to conquer the cosmos. Prediction carries the twin risks of conservatism, with the mere projection of present conditions; and of the illusion that in 2000 Latin America will know peace, happiness, and prosperity.

Nonetheless, we must face the responsibility of building the future from the present. More than just trying to imagine Latin America in 2000, we must consider the concrete steps needed, starting now, to attain levels of social wellbeing consistent with human dignity.

We begin with the following premise: we aspire to a democratic Latin America, with neither marginal sectors nor privileged castes, with equal opportunities, and with per capita income—the means of access to subsistence and culture—reflecting a generally high standard of living, rather than masking huge inequities.

Achieving an improved future demands immediate and concrete efforts to rationalize the process of change, to program measures for development, and to encourage Latin Americans in individual and social fulfillment.

Human beings are the actors and beneficiaries of development. We are witnessing a growing demographic consciousness, in the large sense of concern for man's location and condition on earth. The philosophy of social action is being organized around this same consideration.

LATIN AMERICA'S PRESENT SITUATION

Latin America extends from the Río Grande to Cape Horn and occupies about 21 million km^2, nearly one-fifth of the earth's land mass.

Geography and history are the two great challenges confronting today's Latin Americans. Nature, dominated by the Andean mass and huge jungles, is a major obstacle to both communications and human development. Desert, forest, and mountain barriers isolate populations and make the region more an archipelago than a continent.

Latin America's modern history dates from the rise of the West and its capitalist economy. This system has unleashed enormous natural forces, expanded production by incalculable dimensions, and substantially modified existing life styles—its great sin has been the attempt to bring all people within its dictates. Latin America has played a passive role in the world capitalist system, as a consumer area and a supplier of raw materials. Normal development has been distorted, and the economy has been adapted to the interests and needs of the industrialized nations. It now forms part of Myrdal's "submerged" world—submerged in ignorance, backwardness, and misery. Latin America is joining the other underdeveloped nations which, despite scientific and technological advances, are falling further and further behind the developed countries.

Recent figures put the region's annual population growth rate at 3 percent; growth is slower on other continents with higher mortality or with birth and death rates both low—2.3 percent for Africa, 2.2 percent for Asia, 1.8 percent for Oceania, 1.1 percent for North America, and 0.7 percent for Europe.

Latin American demographic growth rates exceed 3 percent per year in 14 countries; only Argentina, Uruguay, Jamaica, and

Barbados are growing at less than 2 percent annually. Area population will double in just 24 years, and in most of the region's countries, like El Salvador, Costa Rica, Honduras, Mexico, Nicaragua, the Dominican Republic, Venezuela, Ecuador, Panama, Brazil, Colombia, Guatemala, Paraguay, and Peru, the time will be even less. Comparable figures for developed areas are markedly higher—63 years in the USA, USSR, and Japan; 100 years in Finland, Bulgaria, and Europe as a whole; 117 years in West Germany, Belgium, and Rumania. At the present rate, Latin America's 270 million inhabitants will increase to 700 million by 2000.

Economic development statistics are discouraging in the light of these figures. As Luis Escobár has indicated; "Latin America's Gross National Product has grown by an average of 4.4 percent per year, but rapid population increase cuts this figure to just 1.6 percent per capita. The average is not uniform; economic growth in some countries has slackened for reasons unrelated to population growth."

Food production has increased by about 2.5 percent annually during the past ten years, that is, less rapidly than population growth. Per capita daily caloric consumption is beneath FAO [United Nations Food and Agriculture Organization] regional minimums in more than twelve countries, and dietetic disparities between income groups aggravate the situation.

More than 60 percent of those entering the job market lack primary education. Only half of all school-aged children matriculate, and three-quarters of these drop out before completing their studies. Despite all that has been said and done since the Punta del Este Charter, these statistics reveal a disquieting situation.

GENERAL OBSERVATIONS

UN estimates for 2000 put world population around 7 billion, with 80 percent of this number in the presently underdeveloped continents. This unprecedented population growth, intensifying since the second half of the nineteenth century, has motivated endless speculation on such matters as the earth's capacity to house the human race, the availability of cultivable lands and energy sources, and so on. We are optimistic about humanity's prospects; despite its vicissitudes, the world's history is that of human progress. The Malthusian theory, as the noted sociologist and demographer Kingsley Davis has shown, "lacks validity now, and never had any." Human populations are substantially different from animal populations in having created culture, and man's prospects cannot be judged solely on the basis of a naturalistic or biological theory which simply relates population growth to food resources. But population is a grave problem at the regional level, since resources are frequently either unavailable, or unequally distributed between regions.

While a reduced proportion of world population enjoys high standards, four-fifths live in inadequate circumstances. Unjust social and economic distributions perpetuate and intensify the inequality of nations and of human beings, and the nations taking the most advantage of a civilization's benefits are growing less rapidly than those lacking indispensable resources.

SOLUTIONS

In an age when society is battling against death, it is no longer possible to contemplate increased mortality as the answer to food shortages and social ills. Nor is it possible to imitate the European countries which found international migration an escape valve for excess population in the eighteenth and nineteenth centuries, when millions resettled in America, Oceania, and other areas.

Only two possibilities remain—that underdeveloped countries increase productive capacity to meet population growth, and/or that they slow population growth by reducing birth rates.

Simplistic statements and misunderstandings abound with regard to this problem. The matter demands unprejudiced attention in international meetings like this one, where scientists can compare viewpoints and coordinate efforts to remedy the continent's ills in the hope of a more optimistic outlook for conditions in 2000.

In my opinion, there are two critical factors: 1. the meaning of population growth for Latin America; and 2. how to improve Latin American living standards. We oppose the widely held thesis that identifies the population explosion as the key obstacle to Latin American development. We disagree with Robert Mc-Namara when, as President of the World Bank, he referred to its studies and affirmed: "These studies demonstrate that the population explosion, above all, is obstructing growth in poor countries, further separating rich and poor countries, and accentuating the dangerous differences between them." Authorities from both the Americas have made even more emphatic declarations.

Latin America's backwardness, its inability to provide adequately for its population, are products of basic problems and of secondary factors which exacerbate these problems. The profound causes are economic and social, and respond to the continent's role within the capitalist world; they antedate the so-called "population explosion," which only characterizes the last forty years. And these profound causes persist and intensify, as reflected in the treatment of exports by industrialized countries, the constant drain of wealth and capital by foreign companies, the "brain drain", and the persistence of archaic structures which perpetuate traditional patterns of internal domination. Population growth aggravates these problems of stationary or slowly expanding economies, which often include deteriorating agricultural zones.

Ordering the causes in this manner is fundamental for orienting development policies. The continent will achieve little if population is regarded as a discrete and fundamentally medical problem to be solved by distributing contraceptives. Some sectors, disregarding or unwilling to face socioeconomic problems, seek an easy way out by advocating family planning as an isolated means. Their rationale is simple—if the economy is stationary or growing slowly, population growth must be adjusted to fit.

As the distinguished demographer Leon Tabah has rightly noted,

> birth control has provoked the strangest illusions in public opinion. In the United States and Europe, many imagine that merely imposing birth control will resolve the population problem. Believing thus, they often provoke violent and counterproductive reactions, even among those recognizing the need to limit births. But this may be of secondary importance. It has been proved that even when the

environment is favorable to reduced family size, systematic infecundity demands certain prior conditions: higher living standards, extended education, emancipation of women vis-a-vis spouses and society in general, and so on. These conditions are even more necessary insofar as every known contraceptive method requires an effort of self-control, a self-possession to be expected only in those really wanting to avoid children.

Latin Americans are often irritated by the cold rationalism of some family planning experts who, in international meetings, have compared childbirth costs with the birth control materials the same amount would have bought. This does not mean we oppose the use of contraceptives by persons so desiring; neither do we deny couples the right to limit or space their children; nor is our attitude to be construed as hostility to science for its achievements in regulating fecundity; and even less are we discounting the dangers of high population growth for Latin American development.

We only oppose the position that lowering birth rates is the sole short-range alternative for elevated living standards; that Latin America's ills are essentially due to population growth; that population is an isolated problem, and not part of an interrelated group of factors; that only family planning need be stressed, while direct stimuli to economic development are neglected.

A NEW CONCEPT IN POPULATION POLICIES

As a healthy reaction to the above considerations, and following work by Latin American social scientists who have been meeting under OAS auspices since 1967, a new concept of population policy is being developed. This new population policy cannot be formulated independently of an integral development policy, and thus it is not limited to family planning. By this concept; more concretely, population policy must be understood as a coherent set of decisions constituting a rational strategy, adopted by the public sector in accordance with the needs and aspirations of the collectivity, to develop, conserve, and utilize human resources, and thus influence the probable magnitude and growth of population, its age distribution, family composition, regional and rural-urban distributions, and availability of jobs and education, to the end of facilitating economic growth and participation in the responsibilities and benefits of progress. Furthermore; as long as perspectives of international economic cooperation do not improve, especially in the basic commodity trade on which Latin America's economy is largely dependent, development programs cannot meet full success.

A population policy only diffusing family planning methods could not resolve Latin America's problems of economic and social development. Even supposing that these measures were completely effective, a less rapid population growth rate would relieve no governments of the obligation of intensifying policies and programs for economic and social transformation. A population policy can only be successful in the context of other programs and policies involving such areas as land tenure and use; rational exploitation of natural resources; educational reform; more efficient health services; a better trained labor force; increased social, economic, and civic participation; urban and regional development; and, especially, improved income distribution.

FECUNDITY AND HUMAN FREEDOM

Specific considerations related to individual and family health and the right of all couples to determine their family's size in accordance with their present and future possibilities and with the level of well-being they wish to provide for their children are independent of the problems of social and economic development and of high population growth. The state and society, both of which have traditionally condemned those wanting to limit family size, cannot ignore these issues. The state must face the growing demand for information on sex problems and on the means for organizing family life without resorting to criminal practices like abortion and infanticide. In our opinion, Ministries of Public Health should assume the responsibility for providing these medical assistance services which, as induced abortions increase, are as essential as any others they provide.

CONCLUSIONS

1. Latin America urgently requires social and economic development to raise living standards; such development demands adequate planning, with active state participation.
2. The people are the actors and beneficiaries of development. In the light of rapid demographic growth, Latin American countries must incorporate clear population policies into their overall development programs.
3. Population policies must not just restrict themselves to birth control programs, but must be coherent sets of decisions forming a rational strategy adopted by the public sector, in accordance with the desires and needs of families and the collectivity, to influence directly probable population size, age structure, family size, and regional and rural-urban population distribution, to the end of facilitating other development goals.
4. A population policy can only be successful to the extent that living standards are raised and that sociocultural changes strengthen parental consciousness of responsibility for children.
5. The state should channel international birth control aid via Ministries of Public Health or Population Centers, to guarantee the suitability and correct application of methods, and to prevent the use of Latin America's population as a contraceptives laboratory.
6. The State should deepen its demographic knowledge, intensify the training of demographers, and actively foster a generalized demographic consciousness and adequate sex education.
7. To avoid induced abortions, the state should provide couples with medical assistance services through its Ministry of Public Health.

15. EDUCATION AND HOUSING: PRESENT DEFICITS AND PROSPECTS IN THE FACE OF POPULATION GROWTH

ALVARO GARCÍA PEÑA
Population Reference Bureau, Bogotá

INTRODUCTION

Latin American underdevelopment urgently demands profound and socially sensitive examination. While some irreversible features will certainly be discovered, elements of change must be found to alter the picture. Planning, for example, should incorporate ample, sensible, and balanced population policies which could make the development effort, including necessary structural reforms, truly effective. The future must be pondered not simply as an intellectual exercise, but to gain a clearer picture of the present and of current responsibilities.

The Population Reference Bureau, a private entity dedicated to information and education on population and development problems, has prepared this short study as a contribution to the Seventh Latin American Planning Congress. This work stresses two key development sectors—education and housing. First, though, a general analysis will outline the range of deficiencies in other areas.

Viewed in the light of demography, Latin America's development process is irremediably chaotic; and we do not consider ourselves alarmists. This study follows UN median demographic projections, which hypothesize a decline in fecundity levels from

29 to 24 per 1000 inhabitants. To emphasize that the development crisis cannot be solved by treating the demographic variable alone, housing projections have been made with the even more optimistic assumption that a 1 percent growth rate can be reached. Nonetheless, deficits will remain alarming at the beginning of the twenty-first century. Obviously these projections have not taken into account imponderables like scientific advances and new technology which might accelerate development. But the objective of this study is precisely to illustrate the extent of deficits and thereby emphasize the need for reorienting and dynamizing development. Not only is it necessary to speed the process, but effective structural reforms are needed to make it truly integral and beneficial to all groups.

THE DEMOGRAPHIC PERSPECTIVE

According to median UN projections, Latin American population will reach 638 million in 2000—the present 268 million will have multiplied 2.4 times. This calculation is based on the three determinants of population size: mortality, fecundity, and migration. The UN projections assume that mortality will continue to decline slowly, thus augmenting life expectancies; that fecundity will also gradually decline, though not before the 1980s; and that international migration will remain constant.

These changes in fecundity and mortality will modify the population structure. The fertility decline means that children between 0 and 4 years of age will barely double in number, from 44 to 88 million; instead of forming 16.6 percent of the population, they will only account for 13.8 percent. The 5–14 primary school-aged population will increase from 69 to 154 million, or by 123 percent, which is a growth rate slower than that for the population as a whole. The groups with the highest percentage growth, due to present high fecundity, will be the cohorts between 15 and 24 and between 25 and 44, constituting the labor force and the age groups of greatest reproductive power. Together these groups will increase by 158 percent, from 112 to 289 million; they will form 45.5 percent of total population in 2000, as compared with

41.8 percent at present. The group between 45 and 64 will also grow markedly, by 143 percent, to total 78 million by 2000. The highest percentage increase will occur in the 65 and over age group, which will expand from 10 to 27 million.

We are assuming that Latin America's population growth rate will decline from the present 2.9 percent to 2.4 percent. This will mean absolute annual growth of 15 million, while the current figure is just 7.7 million, with a smaller demographic base. Although a decrease in the population growth rate is anticipated by 2000, our population will still be increasing in absolute terms at double the present rate.

This central fact must figure in plans for reorienting the development process to meet demographic pressures of the end of the century. Among the characteristics of the present, explosively expanding population is its urbanizing trend—our population will be predominantly urban by the end of the century. The Organization of American States estimates that about 73 percent of total population will live in cities of 20,000 and over, leaving only 27 percent in the countryside. Urban population will total 466 million, while rural areas will only include 172 million—these figures represent 230 percent and 33 percent growth over present levels, respectively.

To summarize, Latin American population in 2000 will be 638 million, nearly 2.5 times larger than it is today. It will remain young, though less markedly so than at present, since the proportion under age 15 will have decreased from 42 to 38 percent. Of every ten inhabitants, seven (instead of the present five) will live in cities. Assuming that fecundity decreases, the demographic growth rate will slip from 2.9 percent to 2.4 percent. Even so, absolute annual increments will be 15 million.

Thus we have Latin America's demographic reality at the dawn of the twenty-first century. But statistics alone cannot fully depict the human drama, the social conflagrations, the pressures and political spasms of the next thirty-two years. The figures are better understood in terms of the economic and social demands that 638 million Latin Americans will make, and which planners must consider between now and 2000.

THE RANGE OF DEFICIENCIES

How great will be the needs of these 638 million people? How much must we advance, what radical changes must be made in the development process to provide this population adequate food, elementary medical services, jobs, education, and housing? What living standards can be considered acceptable? Should we be content with just satisfying subsistence needs, or should we attempt to increase living standards and improve the quality of life? Such questions are prompted by an analysis of our growing development deficits.

Nutrition

Our calculations for food needs assume that demand for foodstuffs will grow equally with population. Food supplies must thus increase by 140 percent by 2000 just to maintain present low nutritional standards. The demand for cereals, fruits, and milk products will increase by 33 million tons each over 1960 levels. Thirteen million more tons of sugar and meat will be needed. Agricultural experts assert that satisfying this demand alone will require an investment of $111 billion.[1]

To appreciate fully the magnitude of the effort to meet nutritional needs, it should be stressed that 180 million people, 70 percent of the population, presently subsist on protein-deficient diets.

Health

For the future's 638 million persons to enjoy even the inadequate medical care of the present, we will need 383,000 new doctors, 191,000 more nurses, 140,000 more dentists, and 2,042,000 additional hospital beds by 2000. This proportion of doctors and dentists to total population is still only half that of the United States. The unequal distribution between urban and rural Latin America makes the comparison even more unfavorable. In relative terms, we have only one-tenth as many nurses and a third as many hospital beds as the United States. If our goal is North

Table 1   Increase Needed in Agricultural Production

	1980 90% increase* (in millions of tons)	2000 200% increase† (in millions of tons)
Cereals	15	33.3
Fruits	15	33.3
Milk	15	33.3
Meat	6	13.3
Sugar	6	13.3

*IDB projections for 1980.
†1960 projects were used as a base; levels for 2000 were figured proportionally from the IDB projections for 90% increase by 1980.

America's high levels of medical services, in 2000 we will need a total of 880,000 doctors, 1,914,000 nurses, 314,000 dentists, and 5,870,000 hospital beds.

Labor

Full employment in 2000 will require 208 million new jobs; the labor force will have grown by 115 million.[2] It is presently estimated that about 35 percent of the potential labor force is unemployed or underemployed. Reducing this proportion of wasted human capital to 10 percent will demand 118 to 136 million new jobs for 2000.

Agricultural production only grows about as fast as population. Furthermore, per capita food production for internal consumption is declining.

Preparation of medical personnel and provision of hospital beds also progress more or less with population growth, though doctors increase at a slightly faster rate.

Stagnation characterizes the labor market in both rural and urban sectors. Each day more *campesinos* find themselves obliged to migrate to the cities, where they swell the number of unemployed.

These deficits reveal the urgency with which priorities must be reevaluated, new perspectives found, and emphasis put on integral development. Radical solutions are essential to close the ever widening gap between existing needs and their satisfaction. We will now look more specifically at education and housing. Education is the most important factor in development. Housing, for its part, is the sector most closely linked to pressures for higher living standards. In each case, the needs estimated for the 638 million Latin Americans of 2000 are astronomic. And, because of development's misorientation, prospects for satisfying these needs are slight.

Education

The Interamerican Development Bank signaled the critical importance of Latin American education in 1966, declaring:

> . . .human resources are the key to socioeconomic progress. This is especially important for Latin America, a region characterized by abundant physical resources but at the same time scarcity of capital and the world's highest demographic growth rates. These circumstances clearly demand that the growing population be trained, to foster social justice, best utilize available resources, and compensate for the lack of capital. . . Educational improvements are indispensable for the success of any socioeconomic development plan in the region. . . .

In 1963, the OAS study group on education stated: "The Punta del Este Charter foresaw a social and economic revolution which 20 nations have agreed to carry out... The more programs and goals are studied, the more apparent it becomes that education is the backbone of the Alliance for Progress."

What are the perspectives for education in 2000? The number of school-aged children between 5 and 14 will be 281 million, representing about the same proportion of total population as at present. However, the school-aged population in absolute terms will be three times larger. Clearly, all these 281 million children will not be able to attend school throughout their adolescence, but the proportion must and will be greater than at present. Otherwise, the region's economic and social plans cannot be fulfilled. The Alliance goal for 1975 is to matriculate 98 percent of all primary school-aged children; 35 percent of the secondary school-aged population, between 15 and 19; and 8.6 percent of the university-aged population. This growth of school-aged population and expected matriculation augurs a profound crisis for Latin America's educational system. The number of students will jump by a factor of 4.5, from the current 40 million students to an unprecedented 180 million. Primary school registration will quintuple from 33 to 151 million, and secondary enrollment will quadruple from 6 to 24 million. Universities will expand by 600 percent, from 800,000 to 5 million.

These figures suggest another question: what will meeting this enormous educational demand cost Latin American society? How much will it cost to create and equip schools? Where will financing come from for student texts and teacher's manuals? With what monies will teachers be hired?

According to UNESCO's model for annual education costs per student, Latin American education's minimum annual operating costs will be over 13 billion dollars at the end of the century. And UNESCO minimum calculations for the separate category of capital investments to care for 180 million students surpass an additional $17 billion. The $13 billion operating costs for 2000 compares with what 19 Latin American countries actually spent in

Table 2   School Enrollment, 2000

Age	Population in 2000 (in millions)		Percent Enrolled	Number Enrolled, 2000	Number Enrolled, 1964	Percent Increase, 1964–2000
5–14	154.4	X	98%	151.3	33.3	354%
15–19	68.2	X	35%	23.9	6.1	292%
20–24	58.1	X	8.6%	5.0	.8	525%
Total	280.7			180.2	40.2	348%

1960—just $1.6 billion. Average operating costs per student in 2000 will be $73.00; in 1960, actual operating costs plus capital investments averaged only $36.

Another important factor is the teacher–student ratio, which in 1964 stood at 1:25.5. The number of teachers must increase from 1,600,000 to 7,200,000 to maintain this proportion in 2000. Four and a half million of these professionals will teach in primary schools, 1.9 million in secondary schools, and 600,000 in universities. But, since 44 percent of Latin America's teachers lack certification, the problem is not simply quantitative. Low salaries preclude full-time teaching, so many teachers are not dedicated only to the profession. Moreover, good teachers are unequally distributed, and the low overall teacher–student ratio masks huge inequities between private and public, rural and urban, schools. If education is to fulfill its vital role in development, the teacher corps must both grow and profoundly reform itself so that better trained personnel can teach more effectively.

The notorious lack of statistics on school construction and even on the number of available classrooms complicates planning efforts. Nonetheless, we can estimate teacher training needs.

In general, the number of teachers is growing slightly faster than matriculation. Between 1960 and 1964 the teacher corps grew by 7.6 percent annually, while matriculation increased by 6.4 percent. However, secondary school enrollment during this period increased at 11.9 percent yearly, while annual expansion of the teaching staff was only 9.1 percent. Should this tendency persist, secondary education will be in grave crisis by the end of the century. This is even more critical considering that secondary education requires a greater boost than primary if our continent is to compete successfully in the world market for qualified personnel.

HOUSING

Housing for Latin America's 638 millions of 2000 is the second area of social demand which we will examine in detail.

Despite blatantly inadequate housing among Latin America's masses, house construction has been one of the least dynamic development sectors. Inherent weaknesses of the construction industry partly explain this, including such apparently insuperable obstacles as lack of qualified labor and high finance costs. On the other hand, the Interamerican Development Bank notes: "Considerable difference of opinion remains as to the role of housing in economic and social development, and these investments are often considered of secondary importance. Directly productive projects...especially those promising relatively rapid and high returns, usually take priority over long term housing investments, which are considered of lesser return and less certain economic benefits."

This explains why economists frequently consider housing and related social services as virtual luxury items feasible only after significant industrial and economic development. Nonetheless, an opposing notion has arisen recently, which considers housing a *productive* investment stimulating employment and the construction and related industries. Unfortunately, solution of this grave problem has been slowed because most private investors want quick profits which the housing industry cannot provide. The growing housing demand will probably not be met, creating one of the most serious crises of the early twenty-first century.

One method of calculating housing needs divides total population by average household size. Assuming an average household of five persons, Latin America's 245 million inhabitants of two years ago formed 49 million households. Censuses and surveys have allowed experts to estimate that only half these families lived in adequate housing, leaving 24.5 million in deficient dwellings. In other words, in 1965 there was already a housing deficit of 24.5 million units.

This deficit is complicated by the critical factor of migration. A long term and large scale exodus from the countryside has been filling the cities or, rather, the slums. The migrants, more and more of whom are abandoning rural poverty for the glittering image of urban life, have seriously aggravated the housing problem.

Each year about 3.6 million Latin Americans abandon the countryside for the cities, and most wind up in marginal areas. For example, 38 percent of Rio de Janeiro's population, and 50 percent of Recife's, live in *favelas*; and 35 percent of Caracas' population lives in the so-called *ranchos*. In Buenos Aires, the *villas miserias* house 10 percent of the population, while in Lima the *barriada* population has increased from 10 to 20 percent of the total in 6 years. One can imagine conditions in 2000, when *barriada* population will have quadrupled.

It is also significant that half of urban, and 90 percent of rural dwellings lack running water and sanitary services.

How do 122.5 million Latin Americans live in such housing? The image is excruciating—people are jammed together, three or more to a room, and usually in flimsy improvised structures which do not really provide protection from the elements. Electricity and basic comforts are lacking, and running water, sewers, and other necessary services are infrequent. These conditions foster the endemic and contagious disease which is maintaining high mortality rates among certain groups, such as those under twenty. Interamerican Development Bank figures single out diseases directly related to lack of an adequate water supply as the main cause of death in six countries, and the second highest cause in three more. The same diseases are the principal cause of infant mortality in three countries, the second cause in seven, and the third in four. While projecting such factors to the future is difficult, persistence of present unhealthy and inadequate housing will create a grave sanitary crisis for the coming generation.

This is, then, the difficult situation of our cities with their huge marginal districts, and of our vast rural zones with their impoverished peasants. How large will housing needs be in 2000? The calculation is simple. To begin with, the number of families will have increased by 78.6 million, so that 78.6 million housing units will be needed just to meet population growth. By 2000, another 24.5 million units will have deteriorated to the point of replacement. So 96.2 million units will be needed, and this sum does not include the 24.5 million units now in bad condition. Since most Latin American experts have not considered these, our goals are modest. If our figures can be met, only 19 percent of total population will inhabit deficient housing, as opposed to today's 50 percent.

But what are present trends in housing construction? OAS figures indicate that two units per thousand inhabitants per year are being constructed, so only 490,000 units were built in 1965. This represents just 2 percent of existing housing, equal to the percentage which deteriorates each year. If the same rate of two units per thousand inhabitants is maintained through the end of the century, total construction during thirty-two years will equal only 29.8 million units. But, as we have indicated, 72 percent of 1965's housing will have deteriorated by 2000. So that, of the 29.8 million units constructed during the rest of the century, 17.6 million will be replacements, and only 12.2 million units will remain to house the 78.6 million new families. The deficiency is clear, and we could add that the number of families in deficient housing would increase to 90.9 million by 2000. Seventy-one percent of Latin America's population, or 455 million—nearly twice the region's total present population—will live in sub-subsistence housing, in miserable urban *barriadas* or in rural huts.

The tendency to blame all the inadequacies of development on excessively high population growth is an important but controversial aspect of the population development problem. Demographic pressures have clearly "made ever less attainable the social objectives of the Alliance for Progress."[3] Nonetheless, the development programs themselves contain inadequacies which have exacerbated the growing deficits in every aspect of the continent's socioeconomic life.

Let us take the concrete case of housing in 2000 and assume a population growth of 1 percent annually, comparable to that of industrialized Europe and North America. Were this the case, Latin American population at the end of the century would only reach 347 million, rather than the 638 million calculated from a growth rate of 2.9 percent. The housing needs of these hypothetical 347 million would come to only 69.4 million units. Nonetheless, at the present construction rate, only 21.l million units would be completed in the next thirty-two years. A deficit of 41.4 million units would remain even after adding the 6.9 million still habitable units in 2000; 60 percent of the population would lack decent housing.

Assuming both a decline in demographic growth rate to 2.4 percent by the end of the century and constant construction trends, we predict a housing deficit of 90.6 million units. Experts estimate replacement costs for substandard housing at $2000 apiece, according to which $188 billion would be necessary to eliminate the deficit by 2000.

The dilemma is grave. Neither internal nor external capital resources are likely to become available to finance programs of this scale. But something must be done, as it will be impossible to have 455 million people living at infrahuman levels. And these masses will demand action and radical change, at any cost.

The task is monumental and truly revolutionary. Only a coordinated development effort by all sectors, taking into account the impact of demographic growth, can respond to these explosive needs.

CONCLUSIONS

Projection of socioeconomic deficits is at once discouraging and challenging. The gravest aspect is that present population is excessive with relation to the resources available for development, while in many areas present birth rates preclude even minimum subsistence levels. Moreover, our projections are based on the assumption that fecundity will diminish from 2.9 percent to 2.4 percent around 1980. But this is conjecture—1968 is ending, and Latin America is still debating parents' rights to limit family size and state responsibility to provide family planning services.[4] Precious time and opportunities for immediate and long range progress are escaping during this period of indecision.

A spontaneous decline in Latin American birth rates, as occurred in Europe and North America, is unlikely. The region's social conditions are remote from those in which fecundity diminished in the industrialized nations during the past 200 years.

The situation will be even more critical if the UN hypothesis turns out to be incorrect, and fecundity does not diminish by 1980. With present growth rates, 118 million more people would have to be added to our figures; total population at the turn of the century, in just thirty-two years, would be over 750 million instead of 638 million. Deficits would be correspondingly larger, and the implications of underdevelopment greater and graver. All of which leads us to one conclusion—regardless of birth rates, prospects for both present and future are critical. What we have outlined in this study may come to pass; statistics and projections are not science fiction. In any case, transforming the development process would lessen the intensity of crisis, and the key to Latin America's future lies in such transformation.

NOTES

1. This figure, corresponding to a 200% increase, was calculated on the basis of IBD's estimate of a $50 billion investment for a 90% increase by 1980.

2. The figure of 208 million is based on International Labor Organization projected participation rates.

3. General Secretariat of the OAS. Preparatory Document, Caracas.

4. The population growth rate was 2.9% from 1965–1972. UN Demographic Yearbook, 1973 ST/STAT/SER.R/1 (Ed.)

16. PERUVIAN DEMOGRAPHIC POSSIBILITIES FOR THE YEAR 2000

JULIA SALAZAR
Dirección Nacional de Estadística y Censos, Ministerio de Hacienda y Comercio, Lima

INTRODUCTION

The Demographic Analysis Unit of Peru's Dirección Nacional de Estadística y Censos [National Bureau of Statistics and the Census], in collaboration with the Latin American Demographic Center (CELADE), has been publishing studies since 1964. The first part of this presentation, summarizing the findings of the Demographic Analysis Unit, notes Peru's most relevant demographic features; the second section details probable population characteristics in 2000.

Guillermo Abad, Peruvian fellow in CELADE, [Centro Latino-americano de Demografia—Latin American Center of Demography] has projected total population for 2000 by sex and age groups. Results of only one of three alternatives, the extension of the 1960–80 projections which the Direction of Statistics and the Census has accepted as official, are available to us. These figures have allowed us to estimate urban–rural, student, and economically active population for 2000.

THE PRESENT DEMOGRAPHIC SITUATION

Like other developing nations, Peru faces a serious problem of excessive population growth. The growth rate has nearly doubled from 1.2 percent in the intercensal period 1862–1940 (78 years), to

335

2.2 percent for the period 1940–61 (21 years); it is expected to reach 3.0 percent in 1965–70, and population will total 33,500,000 by 2000.

Since economic development shows a tendency to stagnate at existing levels—low levels, inadequate for general well-being—while population can be expected to continue growing at about the same pace at least for the next few years, the situation is critical. High fertility and declining mortality are the demographic factors which have encouraged rapid population growth and created a youthful population.

High and Virtually Constant Fertility

Though the statistical evidence does not enable us to determine fecundity and mortality with any certainty, probable rates for the intercensal period can be indirectly derived from 1940 and 1961 census data (see Charts 1 and 2).

According to these estimates, Peru's birth rate around 1950 was 48.0 per thousand, and the death rate about 26.0 per thousand. Results for the first two methods would indicate under-registration of births on the order of 32 percent, and of deaths on the order of 52 percent.

The second method suggests a crude reproduction rate of 3.2 for the intercensal period. 1961 census data signal a crude birth rate of 45 per thousand, as contrasted with an estimated 50 per thousand in 1940. Past variations have not been great, and natality remains high.

Chart 1   Age Structure of the Population, 1940 and 1961 Censuses

	Percent	
Age	1940	1961
0–14	42.1	43.3
15–59	51.5	50.7
60 and over	6.4	6.0
Total	100.0	100.0

Chart 2   Estimated Birth and Death Rates, 1940–1961

Method Used	Gross Birth Rate (per thousand)	Gross Death Rate (per thousand)
Method of stable populations model	48.3	25.9
Method of constant structure by age	48.9	26.5
Method of comparing censuses by age groups	44.0	21.6
Average rates according to official data (1941 to 1960)	32.9	12.5

Widespread failure to register birth precludes either analyzing annual fluctuations between 1940 and 1961 or distinguishing fecundity levels by political subdivisions. Regional fecundity differences undoubtedly exist—one analysis of the 1961 census found the Coast (excluding the Department of Lima and the Constitutional Province of Callao) to have higher fecundity than the Sierra, while that of the Selva was higher than that of the Coast.

The urban–rural fecundity differential within each region is around 9 percent, except for the Department of Lima and Callao's much higher figure of 34 percent, which indicates that fecundity in the Lima–Callao urban zone is by far the country's lowest.

UN studies show that, with few exceptions, countries and regions divide between "developing" areas, with crude growth rates above 2.0, and "developed" ones, with slower growth.

Metropolitan Lima is clearly Peru's most developed zone. The Survey of Immigration to Metropolitan Lima found a crude reproduction rate of 2.05. The great difference between fecundity levels in the capital and the rest of the country is due in part to Lima's low proportion of illiterates, later marriage age, relatively large proportion of single women, and widespread voluntary limitation of births. The Hall Study revealed use of birth control

Chart 3   Fertility Measurements by Region, 1961

Region	Gross Natality Rate	General Fertility Rate	Relation of Children to Women	Overall Fertility Rate
Coast (excluding Lima-Callao)	44.2	199.2	769.5	6.54
Urban	43.1	187.8	700.8	6.18
Rural	45.2	210.5	337.5	6.80
Sierra	43.0	189.3	755.4	6.15
Urban	40.8	177.2	685.2	5.78
Rural	43.8	193.4	779.8	6.31
Selva	49.1	232.7	926.8	7.18
Urban	47.6	213.3	804.1	6.90
Rural	50.3	249.4	1031.8	7.56
Lima-Callao	36.9	147.8	613.6	4.61
Urban	35.9	140.2	586.1	4.34
Rural	43.4	212.4	848.3	6.62
Peru	42.4	184.5	734.7	6.03
Urban	39.9	165.9	652.3	5.35
Rural	44.6	202.9	815.9	6.70

SOURCE: Dirección Nacional de Estadística y Censos—VI Censo Nacional de Población, Tabla 2 del Anexo.

techniques among 68 percent, 55 percent, and 38 percent of women of the upper, middle, and lower classes, respectively.

Using crude reproduction rate as an indicator of development, only Lima appears developed—the Departmental rate decreased by 5.4 percent between 1940 and 1961. On the other hand, estimated fecundity in the same area declined by about 11 percent in 24 years. Fecundity differs by population groups within Lima, as in other cities, along with education, migratory status, economic activity, and socioeconomic position. In the *barriada* District of El Agustino, for instance, where 36 percent of the women between 15 and 49 are illiterate and 84 percent are migrants, the crude reproduction rate is 3.

Urban fecundity studies by the Center for Social Sampling Research—Centro de Investigaciones Sociales por Muestro—(CISM) confirm our argument. Arequipa, Peru's second city, shows a crude growth rate significantly beneath the national average. Iquitos, in the selva, is less developed than Arequipa and in Peru's region of highest fecundity--its level is well above Arequipa's. And the city of Cerro de Pasco, finally, represents rural fecundity patterns: the birth rate is 54 per thousand, and about 70 percent of mothers past childbearing age have had seven or more pregnancies.

Declining Mortality

Cheap and efficient scientific advances brought a sharp decline in mortality during the intercensal period 1940–1961. Due to extensive under-registration of deaths (as with births, as noted above), precise figures for 1940–1961 are not available. It has been necessary to revert to census figures to estimate mortality during those years. Overall values, as well as a division into two ten year periods, were obtained by comparing generations in successive censuses, with various indirect controls.

Chart 4   Gross Reproduction Rates for Selected Cities

City	Year	Gross Reproduction Rate
Arequipa	1965	2.61
Cerro de Pasco	1967	3.76
Iquitos	1966	3.49
Lima	1967	2.00

SOURCE: Center for Social Sampling Research (CISM).

Chart 5   Life Expectancy at Birth, by Sex

Sex	1940–1960	1940–1950	1950–1960
Males	39.0	33.7	45.6
Females	39.7	34.8	48.0

Estimated life expectancy at birth for the two periods, thus, indicates high mortality relative to other American countries and to the world. Between 1940 and 1960, life expectancy at birth averaged about 39.4 years for both sexes. Though this level is not low, there was nonetheless a pronounced mortality decline between the ten year periods; men gained 12 years of life, and women 13. The difference between sexes was 1.1 years in favor of women in the period 1940–50, increasing to 2.4 years in the following decade.

Crude death rates for 1940, 1950, and 1961 were approximately 33, 26, and 15 per thousand, respectively. Infant mortality rates for the same years have been calculated at 250, 174, and 116 per thousand, respectively.

Accelerated Urbanization

Another of Peru's striking demographic features, common to other Latin American countries as well, is the intense population movement from country to city, and particularly to the major cities. If migration normally acts to better distribute population in terms of resources and economic opportunities, the efficacy of such redistribution is always related to the receiving region's absorptive capacity. The pace and volume of Peru's rural–urban migration, far exceeding the absorptive capacity of the main cities, are creating general underemployment and exacerbating social tensions and problems of inadequate housing and education.

There are various definitions of "urban" population. The most common criterion, lending itself to international comparison, is the size of localities. Peru used a political-administrative definition in the 1940 and 1961 censuses, where district capitals and other centers showing certain urban characteristics were considered urban.

Chart 6 illustrates how urban and rural population levels depend on the criteria chosen. For instance, in 1961 47.4 percent of the total population was considered urban by the census definition; this figure drops to 39.4 percent if urban centers are defined as those with over 2000 inhabitants; with a cut-off of 10,000 and over, the percentage falls to 29.0.

Chart 6   Urban and Rural Population According to Three Definitions

Zones	First Definition (a)	Second Definition (b)	Third Definition (c)
	1961 Census (percent)		
Urban	47.4	39.4	29.0
Urban (excluding Lima-Callao)	31.0	23.0	12.6
Lima-Callao	16.4	16.4	16.4
Rural	52.6	60.6	71.0
Total:	100.0	100.0	100.0
	1940 Census (percent)		
Urban	35.4	25.4	18.9
Urban (excluding Lima-Callao)	25.7	15.7	9.2
Lima-Callao	9.7	9.7	9.7
Rural	64.6	74.6	81.1
Total:	100.0	100.0	100.0
	Rate of Intercensal Growth, 1940–1961 (per thousand)		
Urban	36.8	43.9	43.5
Urban (excluding Lima-Callao)	31.6	40.9	37.8
Lima-Callao	47.2	47.2	47.2
Rural	12.5	12.5	16.0
Total:	22.4	22.4	22.4

a) Census definition
b) Urban population is that inhabiting localities of 2,000 or more on the census date.
c) Urban population is that residing in cities averaging 10,000 or more in the 1940 and 1961 censuses.

The rhythm of urban and rural growth also varies with the definition chosen. According to the census definition, urban growth between 1940 and 1961 was 36.8 per thousand; by either of the other two criteria, growth stabilizes around 44.0 per 1000. Urban growth appears lower with the census definition because many district capitals contain fewer than 2000 inhabitants.

Between 1940 and 1961, Peruvian migration tended toward zones of low altitude (the Coast), and to the North and Center rather than the South. The Northern Departments grew at 2.1 percent, the Center at 2.9 percent, the South at 1.2 percent, and the Eastern Departments at 3.1 percent. Calculations for the demographic baricenter corroborate these trends, signalling population movement from 1940 to 1961 of 20'56" [degrees and minutes latitude] toward the Coast and 10'50" [degrees and minutes longitude] toward the North.

Two important and independent movements become apparent in considering place of origin, according to the 1961 census data and the Survey of Immigration. One is from centers of less than 1000 inhabitants (rural areas) to centers with between 1,000 and 19,999 (semiurban zones); the other involves those leaving the latter for cities of more than 20,000. More than half of all migrants originated in populated centers of over 5000 (1961 figures), while only 6.1 percent arrived from centers of less than 1,000, in which 64.4 percent of total population lives (excluding metropolitan Lima). Seventy-nine percent of all migrants arrived in one stage, almost all of them having come directly from their place of birth.

Peruvian urbanization is megalocephalic, or concentrated primarily in one main city, Lima. The 1961 census puts 38 percent of the country's urban population in metropolitan Lima, and another one-fourth in the 34 cities with more than 12,000 people each. There is extensive migration toward metropolitan Lima; the 1965 study indicated a population 40 percent immigrant. Greater Lima's expanding industry and commerce, and the migrants' desire for improved living conditions, stimulate moves to the capital. Work was one of the main reasons men gave for migrating in this study, while women mentioned family reasons.

Chart 7   Main Reason for Migration to Metropolitan Lima (Percent)

Main Reason	Metropolitan Lima (1965)	
	Men	Women
Work-related reasons (low pay, unemployment, etc.)	53.8	33.7
Family problems (includes health, death of a parent, family break-up, etc.)	19.1	48.3
Study by the migrant or one of his dependents	16.9	10.6
Other (includes social problems, inability to adapt to the environment, trouble with the police, with the neighbors, etc.)	10.2	7.4
TOTAL	100.0	100.0

SOURCE: DNEC [National Bureau of Statistics and Censuses, Survey of Immigration in Metropolitan Lima]

Urban population is concentrated on the coast. Of the 35 cities averaging over 10,000 in both 1940 and 1961, 19 are on the coast, 13 in the sierra, and 3 in the selva.

Population growth was fastest in the largest cities and decreased with smaller city size—though, of course, with significant variations. Only six towns grew more rapidly than Lima–Callao (5.2 percent—Chiclayo, Chimbote, Castilla, Tumbes, Juliaca, and Callaría.

The Economically Active Population

Peru's demographic configuration and its predominantly agricultural economy, in conjunction with the problem of excessive population growth accompanied by incipient economic development, invest its economically-active population with certain noteworthy characteristics.

The age structure of the economically active population is young, and participation of marginal ages is high in comparison with industrialized countries. Forty-two and eight-tenths percent of the male labor force is under thirty (1961); in the United States, the comparable figure in 1950 was 28.8 percent. The overall activity rate in 1940 was estimated at 33.2 percent; in 1961 it was 31.5 percent. The economically active population grew by 2.0 percent per annum in the intercensal period, while total population increased at 2.2 percent. The country's economically active population is composed of 78.3 percent male workers, and 21.7 percent females. Working women are concentrated in agriculture, domestic service, and home industries.

Comparative activity rates by sex and age, using data from both censuses, reveal that age structure has almost no effect on activity rates per age group in either total population or in male and female subgroups. Nondemographic factors account for most of the variations. Among males, these may result from slight industrial development, incipient labor legislation, and growing

Chart 8   Economically Active Population 16 and over, 1940 and 1961

	Figures in Thousands		Overall Activity Rate*	
Sex	1961	1940†	1961	1940†
Men	2,445.4	1,636.7	49.7	52.1
Women	679.2	421.9	13.6	13.1
TOTAL	3,124.6	2,058.6*	31.5	33.2

*Percent of economically active population with respect to total population.
† Estimated values.
SOURCE: DNEC. Boletín de Análisis Demográfico, No. 2.

efforts to enforce school attendance. In the female population, the main differences are due to the census methodology, since an implausibly large number of women in the textile and livestock sectors register as occupied in artisanry.

Peru's predominantly agricultural economy is reflected in low overall participation rates at the provincial level, with high percentages in the primary sector. Activity rates oscillated between 25.0 percent and 29.9 percent—below the overall national rate of 31.5 percent—in 54.8 percent of the 144 provinces enumerated in 1961. Only the Department of Lima has less than 30 percent of its active population in agriculture (15.1 percent).

Chart 9 Average Activity Rates Per Age Group,1940 and 1961 Censuses

Age Group	Total		Men		Women	
	1940	1961	1940	1961	1940	1961
6–14	11.0	3.4	11.6	3.5	10.5	3.4
15–19	49.7	41.2	61.2	54.9	38.0	27.1
20–29	66.8	59.3	91.7	94.3	43.4	25.5
30–34	69.7	59.3	95.1	98.7	45.4	20.7
45–64	68.7	57.1	93.8	96.6	46.2	20.0
65 and over	55.5	36.8	82.5	68.7	35.9	11.9
Gross Activity Rate	39.9	31.5	52.1	49.6	27.9	13.6

SOURCE: DNEC, op. cit.

Chart 10 Distribution of Departments According to Percent of Active Population in Agriculture, 1961

Less than 30%	30 to 49.9	50 to 69.9	70 to 89.9
Lima	Arequipa	Ancash	Amazonas
	Ica	Cuzco	Apurímac
	Junín	La Libertad	Ayacucho
	Lambayeque	Loreto	Cajamarca
	Pasco	Madre de Dios	Huancavelica
	Tacna	Moquegua	Huánuco
	Tumbes	Piura	Puno
			San Martín

POPULATION PROJECTIONS FOR 2000

The Period 1960–1980

The National Direction of Statistics and the Census has estimated population for the period 1960–1980 using the component method, which projects males and females separately by age groups. The calculations are based on likely assumptions for mortality, fertility, and migration, the demographic factors determining population growth.

Two sets of estimates were developed. One assumes constant fertility, and the other a slowly declining fertility; both postulate the same mortality rate. International migrations are discounted, since their intensity is negligible. Depending on which fertility rate is used, the two series differ by about 1,300,000 in 1980.

Annual growth rates for both series remain above 30 per thousand during the entire period 1960–1980. With the first projection, which assumes constant fertility, the rate reaches 36 per thousand in 1975–1980—a high value explained by permanently elevated fecundity. Increase is only less intense in the second projection, suggesting that even a fairly large fecundity decline will not compensate for reduced mortality.

Life expectancy at birth will increase from 54 to 65 years between 1960–65 and 1975–80, with crude mortality rates dropping to half their initial level.

Age structure changes significantly in the first projection: child and adolescent populations increase while the relative weight of youths and adults decreases, lowering the proportion in potentially active age groups. The second projection, on the other hand, signals a stable proportion between 0 and 14, and slight increase in the 15–19 group. The results of the second projection have been declared official by the Direction of Statistics and the Census; they have been used in the following section to calculate urban–rural, economically active, and school-aged populations for 1980.

Extending the Projection to 2000

According to hypothesis II, the population in 2000 would be nearly triple that estimated for 1965, with an age structure still young but with relatively fewer in the 0 to 14 group than in 1980, as follows from the assumption of declining fertility.

In 2000, life expectancy at birth will probably approximate current figures for industrialized nations (71 years), and fertility probably will resemble that of metropolitan Lima in 1965 (crude reproduction rate 2.15). The growth rate will remain nearly stationary between 1965 and 1980, and then decline from about 31 per thousand to 28 per thousand by 2000; that is, fertility will show a moderate decline. Another alternative is possible. Assuming constant fertility between 1960 and 1980, followed by a decline such as the second projection assumed for 1960–80, growth in 2000 would be about 34 per thousand. Existing figures indicate no clear trend toward generally lower fertility regionally; only the Department of Lima shows a decline. On the other hand, if fertility drops rapidly, a growth rate smaller than 28 per thousand would be expected for 2000.

School-aged population is another critical group. Children between 7 and 14 increased from 19.0 percent of total population in 1940 to 20.3 percent in 1960; the projection indicates they should decline to 19.8 percent by 2000. The 1961 census identified 63 percent of the 6–14 age group as primary school students.

Chart 11   Main Features of the Projected Populations for Peru, 1960–1980

Characteristics	1960	1965	1970	1975	1980
PROJECTION I	(5-year averages)				
Growth (rate per thousand)	31.0	33.3	35.3	36.6	
Natality (rate per thousand)	45.2	44.7	44.3	44.0	
Mortality (rate per thousand)	14.2	11.4	9.0	7.4	
Reproduction	3.2	3.2	3.2	3.2	
Life expectancy at birth (ê)	54	58	62	65	
Relative structure (%) (Both sexes)					
0–14	44.6	45.2	46.0	46.4	46.9
15–59	50.0	49.8	49.2	48.8	48.3
60 and over	5.4	5.0	4.8	4.8	4.8
Males per 100 females	101.0	101.2	101.4	101.6	101.8
PROJECTION II	(5-year averages)				
Growth (rate per thousand)	30.0	30.7	31.0	30.9	
Natality (rate per thousand)	44.1	41.8	39.8	38.1	
Mortality (rate per thousand)	14.1	11.1	8.8	7.2	
Reproduction	3.11	2.94	2.76	2.59	
Mortality—Life expectancy at birth (ê)	54	58	62	65	
Relative structure (%) (Both sexes)					
0–14	44.8	45.0	45.0	44.2	43.4
15–59	50.0	50.0	50.1	50.8	51.5
60 and over	5.4	5.0	4.9	5.0	5.1
Males per 100 females	101.0	101.2	101.3	101.5	101.6

Chart 12 Peru's Population Structure

Age Groups	1950	1980	2000
0–14	44.6	43.4	40.4
15–59	50.0	51.5	53.9
60 and over	5.4	5.1	5.7
Total	100.0	100.0	100.0

Chart 13 Main Characteristics of Peru's Projected Population, 1960–2000

	Assumptions Used		Rates Resulting From the Projection (Per Thousand)		
Periods	Life Expectancy at Birth	Gross Reproduction Rate	Natality	Mortality	Growth
1960–1965	54.00	3.11	44.10	13.60	30.50
1965–1970	58.00	2.94	41.83	10.59	31.24
1970–1975	62.00	2.76	39.76	8.21	31.56
1975–1980	65.00	2.59	38.15	6.70	31.45
1980–1985	67.02	2.47	37.07	5.78	31.29
1985–1990	68.75	2.36	35.84	5.13	30.71
1990–1995	70.11	2.25	34.40	4.76	29.64
1995–2000	71.00	2.15	32.93	4.42	28.51

If this proportion is maintained, absolute enrollment will double between 1960 and 1980, and almost double again between 1980 and 2000.

Urban and rural population.   Reduced fecundity correlates with urbanization, although rural women may follow urban reproductive patterns and have fewer children. Lines of parabolic regression, based on intercensal urban growth and the 1960–80 projection, have been employed to calculate growth rates by five-year periods between 1980 and 2000, and to estimate urban population at the latter date.

The figures indicate a population 77 percent urban in 2000 (defining district, provincial, and departmental capitals as urban, and recalling that in 1961 many district capitals had fewer than 2000 inhabitants).

The city of Lima represented 64 percent of that department's population in 1940; the proportion grew to 72 percent by 1961, or by 12.5 percent in 21 years. Accepting this percentage as a rough measure of urbanization and comparing it with the estimated fertility decline of about 11 percent in 24 years would suggest that decreasing fertility is not offsetting urbanization. If urban population follows Lima's pattern of 12.5 percent growth every 20 years, Peru will be only 65 percent urban in 2000, a figure far below that projected.

This observation is substantiated by the varying notions of "urban" in the Department of Lima and the rest of the country, reflected in urban–rural fertility differentials by regions. Furthermore, the projection of total population implicitly assumes a fertility decrease of about 11 percent in 20 years.

The economically active population.   Assuming that rates of economic activity among males in marginal age groups in 2000 will be similar to those of the United States in 1950, and that female rates will equal those of the Department of Lima in 1961, the overall activity rate will be 33.4 percent. Higher female participation rates, following growing participation by women between 15 and 40, appear in the projection of the economically active population for 1960–80; an overall urban activity rate of 32.5 is expected for 1980, and will increase further by 2000.

Chart 14   Population Under 20, 1940–2000

Age Groups	Inhabitants in Thousands			Percent of Total Population		
	1960	1980	2000	1960	1980	2000
0–6	2,428.0	4,204.3	6,878.1	24.2	22.7	20.6
7–14	2,038.1	3,843.5	6,631.0	20.3	20.8	19.8
15–19	1,005.2	1,987.3	3,491.2	10.0	10.7	10.4
0–19	5,471.3	10,035.1	17,000.3	54.5	54.2	50.8

Chart 15   Estimated Urban and Rural Population, 1960–2000

Year	Urban	Rural (Thousands)	Urban Percent
1960	4,674.3	5,350.3	46.6
1965	5,780.8	5,868.8	49.6
1970	7,131.6	6,454.7	52.5
1975	8,875.0	6,993.8	55.9
1980	10,894.8	7,632.2	58.8
1985	13,498.6	8,113.2	62.4
1990	16,762.5	8,379.8	66.7
1995	20,834.1	8,264.4	71.6
2000	25,884.3	7,606.7	77.3

Estimated global activity rates, by sex, for 1960, 1980, and 2000 fluctuate from 49.7 to 48.1 to 48.3 for men, and from 13.2 to 16.7 to 18.3 for women, respectively.

The rate at which males enter economic activity diminishes from 43.5 per thousand in 1980 to 41.5 per thousand in 2000, while the relationship of economically active to economically inactive population varies from 217 to 199 inactives for every 100 actives.

Chart 16   Peru's Estimated Economically Active Population, 2000

(Thousands)

Age Group	Men	Women	Total
10–14	50.9	123.4	174.3
15–19	792.3	637.9	1,430.2
20–24	1,252.2	643.0	1,895.2
25–29	1,240.6	457.6	1,698.2
30–34	1,115.9	315.2	1,431.1
35–39	957.4	231.4	1,188.8
40–44	807.9	176.0	983.9
45–49	637.7	135.7	773.4
50–54	518.7	109.3	628.0
55–59	379.7	82.8	462.5
60–64	251.0	58.7	309.7
65–69	132.3	34.9	167.2
70–74	33.4	16.9	50.3
TOTAL:	8,170.0	3,022.8	11,192.8

CONCLUSIONS

1. These figures augur favorably for Peru's demographic distribution in 2000, given the tendency toward an adult population which does not show up in the 1960–80 projection. This trend implies relatively fewer of school age, and larger proportions of urban and economically active population—always and insofar as the hypotheses, especially that of fertility decline, are substantiated.
2. The complex phenomenon of fertility is linked to industrialization levels. In Peru, existing data only confirm a fertility decline in the Department of Lima, a decline of virtually no national import in the 1940–61 intercensal period. Urban fertility differs little from rural levels in the other regions; there are variations between cities, but fertility in all is higher than in the capital. Later studies may reveal a clear tendency which has not yet defined itself.
3. Accelerated population growth will persist in 2000, when volume will about triple that estimated for 1965; it is pertinent to ask economists whether the pace of economic development will allow the better living conditions which all people hope for.
4. Demographic investigations must continue. They are presently hampered by scarcity of statistical data and of qualified experts. Encouraging information collection and teaching the disciplines most pertinent to these problems should receive top priority.

THE FUTURE OF
IDEOLOGY

5

17. IDEOLOGICAL DEVELOPMENT

CANDIDO MENDES
*Director del Instituto Universitario de Pesquisas de
Rio de Janeiro*

REFLECTION IN THE FRAMEWORK OF DEVELOPMENT: THE TROPHIC PARADIGM

A prospective study of Latin American ideologies requires definition of the present paradigm governing change—an examination
in the context of the past 25 years. This context is conventionally
identified with development, in the large sense of a transition between total social structures. Such transition would originate in
changes in the production process which, in a series of accumulative shifts, would permeate the social, political, and cultural
spheres. The economic changes would follow supercession of the
colonial complex and the ties between Latin America's political
units and the international economic system—ties which have
weakened significantly since the 1930s.

The import substitution paradigm, when it became dominant
throughout the hemisphere, replaced the old economic structure
with another of similar scale, but with radically reoriented
elements. This transition was identified with the development
which, in the immediate postwar period, appeared capable of
spontaneously, gradually, and unconsciously shifting economic
factors from one structure to another. The dynamism assumed in

357

this incrementalist and gradualist perspective was labeled "evolution" and "progress."

The thesis of the permeation of economic parameters through all aspects of society arose in the 1950s. It was strongest in those nations which could achieve this "gratifying" transfer of economic factors by completing import substitution, reordering the productive apparatus to meet internal demand, generating new and large scale social mobility with urbanization and industrialization, and beginning to precipitate social classes out of the old caste society. Such complete and radical reorientation also affected social consciousness. Latin America's general change process is identified with the very emergence of consciousness, in the most profound sense. There could be no intelligentsia, no subject of reflection, where the nation lacked sufficient autonomy to cluster or agglomerate its economic, political, and cultural relations. As long as an external center integrated these elements, decisions were necessarily made in the centers of power, with little attention paid to the peripheries.

Nonetheless, the phenomenon of general change concentrates rapidly. The "canonic" stage continues while change takes place simultaneously in diverse spheres. The counterpoint between change and reflection thus demonstrates a *trophic* sequence—the participants share a common ideology, and the *prise de conscience* accelerates the process. Symbols derived from change, and appearing along with the impact and goal of a new total social structure, complete this phase.

Latin America's ideological production between now and the end of the century will lack this interplay between social events and reflective consciousness. Neither the image of spontaneous change, nor that of developmental continuity, has been or is now dominant. Our study focuses on the dangers of stagnation or retrogression in the "change" paradigm—a paradigm which allowed Latin America's "progressive" ideological constructions, and an eschatological and even inevitable vision of altering the conditions which trapped the area in the old colonial system.

We must characterize the appearance of interruption of the "condition of inertia" which will probably dominate Latin America during this phase.

THE DYSTROPHIC PARADIGM

It is not adequate just to analyze Latin America's growing paralysis and stagnation, which are succeeding the so-called Development Decade's great expectations (onto which was grafted the facile eschatology of the Alliance for Progress). It is more important to realize that this mounting lethargy will generate neither disruption nor crisis.

Even within Alliance eschatology, orthodox change policies responded to the myth, phrased in terms of the nemeses of progressivism and exemplified by Northeastern Brazil's expected social "catastrophe," of political and economic "explosions."

Revolution and anomie are not in fact the only response to stagnation in the wake of efforts at change. Our prospective analysis must admit a third and more likely outcome: that a growing entropy will envelop and "cool" the abortive change process. This is the most probable result of Latin America's present economic, political, and social inertia. Since the future is not devoid of alternatives, we must evaluate the hypothesis that the flow of "becoming" could escape the predicted course of logical sequences resulting from counterposed theses and antitheses within models which order historical and social reality.

The field of future "praxis" must be located in order to specify the suppositions of the present flow while avoiding sequences which, according to the "imperialism" of some models would inevitably predetermine events. These constructions reflect the desire to judge a series of effects from the play of complementary pairs anticipated by the exhaustive logic of their premises. Disruption would be the unavoidable counterpoint to the model's inevitability, which a "counter-model"—always a negation of the initial thesis—would then follow. However, the "aborted change" model for Latin American evolution would:

1. Last indefinitely without intensifying the contradictions which logical analysis would reduce to the skeleton of historical events;

2. Tend to an entropic configuration of this inertia, represented by retrocessive hierarchies and, similarly, a counterpoint between advances and retreats;

3. Show superstructural configurations which would institutionalize a type of minimodels, or small scale rationalizations. This would concentrate effects and allow "closed-circuit" change, removed from the primitive challenge of progress and the trophic sequence between medieval and development structures. The virtue of neocapitalist schemes is their indeterminate elasticity—they can adjust to any viable scale via distinctions between chosen areas and those which remain marginal;

4. Be structured in "enclave economies," the centers of the 1950s' apparent development.

We must conceptualize this aborted development pattern—distinct from the stage of accumulative growth following a "take-off"—by means of the disruptive situations which would be its reverse. We must consider the social anomie which intensifies as repression counters the inability to reach that critical rest period in which development can be stably ordered.

Brazil and Argentina show how this third alternative can persist, even in countries on the verge of take-off and the trophic change pattern which would be mastered by the classic tools of economic growth.

The background for Latin America's intelligentsia thus includes this inertia, this frustrated change in the still-spontaneous panorama of parametric conversion of factors abducted from one social structure to another of similar scale.

The framework for significant and socially-articulated action in these disruption-free regimes of interrupted change will incorporate a counterpoint between: 1. overcoming inertia through planning and much more profound systemic rationalization, and; 2. the effects of social entropy. This entropy results from weakened conditions for change which were wasted in the first frustrated "take-off" attempt; it follows the dissipation of growth potentials which remain viable in the classic "developmentalist" formula.

Though often proclaimed as a follow-through of the 1950s' interrupted process, frustrated take-off is easily differentiated from the traditional development scheme. Post-spontaneous development regimes characteristically combine: 1. rationalization allowed by the inertia of those same factors of compatibility which sparked the previous decade's change formula; and 2. accommodation to entropy, linked to the potential of those same compatibility factors, and its inevitable impact on the scale of change or the unfolding of fructifying disequilibria in growth crises. In addition to planning, all post-development efforts thus involve contained and sometimes miniaturized patterns of change. This third situation simultaneously incorporates mechanisms of containment and change; of controlled or even Malthusian expansion in new correlations which can—reflecting the merging of rationality and entropy—miniaturize the scale of the process, invert the dynamism of macrosocial change, and reverse the levels of concordance between the social superstructures and infrastructures.

THE MODEL OF ABORTED DEVELOPMENT

The new regime's framework of aborted and delayed development is gradually revealing the pattern of inertia, whose features necessarily correspond to the neocapitalist model's social and political impact. This framework was adopted by the technocratic regimes of the 1960s, exemplified by Brazil and Argentina. In accord with the ever more typical strategies for the fortuitous event of "controlled" development, inertia's basic outlines would include:

1. *The pattern of concentration.*   New policies are based more and more on nucleating the development effort, in keeping with the classic thesis that "reinitiation" should be based on the economic sectors which are already most dynamic. These regimes adhere strictly to the doctrine that fortuitous events have compelled initial retreats to presently effective growth poles, pending a new impulse for expansion. All emphasis is thus on "developing the already developed," under the conviction that benefits will propagate and diffuse.

This strategy could eventually reorder the logistics of the prior spontaneous phase's doctrine of "growth nuclei," with its highly flexible policies for structuring national investments. Both old development centers, and their growth potentials, may be reordered in the process. Each stage definitively segregates chosen areas and those marginal to its development effort. The previous stage's pretension to generalize change under the prodding of spontaneity and the demonstration effect is implicitly rejected in the new strategy's divorce from social expectations.

Concentration would eliminate the danger of an internally diachronic vision of national development, which outlives the spontaneous phase. Dissociation between chosen and rejected areas could thus be prevented.

2. *The pattern of disfunctionalization and compartmentalization (in contrast to functionalization and integration).* Though still unclear, this feature corresponds to a general situation of controlled social mobility.

The spontaneous phase, by contrast, supposes:

1. The market economy's growing absorption of groups isolated at subsistence levels;
2. The leading role of accelerated industrialization in the market economy, which necessarily conditioned urbanization and consequently induced an urban-rural counterpoint (agricultural shifts to supply new urban industrial complexes).

This process and the parallel structural alteration were delineated within a productive apparatus which assumed open and irreversible social mobility. Mobility was characterized by functional behavior within an expanding and increasingly dynamic market economy, and by growing participation in the benefits of a complex and productive social system.

Today's framework, by reversing these mechanisms and their related "trends," fits the pattern of inertia; limited functionalism and integration coexist with mechanisms representing their antithesis. These mechanisms are, as it were, induced by the new regime—they saturate the condition of relaxed change, which is separated from all its trophic potential.

This model and strategy thus imply the combination of development mechanisms with those of compartmentalization and reversion, which minimize its defects.

The core of the new regime includes a well-structured complex of "deceptions" and compartmentalizations; a system of communication which contrasts with the old unidirectional and irreversible circuit by which development was linked to a simultaneous process of accelerated socialization. *Lumpenproletariats* resulted from the dynamic disfunctions of this framework. Contained development regimes, though, are fully adapted to long term marginality; the system adjusts to its residues as economically available factor excesses. Mechanisms of integration and marginalization are coupled, along with functionalization and reversion of social processes.

This is apparent from the inception of the new system of access, which controls mobility between the market and subsistence economies through a set of "one-way doors." Colonial regimes can, without crisis, return large numbers of workers newly introduced to the "plantation" economy to a subsistence level. This process is especially facilitated by an elastic labor supply and large manpower reserves. These seasonal and indefinite transfers are of the regime's essence. Available manpower is not definitively absorbed in the most dynamic economic sector; the contradictions do not even become structural crises. The economy is completely open to this endless reservoir, which is subordinated within an "anomic" flow in terms of the sociological and political implications of the levies subtracted from and returned to its care. This pattern's effect on primary activity associated with export commodities shows how neo-Malthusianism can be imposed, and the country's economic space miniaturized, with neither resistance nor crisis. There is no "complementarity" of quotas by which repressing or expelling labor would reduce the functionality of capital, know-how, or labor. And various factors prevent any reaction when the regime's castoffs come into contact with each other.

Anomie acts as a cushion to suffocate these suppressed elements. Inertia is so profound that they disappear without a sign of rebellion, to reappear submissively at times of new and limited expansion.

3. *Inverted conditioners between macrosocial change processes.* This Malthusian development mechanism finds support in the market economy, and its urban pole, in the inversion of conditioners between "industrialization" and "urbanization."

Having outlived spontaneous secondary-sector growth, the neo-capitalist model fortuitously came to stress housing and complementary social investments. Such stimulation, according to the system and its ideology, supposed an itinerant and relatively "external" entrepreneurial factor. Housing investment is a paradigm for the role of ex-centric stimuli in replacing the multiplier effect. These investments, not really part of the system, are only artificial anticyclical stimulants in the face of the paralysis of neocapitalism's mechanisms for reinitiating development. Public investments and investment policies thus find a typical pattern and a response to meet the systemic imperative of repressed mobility in the cities.

The housing plan is not the only alternative to combat stagnation according to neocapitalism's rules of stimulation and therapy. Nor does it suffice to note the motivation from "within" the system, the preoccupation to reduce the social tensions resulting from change. A classic pattern of repressed mobility, lavishly employed by the colonial structure, lies in this reversal of urbanization and industrialization. "Clientelization," in the urban pole, plays the same role as one-way doors between market and subsistence economies in the rural extreme. The neocapitalist model uses broad state patronage to assure generalized equilibrium. Such equilibrium is not restricted to the regime's economic dynamism; conditions demand a true entropy in which general and continuous social mobility is replaced by localized access to benefits and social privilege. These favored enclaves show ever more leveling—in terms of public participation, the imperatives of economic stimulation, and the attenuation of stagnation's social risks.

THE IMPACT OF ABORTED DEVELOPMENT ON SOCIAL CONSCIOUSNESS

The political impact of repressed mobility must be analyzed to complement the discussion of the inertia of aborted development regimes. Effects include: 1. a loss of purpose of the organizations which arose, from the ground up, to mediate spontaneous mobility; 2. consequent overvaluing of the superstructural organizations called to vicariously exercise that mediation; 3. Increased or decreased initiative of the protagonists of continuous mobility, solely as a function of the new and superimposed "clientelization" systems. This will explain some groups' apathy and the hyperactivism of others, completely outside the classical development framework's real and expected dynamisms. Naturally revolutionary groups will be paralyzed by statutory guarantees which invalidate their position in a decaying market or which, by contrast, can marginalize them. Other examples include the aggressive role of sectors classically linked to order and the impunity of groups whose recovery no longer generates counterpretensions or social resistances, but rather echoes in the void created by interrupted and repressed social situations.

These patterns are fundamental for conditioning intelligentsias and, therefore, the ideological production of aborted development regimes. They link the main features of this pattern (which will probably become dominant in the immediate future, since hopes for 1950s'-style spontaneity are fading) with the actual range of ideological effectiveness. In this political context, ideology will depend essentially on the prospects for class and group recovery, given: the conditions of social mobility; the viability of the social vanguards which articulate the behavior of the intelligentsia; and the level of consciousness which the social organization can tolerate, in terms of both exercising the critical function and accepting the role of ideology in change.

The intelligentsia's ideal behavior must be located within the spontaneous change framework, and then with respect to the trophic sequence. Next we must analyze how interrupted development and contained social mobility affect the paradigm. This perspective will permit us to define the axis which will determine future ideological production. Conditioners external to the immediate context will necessarily complement this axis. These conditioners affect both the content of ideas imported to the national system, and the changes in that system resulting from external influences.

The pattern of ideological production, which reflects the loss of change's trophic moment, derives from these factors; thus its divergence from the "canonic" perspective of the 1950s.

All these behaviors will determine the conditions of ideological production and the model which it will follow through the next decades. But ideology will reflect, above all, the crisis of the national growth model, (the prospects of a Brazilian reality) and the consequently reduced chance for a *prise de conscience*. The loss of social memory, with the plundering of the collective consciousness, may follow the collapse of nationally viable change.

The role of ideology must be examined in the development models of power elite regimes—whether these will allow ideological development or whether goal-oriented and repressive governments will eliminate the need for ideology. Power elite regimes would, in the latter case, close a circuit to fulfill social goals non-ideologically, via the cult of rationality.

THE INTELLIGENTSIA'S CONDUCT IN A TROPHIC CHANGE PROCESS

Determinants of the Immediate System

Various features marked the activity of the intelligentsia during the transition from a colonial to a developmental regime. The national reality was discussed in detail, and previous intellectual positions were radically reevaluated. This criticism surpassed normal intergenerational polemics to become a *prise de conscience*, based on a new social perspective resulting from quantitative and qualitative economic changes and from the apparent acceleration of development as a government program.

The phenomenology of the intelligentsia's critical attitude then incorporated: 1. denunciation of the topicality and impressionism of previous ideologies; 2. comprehension of the fortuitousness of the group's insertion at development's "critical moment"; 3. prudence before ingenuous substantiations of this establishment position.

The critical attitude not only judged the past, but also reflected the immediate context of the development effort. A vision was sought in which constant criticism from within would make the intelligentsia an effective collaborator in change and assure fully effective action and consciousness. The intellectual, acting within the power apparatus, would be guaranteed a praxistic perspective and thereby avoid the alienation or detachment that can arise in criticisms developed away from the tensions of action. The intelligentsia could also take advantage of the phase in which spontaneous change assured convergent modifications in all social spheres to formulate an ideology affirming the functionality of reflection. The transition would thus be encouraged by: 1. enlightening the protagonists of change; 2. elucidating their common interests; 3. classifying their role in change.

The process of representing the interests of social groups does not here reach an ultimate situation of strict and localized class recoveries. Nor does the infrastructure clearly delineate opposed social contexts. The transition supposes more ample previous polarizations; it counterposes the old structure's roles and connections of interests with those derived from the nascent development structure and its redistribution of functions. Social consciousness during this phase would simultaneously be: 1. para-ideological, since it affirms an interest prior to its exhaustive configuration as a function of emergent groups' specific demands in a new social complex; 2. concerned with making groups compatible by finding common ground and bypassing dissimilarities and ultimate antagonisms; 3. directed at complementing group cooperation through avoiding a rupture of change's trophism. Social consciousness does not replace trophism, for example, by transforming the momentary *prise de conscience* of real change by qualitatively altering group relations. In the best trophic sequence, ideology retains its inchoate role and accelerates objective change.

Determinations External to the Immediate National System

In this section we will specify the intelligentsia's determinants at the moment most favorable for revealing all its functions.

We have so far described behavior at the time of the intelligentsia's greatest participation in the immediate social system.

But we must also consider the secondary determinants arising in systems external to a spontaneously developing country which is moving toward greater self-determination.

Intelligentsias, even in "canonic" stages, are not isolated from influences outside the national system. To the degree that the nation is articulated within relations of international dependency or conditioning, its ideological production must be influenced by external factors—by the ideologies coined during the evolution of the West's "great society," and by their contradictions and subsequent rationalizations. This reflected influence tends toward inverse proportionality with the capacity for independent reflection at a "canonic" moment or within a "trophic" change sequence.

Such a moment represents the apogee of the underdeveloped country's ideological independence—the phase which corresponds to import substitution. This forms the basis for inferring the influence of the context and of ideologies received from the external circuits to that fostering national self-determination. The conditioners, which still act as supports, include:

The pattern of national ideological independence. The critical moment of underdeveloped countries' transition from colonial to development structures is characterized, in terms of social consciousness, by the particular way in which they achieve national self-determination. This involves the paroxysm of a nonfunctional productive structure which collapses with import substitution–with industrialization and the rise of internal markets. The contradictions in postwar Latin America correspond to a level of self-determination quite distinct from those which characterized Western society in terms of clashes between social structure and system, system and classes, and organization and underlying community. The weakening of metropolis-colony dependency, starting from revolutions for national development, fully reveals the unsuitability of the social change vision characterizing the West's "great society," the progenitor of the colony. This is inapplicable to the stage combining the need for a developmental ideology with key concepts derived from the

West's great visions. Rejected ideologies include rationalized visions of socialism, capitalism, and such reformist versions of the latter as Catholic Church social doctrine. Their inapplicability is substantiated by some basic complaints arising from influence of the context on the analysis required for development:

The principal contradiction. Though the Marxist vision of change is defined by the contextual parameters, it tends to subsume all efforts to affirm a national state within an external process dominated by imperialism and by resistance to its hegemony. The nation's unique role in composing these forces is subordinated to the model's international emphasis; all national behavior has its counterpoint in the larger and more general play of forces in which the state is immersed. The principal contradiction, used to explain the exploitation and conditioning which hinder the rise of a "national will," is always external.

This framework portrays a rigidly polarized and definitive international socio-politico-economic system. It also affirms an idiomatic nationalist perspective—a representation of the interests linking groups and classes in a peripheral country which pretends to independently affirm its dynamisms by overcoming the relative inadequacy of internal resources. (Within certain limits, this mobilization can occur without infringing on the external system's lines of force.) A developing economy can incorporate these groups and classes, at its core or periphery, without being affected by their contradictions. But, according to the doctrine of the principal contradiction and rigid polarities, no other contradictions would be perceived; the model's internal and external play fail to coincide, and may even contradict one another. Particularly symptomatic is the opposition between the role magnification which nationalism afforded the internal bourgeoisie, and orthodox Marxism's nonrecognition of this phenomenon. Or, on the other hand, the Marxist emphasis on *latifundia* as forces braking role magnification, as against their derived importance in nationalist analysis.

The latter vision, while deemphasizing the economic power of *latifundia*, is more sensitive to income redistribution and to mechanisms of guarantee. When these mechanisms were subsumed in the nationalist superstructure, in a decisive instance of its behavior, they also passed into another social dimension.

Gradualism. The canoic growth period rejected both the thesis that comparative backwardness was the structural phenomenon responsible for stagnation, and the notion that underdeveloped countries were just beginning the transformation into complex and mature societies. No longer was it assumed that the gap between the extremes was just a problem of comparative distances within which idiomatic phenomena like nationalism or statism were only "infantile illnesses" of a long maturation process. "Progressism" is necessarily the ideology of a change strategy accommodated to bounds set by the stimuli, the mobilization of acceleration factors, and the evolution and end point already contained in the embryo. Here the outcome is expected to emerge from already-defined historical paths. The regime, already foreseen as a system, would presumably be predisposed to make development a simple play of sums on the social functions of increasing productivity, reproducing investments, and rationalizing the socioeconomic apparatus. A communitarian preoccupation thus accompanies the neocapitalist strategy. Underdeveloped societies are treated as if they were based on the settlers who formed the "great society," rather than the groups which actually constitute them. The colonial structure's particular mechanisms, its play between subsistence and market economies, and the latter's urban–rural counterpoint, are ignored.

Intermediate communities. This complaint may explain why underdeveloped countries reject the Catholic Church's social doctrine, especially as expressed in the directives preceding the 1961 *aggiornamento.* This doctrine implicitly supposed the natural organic quality of all forms of social life. Human conduct would pass through all intermediate communities from family to state, and these communities would fashion the modes of social reform. The acknowledged failure of Latin America's Christian Democratic parties may derive from their obedience to this vision. Through it they became separated from the real play of social contradictions, from adequate appreciation of the forces and the level of opposition needed to remain effective. Reality involves more than full social saturation via class articulation and the adjustment of demands for amelioration on the basis of an essential and spontaneous interchange between latency and organization. The proletariat, for example, cannot accept the principle of pluralistic unionism which originates in the doctrine of intermediate communities. This thesis overlooks the colonial structure's requirement of labor unity for effective labor-capital confrontation. No matter how its proponents protested to the contrary, this ideology would assume a reactionary perspective by insisting on the state's supplementary role in an economic take-off, instead of understanding its function as the dominant and almost unique entrepreneur. Christian Democratic ideologies cannot continue to imagine the underlying community's permanent self-organization or the definitive withdrawal of the mechanism of state action before a spontaneously organized social infrastructure; neither is possible in the colonial complex.

The pattern of asynchrony.   Articulation with foreign ideologies involves more than the complaints arising from specific disjunctures between social contexts. For an underdeveloped country, winning internal time also implies a new distance from the centers which traditionally conditioned its ideologies reflected in the growing asynchronism of its analyses. Traditional influences on colonial regimes are not only unidirectional; they also convey a one-sided "social time." Such partisanship is characterized more by conservation of contents and models which are already obsolete in the metropolitan center than by their delayed reception.

In phases close to the critical moment of change, asynchronism gains meaning through the growing external sensitivity to the underdeveloped country's crisis, which may even include appreciation of its historical significance. Such diachronism is easily established; it allows the primary norms of a given phase to become "changing" stereotypes when structural conditions are altered, as well as at the critical moment when they could play a creative role.

This basic time disequilibrium underlies the difficulties encountered by aid programs in ordering the problems of underdeveloped nations; in emphasizing either social or economic development; and in generating strategies to relaunch change. Discrepancies can be aggravated with reciprocally interacting asynchronisms. This phenomenon characterized, for instance, the imposition of planning to condition international cooperation. Originating in the countries benefitting from the process, it took a great effort to sensitize financing agencies—traditionally fearful of centralizing or "statist-oriented" action. But planning was ultimately adopted to inform aid programs so quickly and with such technical incompetence as to cancel any chance of real effectiveness.

The pattern of operationality. To the extent that under-developed countries gravitate toward their own social time, relations with the external nexus are no longer limited to divergence, rejection, or imbalanced appropriation. A qualitative alteration may result: by considering what is accepted rather than what is rejected, it may be possible to clarify the gap between specific ideologies' external effectiveness and their applicability to the colonial structure. All this indicates a positive reaction to the enveloping ideological context, and thus to part of the international system in which the developing country is suspended. By seeking appropriations fitting its own historic time, the country searches for the usable amid the loss of alternatives which characterize collapsed change. Thus the resistance to importing all the premises, theses, or debates of an ideological perspective, though "pragmas" are retained. Concern focuses on styles and principles which will not depend on the eligibility per se of models of the historical process, but rather on the concrete difficulties of implementing them. The urgency of the task generates an attitude opposing further discussion of basic theses; these are just accepted, and the focus shifts to the strategic problems of implementation. Effectiveness is assured as far as is possible, but thorough analysis of ideological contents is postponed. Clearly utopian ideologies for changing the status quo—like socialist theses in contemporary Latin America—would debate means and strategies of implementation rather than contents. These ideologies increasingly manifest a regression of debate from thesis to strategy, and from strategy to dogma, which correlates with the confinement of change and ever-diminishing expectations of developmental success. This is the "operationalist" pattern by which Latin America's utopian change advocates are now generating discussions of alternative models, beginning with the influence of exemplary experiences like China and Cuba.

Prospective Behavior of the Latin American Intelligentsia

So far we have focused on the intelligentsia's activity in a trophic process or at a canonic moment of change. We defined contexts which would call forth its latent repertory in order to develop a paradigm with which to analyze the subsequent stage. We can thus evaluate the intelligentsia's activity when the canonic moment is lost and inertia sets in—a pattern which fits Latin America's immediate future. A framework of economic paralysis, with parallel regression in other areas of the social complex, now conditions the intelligentsia. These circumstances are heralded by the dissolution or rupture of change's most sensitive layer, consciousness. To study Latin America's intelligentsia at the end of the century, we must establish its position and its behavior and position within this new social model, and analyze the model's effects on: 1. exercising the critical consciousness in change; 2. ideological production; 3. the generation of social symbols; 4. the formation of vanguards for disseminating and programming ideologies; 5. institutionalizing the intelligentsia's function within the power structure.

For all these aspects, we must determine how the intelligentsia—and consequently ideological production—will react in regimes of contained change. These are characterized by:

1. *Neocapitalist development models,* emphasizing conservation of the traditional capital ratios and absorption levels of the subsistence economy by the market economy; and

2. *National decision-making* by a mixed, or simply military, "power elite" regime with growing ideological homogeneity (for example, Brazil's *Escuela Superior de Guerra* [War College] in 1964), and a divorce of economic change from political reaction. The political process opposes the kind of development which

would be reflected in decentralization, diffusion of decisions, and growing collective participation. New constitutions even overcome the formalities of traditional representative democracy by: a) eliminating checks and balances and initiating clear executive ascendancy; b) inhibiting decentralized decision-making (the "diffusion" of power) by destroying the vestiges of federative systems and instituting authoritarian centralism through control of the security apparatus and financial power, and above all by dominating planning; and c) ending any concern for formal legitimacy by restricting the number and significance of elections.

3. *Contained social mobility and political regression.* These inevitably deaden the trophic period's characteristic spontaneous amelioration for diverse groups and classes. The regime will replace the intermediate communities, in a large sense constituted by unions, with a generous welfare organization. A planned program might initially reduce tensions. However, the process would necessarily be limited by the economic model's possibilities and the pattern of contained mobility. Other organizations, independent through their nonsubmission to the state apparatus, will supersede the power elite's hyperorganization in mediating the remaining distorted mechanisms for amelioration. Given Latin American society's traditional weakness in confrontation with the state, especially apparent in the history of its unions, this role will fall almost exclusively to the Catholic Church. A confrontation between the technocracy, incarnated in its military head, and the Church hierarchy, is implicit in the dynamic of power elite regimes, though it is modulated by their opportunities for initiating economic development. Had the Church's officialist tradition not already been affected by Vatican II's *aggiornamento*, its new role as spokesman for repressed or annulled unions would today force the change. This vicarious function, originating in political regimes of contained mobility which destroy the intermediate communities for expressing social interests and aspirations, will give the Church a mixed character. Church action will initially "legitimize" the demands for social recovery still susceptible to channeling within the system. But it cannot avoid personifying the pole of challenges to aborted development and the power elite regime in the confrontations which may follow the collapse of contained change and the rise of overt neo-Malthusianism.

The impact of the abortive change paradigm's economic, political, and social determinants will come to define the intelligentsia's behavior; this model seems destined to dominate Latin American politics between now and the end of the century.

The Immediate Panorama of Frustration of the Critical Function

The main effect of interrupting the development of social consciousness will be loss of practical conditioning for critical analysis. The national development project assumed self-criticism by an intelligentsia acting within the system; this will disappear. Value judgments in the former situation implicitly supposed correction of flaws within an untouchable general framework of goals. Moreover, the intelligentsia was tied to praxis by its very criticisms; it could and did experience the full range of concrete tensions.

Difficulties are to be expected in formulating alternatives to abortive development. These will arise from inattention to the principles allowing a true dialectic in the critical function, which demand that the intelligentsia actually experience the scheme's evolution. During spontaneous development, obligatory reference to the objective conditions did not necessarily confine the range of alternatives; this is not true in the new phase, with its mechanism of cumulative causation necessarily mediated by the development project. Success would buttress a paradigm for transforming reality, in the light of which all other change factors would be reordered. But failure reinverts the conditioners: even within change, viability is restricted as the project narrows. Growing impotence would dominate the realm of concrete tensions; the play of development opportunities and their reordering before wasted potentials, or within the terms of cumulative causation, could only influence action within the basic limits of the project or its collapse. At the critical moment of paralyzed spontaneous development and the beginning of regression, underdeveloped countries attempt repairs in the basic strategy to reinitiate development. New situations and changed contexts impose new patterns of viability. Pure normativity and ideological analysis are considerably limited. Underdeveloped countries are now experiencing these situations in which the future is narrowed; very strict rules of the game govern the praxis by means of which ideologies can become effective. The intelligentsia's activity thus does not accommodate itself to the aspirations of "impure" social groups, which seek change from outside the viability or agony of national development. Ideology is suspended in a given project; its effectiveness is wholly dependent on a pragma. Likewise, pure normative positions, and the contents of summary negation, cannot free themselves from the inchoate role which always characterizes the radical wing of the change. The great danger in "opposition" behavior in Latin America's power elite regimes is that, in situations of relaunched change, they settle for summary and aprioristic substitution of models without regard to viability or effectiveness. This accompanies the failure of groups to assume the understandably traumatic critical function of formulating valid antitheses to current situations. Feasible alternatives demand full acquaintance with the prior development project and an attitude of historical continuity with the concrete and national—rather than summary rejection of the context or its psychologistic relegation as no more than a facade which obscures the deep predispositions or the real constituents of the national situation.

Thus the critical cutting edge was eliminated that provided effective complementarity between thesis and antithesis, situation and opposition, and the content of the development project and that of the counterproject. When the critical function terminated, moreover, ideology was replaced with mere affirmation of antagonism and enunciation of logical propositions to reorder reality. The intelligentsia's functional displacement is apparent; in terms of sociological supports, its new role as mere antagonist objectively encloses it in a fatal alienation. The intelligentsia in this period is formed:

1. By a group of students identified by their contradictory position which involves; a) the very rigidity of the colonial regime's educational system, incorporating the infinitesimal fraction of the collectivity (less than 1 percent) which can overcome the enormous selective pyramid of the secondary schools, and b) the tendency, excepting classic cases of distortion, to transform their "privilege" of education into development's scarcest economic

factor, knowhow. More than any other group, students enjoy the chance of a conservative insertion into the system; 2. By a group of exiled intellectuals. The consolidation of power elite regimes in Latin America showed an unprecedented switch from the traditional activity of personal enemies to that of entire ideological strata. As in Brazil and Argentina, this behavior affected the most articulate university leadership, as well as the union, military, and liberal professional vanguards which formed the developmentalist intelligentsia of the 1950s. Latin America's ideological representations of social reality and social change are likely to feature increased "radicalization" and "millenarianism" between now and the end of the century. 3. By a utopian religious stratum—a group conditioned to vicariously demanding improved conditions for intermediate communities. Due to its social disarticulation, it will tend toward the utopian perspective characteristic of social revolutionism.

The Elimination of Ideology

There is a noteworthy contradiction between power elite regimes and the social necessity of ideological production. Ideology is crucial in the self-analysis of change and for engaging groups and classes which participate in overcoming the colonial structure. Ideology is necessary insofar as the national project depends on the relative compatibility of these protagonists. It loses all meaning when development follows a model originating in the direct adherence of an elite unconcerned with legitimacy or with generating collective support. This is especially true when, as in today's Latin America, the leaders share an ideological position, so that the choices of model and program come built-in. The model's effectiveness is thus entirely dependent on its performance, rather than its representation or symbols; ideology necessarily disappears.

Disuse of Symbols

Contemporary power elite regimes lack any capacity for political symbolization—essential for the consensus to which they are structurally destined. Their characteristically incoherent homogeneity lies in the representations of the world of Castelo Branco's or Onganía's technocracy.[1] These views derived from similar dogmatic premises for analyzing their countries' realities and led both regimes to make the cult of rationality both their ideology and the ruling criterion for the political process they now control. Rationality unified this group's representational homogeneity, which arose prior to its historic formulation. It has also been transformed into an ideology which, in itself, has sterilized its full social function. In 1964, Brazil's "power elite" was obliged to move toward the politics of symbols and consensus. But the dogma of rationality, of which it was already prisoner, precluded this step. Barred from moving forward, the regime fell back on the cult of performance—the production of consensus being replaced by the "heroic" assumption of the "ethic of unpopularity."

The Paralysis of the Vanguards

The power elite regime's pattern of contained mobility attenuates or eliminates recovery channeled through the spontaneous coparticipation of class organizations (the unions). Not only do unions lose significance for the intelligentsia; above all, their urban working class base loses its force. Clientelization projects the urban working class into the center of anticyclical policies for correcting unemployment with so-called social investments and localized redistributions of national income. Above all, specific benefits to this working class are chosen over a contained but effective welfare state (rather than the old paternalism), which would defend the interplay of social ordinances necessarily induced by the power center's "pleasing" behavior. The result is dulled worker demands for increased benefits. Labor's quiescence will tend to be directly proportional to participation in relaunched development. It will also correlate with the regions and sectors united by new productivity patterns resulting from the concentration and reordering of markets.

The resulting modifications of scale will intensify the objective segregation of salaried groups in the new development poles. These groups will receive more and more internal benefits from the tensions of the chosen area and contained dynamism. A nationwide formulation of contradictions, applying to all the groups caught up in the 1950s' spontaneous change, is unlikely. Contained mobility will segregate the urban worker from the social vanguard, while anomie separates him from the *campesino*. The play of one-way doors between subsistence and market economies means that the continual insertion and return of the agricultural labor reserve generates no social articulation. No power of collective change could provide the conditions under which the peasantry would support an ideology. Power elite regimes encountered no resistance in the rural areas of the most complex underdeveloped countries, like Brazil and Argentina. More important, anomie intensifies when the market economy contracts; *campesino* organizations simply disappear. Then neither reaction nor change is likely. The rural masses' eventual return to the market economy is defined by the neocapitalist system's strict rules of the game, and occurs within its demands for regulated expansion and selective incorporation of labor.

Limitations on the urban middle class clearly reflect the pattern of contained mobility and the consequent internal disintegrations of urban society's core, achieved by redistributing national income according to compartments and hierarchies. The proletariat's new "welfare state" increasingly confronts, or even opposes, the loss of acquisitive power in fixed income sectors of the middle class. These groups lack protection from the neocapitalist model's selective processes of inflationary risk. The middle class may thus display growing "massconsciousness," represented by direct mobilization—in the heart of the collectivity—of individuals affected by localized social decline. This class becomes the protagonist of the mass mobilizations and protest which may grow increasingly important between now and the end of the century. It provides resonance for "untouchable" groups like students and the revitalized Church. However, its mobilization must be distinguished from that of classical vanguards in which the intelligentsia's critical and ideological function was extended by emergent groups and classes. These vanguards arose out of the union apparatus's growing articulation—from the organization, rather than the disintegration, of their creative spontaneity. Such formations were thus distinct from the recovery-oriented role of middle class individuals "not structured" in social life.

Deinstitutionalization of the Intelligentsia

The intelligentsia gradually loses its ties to the change process. It passes through a phase in which it only stimulates mobilization; finally, with neocapitalist development models and their theoretical counterparts, mobilization is separated from the last trophic element—acceleration of change from within a social system. Reflection only focuses on the specific regime, its needs and techniques. The intelligentsia's activity reduces to strict analysis of the conflict's short term logistics; the discussion of alternative change programs may even be abandoned. Such operationalism transforms the polemic of change into an ever narrower discussion of subversive techniques, paralleling the power elite's performance cult, planning, and goals. The objective conformation of consciousness in this stage conditions the reception of external theses and debates, the basic elements in contemporary society's polemics between models. The rupture of the Latin American left with classical and nonclassical orthodox Marxism illustrates how operationalism increasingly shapes the process. Thus the search for institutionalized techniques like the cultural revolution to parallel operationalism's merely dogmatic configurations. The vicissitudes of OLAS's thematic are best understood in this framework—its wide role as model and theoretical premise did not allow it to forsake just the debate over metropolitan variants of socialism. Radical sectors are more and more suffering a reduced polemical scope caused by their basically "operationalist" position. Instead of considering the ties between the party and communitarian spontaneity in forming the "people's army," polemics are tending toward entirely reduced discussions of operational tactics through analyses of urban variants on the guerrilla. At the end of this regression, when a closed and idomatic model matches each confrontation with its own "situation", an inverted form of the original praxis recurs. The subsequent step depends on the unfolding of tensions in the neo-capitalist model. This signals absolute topicism—consciousness, a prisoner of events, can neither advance nor actively confront present trends.

THE INTELLIGENTSIA'S PROSPECTIVE BEHAVIOR

Determinants of the Context

Analysis of the future of Latin America's intelligentsia must consider the interchange between the national system and the external parameters. These determinants which complement the immediate conditioners of reflection, can be analyzed from both subjective and objective poles.

1. *The subjective extreme* involves the direct influence of mental contents derived from external systems as per amplifications or reductions in the already mentioned canons of idiomatism, asynchrony, and operationality; 2. *The objective pole* concerns the system's national supports, as altered by neocapitalist development strategies. It includes this model's problems of economies of scale, integration, and reordering productive forces, the solutions to which may weaken the national framework.

Within the subjective aspect, the formally utopian character of ideology intensifies. This tendency is apparent in several ideological styles which have persisted since the 1950's crisis of spontaneity, and which are becoming ever more pronounced and dubious as power elites cement themselves in Latin America's most complex societies: millenarianism, radicalization, and idealization.

1. *The millennial vision* of violent change corresponds to the violence with which the intelligentsia's social supports were removed in Brazil and Argentina. This position incorporates the compensation and projection with which the intelligentsia reacted to its summary and unprecedented separation from national decisions.

The millennial vision inverts the traditional sequence. Though the intelligentsia's reinsertion into reality is indicated, they intervene less and less in the now-distant context. Rationalizing inactivity should just be a beginning, and not an end point. But the activity of the exiled intelligentsia slows, rather than intensifies, as it searches for new articulation with the original context. Chiliasm is the first symptom—the belief that some unexpected and isolated action, occurring in a context already saturated with contradictions, will trigger change. Even though utopian, this pattern is a variation on concrete intervention; the system could fall with two or three opportune pronouncements or returns by representatives isolated by the power elite. The country would instantly respond to the clarion call of their reappearance, and the true social and economic order—only incidentally perturbed by technocratic military governments—would quickly re-emerge. The chiliastic aspect is apparent in the analytical divorce of these eruptions from the system's internal logistics and dialectic. The viability of such a sudden denouement is totally assured by this picture of a system verging on explosion. Its contradictions would be fully matured; no more than symbolic gestures of "return" would destroy the dependent power.

2. *Radicalization.* The growing orthodoxy of the intelligentsia's subjective vision and its aspiration to social effectiveness is understood by the same divorce of social consciousness from social change. This situation generates increasing desires to impose a plan regardless of time and of contextual limitations; the breach with effectiveness grows ever larger. The rupture with viability, moreover, implies substitution of growing radicalization for a strategy which, in most cases, further exaggerates the gap with effectiveness.

3. *Idealization.* The remoteness of the intelligentsia's models from the reality in which they would act is another consequence of lost praxis. The utopian attitude is fully alienated; it lacks any effective social role. The intelligentsia's formulations regress to the starting point of ever more formally rigorous theses and contents, with ever less correction from reality. Models will become idealized to the degree that the intelligentsia immobilizes itself through simultaneous withdrawal from actual circumstances, and refuge in a strategy of eventual return to full activity, in a melancholy and fulminating moment.

The Subjective Element

A complete change from the ideologies characterizing the canonic phase of development thus seems likely. The distances and gaps which earlier affirmed autonomous social time and ideological production in countries moving toward qualitatively changed social structures will probably diminish. The previous climate allowed an authentic national development ideology; the new conditions suggest:

1. *Reduced national individuality.* Rationalizing change and attempting to reinitiate contained development will initially facilitate the direct appropriation of external models by the national decision center. Growing idealization will characterize the orthodox reiteration of opposition; the status quo will respond in kind through the cult of rationality's dominant tone of formal rigor. Rather than emphasizing programmatic contents, power elite regimes stress the instrumental perspectives of models—how to implement them for post-spontaneous development.

2. *Reduced asynchrony.* The rationalization which characterizes repeated change necessarily blurs the distinctions between stages of historical evolution. One can vaguely discern the reciprocal interaction mentioned above within the new project's focus. Both the internal sequence of stages and fluxes with the external context are ordered; real transactions are initiated between the systems. External dependency increasingly conditions the development strategy. Rationality implies a built-in perspective by which the extent and rigor of this dependency make the new process's stages more and more compatible. Blurred stages of historical evolution are reflected in increased synchronism; the distances between plans—their different starting points for reinitiated change—are reduced. There is growing exchange between the internal and external conditioners of aid. Ultimately the two times—that of the immediate system and that of the external context—would be fully integrated. The result would be progressive and inevitable inversion of initiatives and conditionings between what were previously called "immediate" and "complementary" systems.

3. *Exacerbated operationalism.* The current process, intensified by enthusiasm for rationalizing the new project, is complemented by accelerated degradation of contents in antagonistic representations of reality. The critical edge of effective theses is replaced by exaggerated concern for means. Focused on a specter of intermediary conduct and with growing logistic content, opposing theses are increasingly remote from the axes or parameters of effective action. An escape from formalism and preconditioned conducts could make the intelligentsia effective once again; this process can occur even within its present self-deception and separation from the power elite's project. Creative spontaneity would again become possible.

The Objective Extreme

National viability is further limited within the current model for relaunching development. The loss of initial national viability and alterations of scale, reordered growth poles, and the tendency toward integration, all affect ideological production. We must investigate these activities.

The objective pole reflects the loss of the national axis as a base for restoring social consciousness. This loss is obvious insofar as consciousness derives from the development model's prospective base, the immediate reference point of which is a plundered national identity or national poles. Social memory is affected by the growing gap between meaningful actions to allow an effective, culture-generating social challenge, and the sentiments of national identity underlying the present moment of reinitiated change. The data which define awareness, arising prior to spontaneous development, change with the project's full viability and its national tone. Goals would still correspond to an ingenuous phenomenology of national identity, not yet mobilized by an effective effort at self-determination. Social memory would be stuffed with the iconography of the splendors of change.

Thus would begin the impact of development in the entire repertory of literature, songs, and popular iconography. It would even regenerate the epic, in which national themes ultimately dominate.

Insertion in a New Supranational Context

The postwar period's characteristic loss of the national center for development has engendered disarticulation, as well as projecting the aborted development regimes which succeeded the change phase of the 1950s into new and extended systems. Even in the context of ideology, complexes tied to external dependency are less and less permanent. To the degree that relaunched development is assured success in today's neocapitalist framework, these complexes are no longer even secondary conditioners.

The new change pattern implies altered economies of scale and changed labor and capital proportions; these necessarily modify the former strategy of national development poles. The need for continental integration generates this situation and the double option of forming the "common market" as an obligatory overflow of and complement to national development; or unforeseen establishment as a goal of reinitiated change, on the basis of national affirmation in the 1950s.

In the second case, reinitiating strategies would necessarily maximize possibilities for reordering the hemisphere's economic and political framework. This would allow an influx of resources and effective use of the colonial regime's remaining endogenous potentials, severely weakened in the last decade. Internationalizing development is more than a strategy to reinitiate the effort and overcome new vicious circles and the deficiencies resulting from spontaneity's collapse. Though conceived as no more than internationalized planning, this perspective may run up against the same obstacles on a larger scale. These may include the confrontation between autonomy and dependency which arose during the spontaneous change phase and persisted into the 1960s, to the benefit of national affirmation.

The common market is not forming as a means for expanded neocapitalist development in an economic and political vacuum. Perhaps the most profound effect of the stagnation which has characterized the advent of national power elite regimes is that external capital has moved to create a complementary, clandestine, and supranational economy. Foreign capital had previously integrated this market with no thought of a rationale or a continental decision center which would preserve the essentials of self-determination. The collapse of nationally viable development with the crisis of spontaneity did not necessarily imply loss of pretenses to ultimate self-determination, barely altered in scale, among the countries whose space for change moved beyond their frontiers. In the meantime this is a concrete and difficult option in terms of the necessarily transcendental and uncontrollable capital influxes linked to neocapitalist strategies of maximization. The nation's remaining perspectives as a decision-making center must be defined in this image of a continent quickly integrated by long term corporate strategies. The state would be subordinated to a decision structure opposed to any new economic complex outside its control.

There is some risk that the integrationist ideology will not naturally appear as the redoubt of effective hemispheric inter-dependency. The common market did not reconcile new dependency with the residual autonomy of areas marginal to the enlarged dimensions of continental neocapitalism's strategic nuclei. These areas sheltered the remnants of national econo-mies. The decisions to "relaunch" Latin American development have almost universally generated this latent antagonism. Positions are gained or surrendered with each choice; the long-run effects will be decisive for such crucial problems as the level of incorporating subsistence economies in the market structure; the capital ratio of national industries and endogenous savings; and the role of public capital in the process's strategic nucleus, or in providing the external economies required by new decisions and possibilities. This context, and the ideological polemic it engenders, may have great impact between now and the end of the century. The interplay between the collapsed system and the new international framework could generate alliances entirely unexpected in the old focus of national tensions. For instance, the left's perspective of external domination has been subordinated to the rule of the principal contradiction. But, in their new political struggle, they might be led to the same orientations—though not the same range of priorities—as the national security ideologies toward which the power elite regimes are tending. The scale changes required by neocapitalist development may lead to a reinsertion of now antagonistic forces and groups in the weakening national dimension of regimes like Brazil and Argentina. Marked "distortions" would characterize the new local intelligentsias arising after the collapse of national development projects in a continental context. These would include forced convergence of the nationalist and national security extremes, joined by common opposition to an internationalization which could expropriate all decision making power over Latin American change.

CONCLUSIONS

Our framework allows several conclusions concerning Latin American ideological production in the light of: a) the characteristics of social consciousness in the current dystrophic change framework; b) the impact of aborted development on the intelligentsia's functions (developing a critical attitude, elaborating ideologies and symbols, organizing social vanguards, institutionalizing consciousness and self-criticism within government; c) secondary determinations from the context, subordinated to the change structure and its supports, and including the impact of external ideologies, and alterations from new models and new relationships of external conditioning and dependency.

These alterations can be classified under four headings:

1. The tendency toward parallel loss of social consciousness and elimination of the intelligentsia's functions in a dystrophic change process, manifested by: a) substitution of operationalism for true ideological production (the exhaustive thematic appreciation of reality); b) development of "utopian" representations of reality (millenarianism, radicalization, idealism), c) elimination of the very need for ideological production. The old change paradigm disappears when social demands are made compatible; support for change now comes from groups and classes seeking to overcome the colonial structure; d) disuse of symbols. Power elites, the heirs of spontaneous change, will assume an attitude of "rationality." The previous phase was characterized by simultaneous alterations in the economic structure, increases in national political self-determination, and diffusion of power.

Though the new regime brings heightened national mobilization and a convergence of oppositions toward consensus politics, its ideology of rationality cancels all symbolic urgency. Having abandoned mobilization politics, the power elite can only make a limited effort for indirect adherence to its change model. Appeals are channeled through the cult of performance and the topical manifestation of results. There is no reference to the "redoubt" level of nationalism and its prospective recognition in the collective change task; e) paralysis of the vanguards and their role of diffusing ideologies by means of the new patterns of contained mobilization. While rural workers are isolated by the intermittent play of the market and subsistence economies in absorbing excess labor, the urban proletariat's quiescence derives from its susceptibility to localized favoritism. Policies to reduce social tensions, conforming to doctrines of localizing progress and concentrating development poles, ensure contained mobilization; f) deinstitutionalization of the intelligentsia, whose role is necessarily submerged in power elite regimes' "technocratic" perspective.

This framework makes the intelligentsia obsolete; its role gradually vanishes. Criticism, tending more and more to mere antagonism, recedes into purely instrumental discussions of the logistics and scholastics of ending the status quo. Institutionally, universities fill the vacuum left by the old intelligentsias.

This condition persists as long as the new regime's supposed neutrality toward social interests restricts debate to matters of scientific consistency and logical rigor. The university can challenge the power elite by "dialectizing" its new institutional role and reviving the critical function. This is possible if it breaks out of its ostensible role of evaluation to show the system's true conditioners, or the substrata of the regime's rationality. Polemic, in whatever form, is a locus of criticism. In these regimes, polemics accompany dislocations between the practice of opposition (and the classical ideological compromises bringing compatibility) and the consensus served by an "absolutist" rationality; these are now to be purged of ideological content in the institutions whose supposed function is analyzing the political command's scientific propositions.

2. Co-option of the intelligentsia's function by the growing and cyclical antagonisms of the power elite regime's new and "untouchable" actors. Students, exiled intellectuals, and the "socially sensitive" Church subsequently come to share the intelligentsia's basic function, which was lost in the trophic moment of change (along with all simultaneity between the different planes of direct change or between this and social consciousness). These groups, more and more antagonistic to the new regime, are infused with a social revolutionary spirit.

The purely normative rhetoric which would now characterize these actors contrasts with their praxistic perspective—a median between action and consciousness—in canonic stages of change. More important, the demands of these groups—marginalized in terms of social power and of insertion in an effective framework of social benefits—would feature certain intransigence. The context of their "separation" would highlight the students' role in the critical moment of manifesting social opposition, and the clergy's ever more intense and inclusive vicarious representation of contained social mobility, which lacks spontaneous modes of expression.

This new Church role will make it more and more antagonistic to power elite regimes and their decisions on popular participation in change. The Church's vicarious function will tend to outweigh its classic role in society's dominant stratum, inherited from the colonial period. Though relatively few clergymen will rally to this reformist orientation, their actions will have increasing social impact as they are bombarded by expressions of repressed social desires. These, in turn, will arise in direct proportion to the regime's performance limitations. These "untouchable" groups are dissociated from social consciousness. Though they will tend toward cyclical activity, this will not preclude their eventual role as vehicles for the cumulative expression of social opposition. This is especially true insofar as they can channel opinion from such diffuse social groups as the urban middle classes of underdeveloped countries, which can only be aggregated in terms of direct mass confrontation. This type of alliance would permanently radicalize power elite regimes; their survival would demand diametrically opposed policies of economic change and political regression. The symbolic suppositions by which the power elite established itself, without recourse to traditional legitimization, might also be affected. These regimes bypassed popular suffrage to the degree that they developed indirect forms of legitimization through their apparently positive function for the social order and its institutional apparatus. In this framework, even the Church buttresses the symbolic function of maintaining the existing order. Such arrangements typified conditions when the military left a backstage role to assume direct political leadership.

Most significant in this context is the socially aware clergy's role in "desacralizing" the status quo and its symbolic suppositions of stability. Withdrawal of Church backing thus represents much more than a quantitative loss of support. The clergy, in a serious blow to stability itself, can be decisive in qualitatively modifying the perspectives of protest initiated by another "untouchable" actor, the students. The "untouchable" actors' first profanation of the status quo may be followed, for example, by middle class support—even though this reverses its classical behavior as a model of order and social tranquility. Most important is the "untouchable," "radical" clergy's function of desacralizing the notion of order; and, in a second "profanation," the middle classes' anonymous support for the student confrontation.

3. The tendency for social consciousness and the immediate social system which conditions it to regress. Even when trophic change stops, social stagnation alone will not eliminate the intelligentsia's social functions and arouse the substitutive behaviors mentioned under heading 2. But "reinitiated" change can cancel the national context of consciousness. Endogenous viability, necessary for a plenitude of ideological activity, is lost in this framework. Degradation affects all deviations from the ideal national axis—idiomatic resistance to contents imported from secondary constellations, and even to adoption of the external historical context, disappears. Antagonism is ever more confined, and focuses on instrumental aspects of subversion rather than alternative models or the dominant antithesis. At this point spontaneous innovation can only be reinitiated by extreme

exacerbation of operationalism. This occurs, curiously, through an inverted praxis; reality is re-encountered through confrontation and radical antagonism. The effective continuity of behavior can then transcend the degraded debate of revolutionary scholasticism by new techniques of confrontation which, unexpectedly, violate the system's implicit rules for political and social activity.

4. Tendency toward contradiction between the weakening immediate social system and the substitutive secondary system. Strategies to reinitiate development affect economies of scale and demand the polarization of development eventually to maximize returns and encourage new capital inflow. These in turn require a reorganized national economic space. The contradiction from which spontaneous postwar development began is reflected, in this enlarged context, in the inversion of supports for ideological production. The secondary constellation of international dependency passes to the foreground with reinitiated development; the immediate conditioning system is weakened. The insertion of old national regimes in a constellation which was previously only secondary can invert old antagonisms. This framework may generate new common denominators to aggregate forces which, in the context of national development, were inevitably antagonistic. Forces would be reordered, and their historic roles redistributed in new points of contact. This process would be based on new fundamental contradictions and on new incompatibilities and proximities among groups previously tied to the national context. But the difficulties of such realignment must not be forgotten. They include: a) the rigidity of group antagonisms, reflecting a classic discontinuity between political representations of reality and the actual circumstances of reinitiated development; and b) the difficulties of relating the new international scale to the effective level of contradictions. These problems, apparent in the last five years, reflect different degrees of growth and economic differentiation in the spontaneous phase, and their subsequent regression.

NOTE

1. Castello Branco and Juan Carlos Onganía, military presidents of Brazil and Argentina, respectively, at the time this was written.